3/07

WELFARE
REFORM
IN
PERSISTENT
RURAL
POVERTY

RURAL STUDIES SERIES

Leif Jensen, *General Editor*
Diane K. McLaughlin
and
Carolyn E. Sachs, *Deputy Editors*

The Estuary's Gift:
An Atlantic Coast Cultural Biography
David Griffith

Sociology in Government:
The Galpin-Taylor Years in the
U.S. Department of Agriculture, 1919–1953
Olaf F. Larson and Julie N. Zimmerman
Assisted by Edward O. Moe

Challenges for Rural America in the 21st Century
Edited by David L. Brown and Louis Swanson

A Taste of the Country:
A Collection of Calvin Beale's Writings
Peter A. Morrison

Farming for Us All:
Practical Agriculture and the Cultivation of Sustainability
Michael Mayerfeld Bell

Together at the Table:
Sustainability and Sustenance in the American Agrifood System
Patricia Allen

Country Boys: Masculinity and Rural Life
Edited by Hugh Campbell,
Michael Mayerfeld Bell, and Margaret Finney

WELFARE REFORM IN PERSISTENT RURAL POVERTY

Dreams,
Disenchantments,
and
Diversity

Kathleen Pickering   *Mark H. Harvey*
Gene F. Summers   *David Mushinski*

THE PENNSYLVANIA STATE UNIVERSITY PRESS
UNIVERSITY PARK, PENNSYLVANIA

Library of Congress Cataloging-in-Publication Data

Welfare reform in persistent rural poverty : dreams, disenchantments,
and diversity / Kathleen Pickering. . . [et. al.].
p.   cm. — (Rural studies series)
Includes bibliographical references and index.
ISBN 0-271-02877-7 (cloth : alk. paper)
1. Rural poor—United States—Case Studies.
2. Public welfare—United States—Case Studies.
3. United States—Rural Conditions—Case Studies.
I. Pickering, Kathleen Ann, 1958– .
II. Series: Rural studies series (University Park, Pa.)

HC110.P6W43 2006
362.5'5680973—dc22
2006014262

CONTENTS

Figures

ACKNOWLEDGMENTS

This study is the product of many individuals in many communities, and we would like to express our appreciation to them all. Most especially we wish to thank the numerous individuals who accepted us into their homes and graciously shared their experiences as participants in various Temporary Assistance to Needy Families (TANF) programs. Without their generosity and forthright responses to our questions this research would have been impossible. Through their cooperation we are able to prepare this monograph, which we hope will convey their concerns and those of millions of other TANF participants. In addition we wish to acknowledge our indebtedness to our interviewers and to community residents who assisted us in the conduct of our fieldwork.

We wish to acknowledge our gratitude to Robert Lee Maril for his guidance in the overall design of this research. His expertise, garnered from years of ethnographic research in low-income communities in Texas and Oklahoma, was extremely valuable. To the many faceless, and sometimes nameless, toilers in the offices of local, state, and national agencies who produced for us hundreds of data tables from administrative records, we want to acknowledge our great debt and deep sense of gratitude.

In Texas, Mark Harvey thanks his interview assistants, who shall remain anonymous, for their invaluable assistance. He also thanks Sabino Garza and the staff at Community Action, Social Services, and Education (CASSE), Blanca Juarez and the staff at Colonias Unidas, Amada Villarreal and the staff at Community Resource Group, and other workers at numerous community-based agencies who should also remain anonymous for providing information and putting us in contact with TANF participants. He also thanks Romelia Cardoña, John Flores, Eduardo Fuentes, Yvonne "Bonnie" Gonzales, Kelley Goran, Troy Heller, David LaGrange, Gloria Franco Lopez, Ricky McNeil, Elizabeth Cristina Miranda, Patricia Richards, South Texas Community College, and Southwest Texas Junior College.

In South Dakota, Kathleen Pickering thanks Jean Bedell-Bailey, Annabelle Between Lodges, Elaine Rodriguez, Janet Routzen, and Heather Schwartz for their interview assistance. She also thanks Connie Horse Looking, John Hotz, Terry Albers, Joyce Wheeler, Angie Eagle Bull, Elsie Meeks, Tina

Merdanian, Mark St. Pierre, the business owners in the Pine Ridge Area Chamber of Commerce, Marlese White Hat, Nora Antoine, Dr. Bordeaux, Lydia Whirlwind Soldier, Sandy Bordeaux, Matilda Black Bear, Monica Drapeaux, Monica Terkildsen, Joe Blue Legs, Imogene Stoneman, Betty O'Keefe, Jill Sells, Richard Sherman, and Viola Burnette.

In Kentucky, Gene Summers thanks Michael Loiacono, Stella Marshall, and Beverly Woliver for conducting the participant interviews and Peggy Barrett, Nelson Bobrowski, Mary Bowman, Kathy Brannon, Rev. Jamie Brunk, Ronnie Callahan, Joyce Corder, Marilyn Frye, Judge Jimmie Green, Judge Jimmie Herald, Lorette Jones, Juanita Kidd, Saunda King, Rev. Jerry Lacefield, Sister Lorraine, Bruce Murphy, Susan Ramos, Jeanette Rogers, Paul Sizemore, Charlotte Smith, Susan Stepp, Dr. Larry Taylor, Dr. Peg Taylor, Harold Terry, Tanya Treadway, Cal Turner, Lorrie Turner, and Audry Waters for their help with local affairs.

In Mississippi, Gene Summers thanks Mary Tullis for interviewing the TANF participants and Lilly Barner, Clanton Beamon, Tissi Brock, Ann Brown, Rev. Robert Brown, Yvonne Browne, Julia Carpenter, Jean Carson, Linda Day, Anita Hayes, Coy Henderson, Ethel Jean Hill, Ed Wilburn Hooker, Dr. Tony Honeycutt, Dr. Perry Jenkins, Janet Land, Dr. David Lee, Henry Lucket, Diane McCool, Jim Murphy, Judge A. Nelson, Dr. Auwilda Polk, Sylvester Roberts, Mickie Rodgers, Cynthia Stovall, and Clementine Williams for their assistance in numerous matters regarding their communities.

David Mushinski would like to thank Valerie Kepner, CSU Economics, for all of her help as a graduate research assistant and Stella Coleman of the Social Security Administration for data regarding SSI use in the counties and states in the study.

This study was made possible through the financial support of the National Research Initiative of the Cooperative State Research, Education, and Extension Service, USDA, Grant No. 0190121, an Annie E. Casey Foundation Grant No. 201.1855, a grant from the Southern Regional Development Center at Mississippi State University Subcontract No. 01800 280211-01, a Rural Poverty Dissertation Fellowship from the Rural Policy Research Institute's Rural Poverty Research Center, a National Science Foundation Career Award No. 0092527, and the Monfort Family Foundation's Colorado State University Monfort Professorship.

INTRODUCTION

Since enactment of the Personal Responsibility and Work Opportunity Reconciliation Act of 1996 (PRWORA), policymakers, agency administrators, community activists, and academics from a broad range of disciplines have debated and researched the implications of welfare reform in the United States. A tremendous body of literature has developed over the last seven years in an effort to assess how effectively welfare reform has accomplished the goals of PRWORA. Quantitative analyses relying on nationwide data sets focus on participants in more populated areas because most welfare participants live in those areas. Proponents of welfare reform have tended to focus on participants who, because they already had the skills, abilities, and opportunities to become employed, have easily made the transition to work.

This monograph focuses on a group of welfare participants who live in rural pockets of extreme, persistent poverty where there are few job opportunities because local formal economies and labor markets are generally weak, systems of education are poor, transportation is difficult, child care is hard to come by, and levels of human capital are extremely low. The weakness in local economies may be seen in unemployment rates in these areas, which generally exceed those observed during the Great Depression. Because of the weakness of these economies, the types of formal market relationships found in more mainstream economies in the United States are not present. Instead, extensive networks arising out of local social and cultural relationships provide support, determine outcomes in local labor markets, and generally affect implementation of welfare reform in ways that might seem unexpected to mainstream society. The qualitatively distinct nature of the local economic, political, and social conditions in these areas dictate the need for an ethnographic focus on welfare reform in areas of deep, persistent poverty.

This study focuses on eight counties that have been among the poorest in the United States for decades. These rural areas, described as "pockets of persistent rural poverty" (Partridge and Rickman 2005), differ in many ways from the places in which the average welfare participant lives, and apart from their poverty, from each other as well. Shannon and Todd counties in South Dakota are within the boundaries of the Pine Ridge and Rosebud Sioux (Lakota) reservations, respectively, with an almost exclusively Native

American population, a particular history with the land that precedes the creation of the United States, and a distinct social and cultural perspective. Owsley and McCreary counties in Kentucky lie in the Cumberland Plateau of the Appalachian Mountains, which has long depended on extractive industries for employment and has long been associated with poverty and isolation, despite an almost exclusively white population. Maverick and Starr counties in Texas are in the Rio Grande borderlands of the United States and Mexico, a historically contested territory conquered by the United States in the Mexican-American War in 1848. With populations that are almost exclusively of Hispanic origin, the counties are marked by high concentrations of non-English-speaking immigrants, numerous *colonias* or unincorporated housing developments, migrant farmworkers, and attitudes around family life that flow in large part from the Roman Catholic religious tradition. Finally, Holmes and Sunflower counties in Mississippi rest within the Mississippi Delta, with large African American populations, whose ancestors were part of the violent systems of slavery and Jim Crow until only forty years ago. All these communities experienced various and unique forms of social, political, and economic oppression and exhibit distinct interactions between gender, race, ethnicity, and class that influence the implementation and outcomes of welfare reform (Duncan 1996; Savner 2001, 101).

This monograph combines quantitative and qualitative pictures of these rural areas to explore how economic, social, and political conditions influence the implementation and outcomes of welfare reform under PRWORA. This exploration engages the most commonly raised questions about welfare reform. Did caseloads decline and if so, why? What happened to those who left welfare? How are current and former welfare participants, their families, and their communities faring under the new policies? We first paint a picture of these places based on quantitative measures of caseload declines, labor markets, and poverty. We then examine the details of the lived experience of welfare reform by adding qualitative ethnographic materials to the analysis. Through the voices of participants and other members of their communities, we show how caseloads, labor markets, and poverty are intricately enmeshed in culturally constructed local alternative survival strategies. We show how the promise of local administrative control through devolution was accompanied by benign neglect, profiteering, political maneuvering, and social exclusion on the one hand and a commitment to improving access to services on the other.

The economic conditions in all of these counties are unlike those experienced by the vast majority of people in the United States. The rich, deep, pervasive market economy taken for granted in the rest of the United States does not, and may never, exist in most of these places. Instead, distinct logics of socially embedded rights and obligations, driven by factors other than hours and wages, provide the essential ingredients for survival in these communities. While some of this economic activity is reducible to dollar values and clock time, much of the breadth and dynamics of these economic relationships cannot be expressed in monetary terms. As a result, there are many unacknowledged and misunderstood aspects of survival in a world of poverty that can only be explained through the rarely heard voices of those living in these contexts (Besharov 2003, 12; Newman 1999). Our findings show extensive participation in formal and informal work and network-based reciprocal exchange that expose as false the dichotomy between the morally deserving "working poor" and the undeserving "welfare poor" put forth by proponents of the more punitive elements of welfare reform.

Following Braudel, we refer to the economies in these areas as "everyday economies" because they blend activities and resources to meet the needs of material life in the context of unrelenting poverty, played out through the "humble lives at the foot of the ladder," far from the decision-making centers of global capital, far from the privilege to choose (Braudel 1981, 562–63). By observing these small, everyday details of economic life indefinitely repeated across apparently disparate regions of poverty, their apparent dysfunctionality is ultimately explained not as an alternative to modern capitalism but as an experience of it (Braudel 1981, 560). Sporadic and unprotected wage work, fluctuating public benefits programs, subsistence and self-provisioning, home-based enterprise, and family support all move fluidly across the artificial boundaries of formal and informal, cash-based and "free," legal and illegal, employed and unemployed. The socially based nature of these everyday realities also demands that research on the effects of welfare reform account for the broader context in which poor families live and reflect the perspectives of the poor themselves (Blank 2002, 1119; Foster and Julnes 2001, 128; Seccombe, Walters, and James 1999, 204; Newman 1999). While the alternative aspects of these everyday economies may initially appear removed from mainstream experiences, it might be wise for us all, given the national trend toward a postindustrial economy, to become more familiar with the logic and practice of economic activities organized outside a market paradigm (Beck 2000; Peck 2001; Taylor 1996; Larson 2002; Staudt 1998).

Given that PRWORA devolved responsibility for welfare reform to the state level and below, there is tremendous variability in how reform has been implemented, making it difficult to make blanket assertions about its impacts. Reform in these areas of persistent poverty can only be understood in reference to the distinct political, economic, and institutional histories of the states in which they are located. For example, among the states included in this study, the policies of the program known as Temporary Assistance to Needy Families (TANF) vary widely. The Kentucky TANF program is relatively progressive in contrast to those of other states with regard to the level of cash assistance, access to education and training, and access to work-support services and transitional assistance. Likewise, South Dakota's cash assistance available to families who are not living in public or shared housing is extremely generous. At the opposite extreme Texas and Mississippi are among the states with the lowest benefit levels in the country, the toughest work requirements and sanctions, and the most limited access to education and work-support services.

Similarly, structures of welfare administration vary markedly across the states in the study. For example, while workforce development policy in South Dakota is set by one statewide workforce development board, the state board in Texas is divided into twenty-eight regional boards, which have some degree of autonomy in determining local policies applied to TANF participants and low-wage workers. By focusing in depth on four states and how their policies are implemented at the county level, this study complements the limited number of policy studies which attempt to compare state variability in administration in a systematic way (Blank 2002). The daunting challenges of welfare reform encompass issues of race and bureaucratic stringency, internal political favoritism and factionalism at the local level, and the tensions between adequate flexibility to meet local needs and the excesses possible with inadequate national oversight.

Regarding our findings, no county in this study experienced the widespread and dire impacts of welfare reform on material well-being predicted by its most critical opponents (Edelman 1997). In short, for most participants the negative impacts of PRWORA were largely limited to increased administrative and logistical frustrations. This is largely explained by the fact that the low benefits available through AFDC/TANF in these states were never more than supplementary or temporary sources of income for most recipients. As Kathryn Edin and Laura Lein (1997) found in the pre-TANF urban context, families who used welfare relied much more heavily on income from work, networks of family and kin, and the more substantial in-kind forms of public assistance of housing and food stamps. It is also explained by the fact that most respondents, like most people who ever use welfare, used it only temporarily to deal with short-term emergencies (Bane and Ellwood 1994). That said, the impacts of TANF in these counties were not benign. We did find that the reliability of TANF as a means of dealing with emergencies was largely inadequate and while it rarely caused incidents of extreme material hardship, it also failed to prevent them.

It is also crucial to note that other elements of PRWORA did in fact result in direct and significant negative impacts on family well-being, including homelessness and hunger among the small percentage of our sample that was worst off in terms of the strength of their private networks. The welfare system was the primary safety net for these families, and they fell through the holes ripped in it by welfare reform. There is no way to assess the extent to which such families were under- or oversampled in this study.

Additionally, among those families who negotiated the new policies without negative impacts on *material* well-being, many reported loss of access to educational opportunities such as GED classes and community college. Some were literally pulled from GED classes to perform "voluntary" community service cleaning bathrooms and offices.

Ultimately, our findings must be interpreted in light of the purpose of the welfare system in the United States in general and, more specifically, the Personal Responsibility and Work Opportunity Act of 1996. Welfare in this country has never been about reducing poverty or eliminating its hardships. Rather, U.S welfare policy has always been designed to enforce work and keep all but the most desperate families off the rolls (Piven and Cloward 1971; Peck 2001). The hardships experienced by the families interviewed for this study were less the effects of changes to an inadequate welfare system than the interaction of those changes with far more significant and long-standing political, economic, and social relationships that barred them from full participation in mainstream institutions. Welfare did little more than allow these families to pay a utility bill, buy diapers, baby wipes, or some clothes for their children. It is therefore not surprising that in most cases reduced access to such paltry assistance did not produce dire results.

Similarly, reform did not deliver the job opportunities and work supports promised by some proponents (Haskins 2001). The families and community leaders interviewed here expressed disillusionment with what many had seen as the promise of PRWORA to deliver new opportunities. The rhetoric of reform created expectations that participants would receive substantive assistance with education, training, and job placement. For the most part, those expectations were not met. Indeed, opportunities for education and training, and thus finding good work, appear to have existed in larger measure in these communities under the so-called welfare trap of Aid to Families with Dependent Children (AFDC) than exist under TANF (Julnes, Hayashi, and Anderson 2001, 128; Seccombe, Walters, and James 1999, 204).

Even though the poverty in these counties is exceptional, and the economies exceptionally weak, the conditions are nevertheless similar to the circumstances faced by other impoverished groups in the United States generally. People who have long been marginalized in the mainstream U.S. economy are often found living in pockets of poverty within broader urban areas with vibrant economies. Indeed, the urban poor are often located far from available jobs in suburban areas (Wilson 1996; Newman 1999). An outside observer looking at the economy in the urban context might miss these pockets of poverty and thus fail to understand their isolation from the mainstream economy in the area. For example, it is easy for a politician to tour a suburban area, see a "Help Wanted" sign on a fast food restaurant, hop out of his limousine, and argue that jobs are available to people on welfare without appreciating the difficulties that people on welfare encounter in getting to and holding a job. We might view the counties we consider here as such pockets stripped of the surrounding, and obfuscating, economic vibrancy. In this sense, the lessons learned here have broader applicability.

Data Collection and Interviews

Respondents for this study were obtained through a nonrandomly selected sample of eight nonmetropolitan counties with long-standing rates of extremely high poverty. The counties were selected from the four major pockets of persistent rural poverty in the United States. These are Native American reservations, Appalachia, the Rio Grande Valley, and the Mississippi River Delta. Persistently poor counties are defined by the U.S. Department of Agriculture (USDA) as those exhibiting poverty rates of 20 percent or higher for the last four decennial censuses. While these pockets of poverty lie within the boundaries of numerous states, we chose to select from only four (South Dakota, Kentucky, Texas, and Mississippi) in order to examine state-level variation in TANF administration. Within each state, the two persistently poor rural counties with the highest poverty rates according to the 1990 census were selected for in-depth case study to monitor the impacts of work-oriented welfare reform. These were Shannon and Todd counties, South Dakota; McCreary and Owsley counties, Kentucky; Maverick and Starr counties, Texas; and Holmes and Sunflower counties, Mississippi.

To capture the particular experience of welfare reform within the context of extreme rural poverty, we applied a combination of qualitative and quantitative methods. The surprisingly limited secondary literature on any of these specific counties indicated the need for close ethnographic treatment of these communities. To trace the initial and longer-term impacts of welfare reform, we conducted two sets of qualitative interviews. Between February and October of 1999, we conducted in-person interviews with a total of 73 current and former TANF participants and 80 agency personnel, community leaders, and business owners within the states and counties. Between April 2002 and October 2003, we conducted a second round of in-person interviews with another 175 current and former TANF participants and 168 agency personnel, community leaders, and business owners.

We selected the TANF participants through a snowball sampling technique. Interviews were conducted or facilitated by residents of each county who had experience working in the community, but were not employed by a state or county welfare agency (for the key characteristics of the TANF participant interviewees, see Appendix A). The interviews consisted of questions from two standardized but open-ended questionnaires. The participant questionnaire covered experiences with TANF, education and work history, and impressions of their communities' responses to welfare reform. The community leader questionnaires covered local programs, responses to welfare reform, and economic development efforts and were further customized for social and human support service workers, educators, and business leaders. Interviews lasted from thirty minutes to over five hours. The flavor of the participants' perspectives is conveyed through their direct comments whenever possible, but names are not used to protect confidentiality.

Data were also collected from national data archives such as the U.S. Census of Population and Housing, state and local government administrative records, and records of nongovernmental organizations for the period 1990–2002. The secondary data collection examined demographic, economic, and social conditions in these counties over the period immediately prior to and after welfare reform. Because of the small population size within each of the counties and because the participants interviewed were not selected in a fashion that permitted statistical analysis, many of the empirical methods used in national studies of welfare reform were not possible or practical for this study. The quantitative analysis also presents data on the clusters of persistently poor rural counties in which our case study counties are embedded. The clusters are comprised of counties that are contiguous to our case study sites as well as those which are contiguous to all of the counties that fall along a straight line drawn between the two sites in each state. South Dakota was the one exception to this selection rule, where all the rural counties in the state containing a reservation were selected. Data on the clusters represent more general conditions in the pockets of rural poverty (see Appendix B for a list of all counties included in each cluster).

Organization of the Monograph

The monograph is structured as follows. Chapter 1 describes the nature of the regions and counties involved, explains the basics of welfare reform and what it replaced, and explicates the theoretical framework applied in this study. Part I analyzes what the numbers tell us about welfare reform in these eight persistently poor counties by comparing them to each other as well as to their respective states and the nation as a whole. Each chapter addresses one of three key questions about welfare reform. Chapter 2 looks at what the numbers reveal in relation to caseload trends. Chapter 3 explores what the numbers indicate happened to those participants who left the programs, and whether or not they were absorbed by local or regional labor markets. Chapter 4 examines statistical evidence for indications of how current and former TANF participants are doing in the wake of welfare reform in relation to poverty, family well-being, and community strength.

In Part II, we turn to the qualitative evidence to examine how the statistical indicators are either supported or contradicted by what the people on the ground told us about welfare reform, local labor markets, and the well-being of their families and communities. These chapters present the reader with a picture of the real opportunities available to TANF participants and the constraints associated with implementing TANF from the perspectives of participants, TANF administrators, county leaders, and other community members. Chapter 5 examines in-depth the effect of TANF on reservations in South Dakota, focusing on the Pine Ridge (Shannon County) and Rosebud (Todd County) reservations. The findings highlight the special social and political influences on labor markets in this area; the best and worst of interagency collaboration within the complexities of overlapping tribal, state, and federal jurisdiction; the often ambiguous and contradictory status of women and children within a native society impacted by a century of modernization policies; and the social, economic, and political alternatives to market ideology that are asserted within the broader context of these Lakota communities. Chapter 6 examines the experiences of TANF in Owsley and McCreary counties in the Cumberland Plateau of Appalachian Kentucky. Among our case study states, Kentucky TANF policy was more liberal with regard to education. Combined with strong community leadership, high levels of community involvement, and interagency cooperation and facilitated in part by small, racially homogeneous populations, this liberality produced some positive responses to welfare reform. Chapter 7 examines welfare reform in Starr and Maverick counties, Texas, in the context of increasing in-migration and trade across, and development along, the Texas-Mexico border. Findings highlight the widely overlooked role of local administration and implementation practices on caseload dynamics and participant outcomes; the interaction of state and regional politics with federal evaluation criteria in determining where, when, and how welfare reform was imposed; participant experiences under the "Choices" work-first program; the specific labor market hardships encountered by those who left TANF for work; and the key role of border institutions in mitigating the potentially harsh impacts of welfare reform. Chapter 8 focuses on the Mississippi Delta. In Holmes and Sunflower counties, where devolution took the form of unguarded privatization, bureaucratic stringency, and cost shifting, welfare rolls plummeted but household hardships increased, leaving poor families to find employment in a shrinking and segregated labor market with minimal training or support for education.

Chapter 9 brings together the quantitative and qualitative pictures of TANF in these pockets of persistent poverty to examine similarities and differences in welfare reform across the focus counties, and to appreciate both the dreams and the disenchantments experienced by these communities, as well as the amazing diversity across places that are lumped together as uniformly poor.

Overall, the nature of the local everyday economy, relationships of family and community, local administrative variability, and the potential dark side of devolution emerge as critical contexts for understanding the full import of welfare reform.

ONE

Rural Places, State Welfare Policies, and Theoretical Bases

Broad institutional structures condition the implementation and impacts of welfare reform. Each of the areas included in this study share one fundamental experience: they have not been integrated into the contemporary global capitalist system of accumulation in a way that benefits large segments of their populations. They arrived at that condition, however, via very different routes. The contemporary Native Americans of South Dakota are descendants of a people oppressed by the "manifest destiny" and military might of the U.S. federal government. Dispossessed of lands and livelihood, they have long been isolated on remote reservations. The African Americans of the Mississippi Delta are but a handful of generations removed from slavery. Many still recall legally segregated schools, bus stations, lunch counters, and bathrooms. They continue to face enormous barriers today to full participation in key institutional spheres, particularly education (U.S. Commission on Civil Rights 2001). The Anglo poor of Appalachia are a people left in the wake of the decline of the coal mining industry and the "company towns" it supported. Finally, the poor of the Rio Grande Valley are, by and large, immigrants or the children or grandchildren of immigrants, many of whom were pulled into and pushed out of the United States as needed according to the demand of U.S. farmers for cheap labor.

In the Delta and the Valley, histories of economic hyperexploitation, political marginalization, and racism largely explain the persistence of poverty. The legacy of the company town and the unique economic and political arrangements that accompanied it underlies Appalachian poverty. Native Americans, who were never integrated into the white economic system beyond appropriation of their natural resources, continue to suffer extreme exclusion from mainstream U.S. institutions. In all four cases, systems of political paternalism were established through which outsiders, be they the federal government, white plantation owners, absentee coal magnates, or large ranchers, directly and tightly controlled access to jobs and government programs and benefits. While the political situations in these areas are far more complex today, largely as a result of the civil rights movement and the rise of indigenous persons to local positions of power, the legacy of paternalism remains alive and well, affecting efforts at economic development and, in our case, the implementation of welfare reform.

Rural Diversity

All the counties in this study are rural in that they are not part of a metropolitan statistical area (MSA) and do not contain places with populations over 50,000. All of them also lie within pockets of extreme and persistent poverty. Within these broad bounds there is also immense variation in terms of history, culture, social organization, and economic base and development.

History and Culture

What is now the state of South Dakota was once a portion of the Great Sioux Reservation, the aboriginal territory of seven bands of Lakota speakers as well as several other tribal groups, recognized through the Fort Laramie treaties of 1851 and 1868. The discovery of gold within Lakota territory, the subsequent illegal seizure of Lakota lands in the Black Hills, and the victory of an allied force of Lakota and Cheyenne over Custer at Little Big Horn in 1876 led to political pressure to further reduce Lakota lands in 1877. The Great Sioux Agreement of 1889 subdivided the Great Sioux Reservation into six smaller Lakota reservations and seized for the U.S. public domain another 11 million acres of Lakota lands reserved by the Fort Laramie treaties. A combination of resource appropriation and military-style oppression defined the thirty years of Lakota experience after South Dakota became the fortieth state on November 2, 1889.

The Pine Ridge and Rosebud agencies were established in 1877 and 1878 respectively, more than a decade before the state of South Dakota existed, and the exterior boundaries of the Pine Ridge and Rosebud reservations were established by the Great Sioux Agreement in 1889. Shannon County, completely encompassed by the borders of the Oglala Lakota's Pine Ridge Sioux Indian Reservation in southwestern South Dakota, and Todd County, encompassed by the Sicangu's Rosebud Sioux Indian Reservation, have experienced extreme poverty since they were created in the early 1900s.

Since their inception, the economic resources of the Pine Ridge and Rosebud Indian reservations were never adequate to meet the needs of the Lakota people. In this context, the need for social services on these reservations has consistently been great over the last one hundred years. Beginning with treaty annuities and rations obtained in exchange for major land cessions, there has been a series of federal programs aimed at alleviating the harshest conditions of poverty there (Biolsi 1995, 23–25). The federal government has always played a heavy hand in determining the content, scope, and beneficiaries of any economic development carried out on these reservations. Although the Indian Reorganization Act of 1934 granted nominal self-governance to the Oglala Sioux Tribe and the Rosebud Sioux Tribe (Biolsi 1995, 86–98), genuine self-determination was not a legislative option for the tribes until the Indian Self-Determination and Education Act was passed in 1975 (Castille 1998). Over the last twenty-five years, these tribal governments have started to take the reins in planning and implementing economic development strategies that will in fact benefit Lakota people, but the process has been difficult and complex (Pickering 2000a).

Welfare reform was imposed on the Pine Ridge and Rosebud reservations within the local context of complex and intertwining economic, political, and social concerns. This local context has raised some unique questions in assessing the impact of TANF on Indian Country (Berman 2003; Biolsi et al. 2002). TANF is the latest in a long line of programs aimed at reducing the costs of welfare on these reservations. TANF work requirements combine with family dynamics and ethnic tensions in the context of a community already burdened with high rates of poverty and unemployment (Pickering 2000a).

The Kentucky counties included in this study, McCreary and Owsley, are located in a pocket of persistent rural poverty that envelops the southern Appalachian Mountains and runs through a huge swath of Eastern Kentucky, the Cumberland Plateau. More than two hundred million years ago the Cumberland Plateau was a high plain that had risen from the floor of an even more ancient sea bed. For millennia, lush vegetation grew, died, and piled up in this enormous bog, turning first to peat and then to coal. Eventually, streams carved out deep valleys, creating sharply serrated mountains and exposing the thick seams of coal.

This is Daniel Boone country, where European settlers wrested the land from Native Americans and established thriving agricultural communities in the rich valleys (Billings 1988; Billings, Blee, and Swanson 1986). But the curse of coal descended upon the region in the mid-nineteenth century. Ruthless coal and timber corporations extracted the valuable resources and left the descendants of these fiercely independent settlers in bleak and demoralizing poverty (Caudill 1962; Schwartzweller, Brown, and Mangalam 1971; Tickamyer and Tickamyer 1987; Duncan 1992, 1996).

Located within the boundary of the Daniel Boone National Forest (which takes up about 85 percent of the county's land), McCreary County remains geographically isolated today. Such spatial isolation should not, however, be equated with the continuation of the "hillbilly" stereotypes of mountaineer life. Molded plastic deck furniture has replaced handmade rockers and cane-bottom chairs, and satellite dishes far outnumber the dog houses. Late model cars and pickup trucks stand in the driveways, and front yards are no longer "used parts departments" waiting to be scavenged when vehicle repairs are needed. Roadside ditches no longer serve as the county dump. The vast majority of the homes are well maintained, although modest in size. Mobile homes appear everywhere, mixed in with on-site constructed brick homes and frame houses with vinyl siding. Most of the people of McCreary County live modestly, but they take pride in what they have. Urban ways are familiar to most McCrearians, but they prefer the rural life style.

Owsley County is similarly isolated in space and perhaps more so in institutional terms. One county official jokingly said, "There are two Kentuckies—Bluegrass Kentucky and Appalachian Kentucky. Owsley County is neither." It is tucked away in the western foothills of the Cumberland Plateau and on the eastern fringe of Bluegrass country. The eastern and southern areas of the county begin to resemble the mountaineer country that lies farther to the east in the coal fields with steep mountainsides and deep valleys. But in Owsley County the mountains are not so tall, the valleys are not so deep, and the creeks are not so torrential.

Local pundits say that Owsley County lies between the mountains and the bluegrass and gets the benefits of neither. The fact that it has one of the highest poverty rates in the state and the nation gives some credence to the claim. State politicians reject the county's requests for development assistance because it neither qualifies for state aid to address the ills of coal-mining country nor meets the requirements for the large investments in industrial and urban development that are bestowed upon the communities of bluegrass country. To participate in the harvests of these investments residents of Owsley County must commute or migrate. Meanwhile, conditions in Owsley County change slowly, despite major efforts by local leaders to generate economic development.

Among the peoples and places of Texas, there exists enormous variation; yet the Rio Grande Valley is clearly the most distinct part of the state. Marking the line that either connects or divides Texas and Mexico, it is home to a hybrid culture that is as much Spanish and Mexican as it is "American." According to the census, over 80 percent of the overall Valley population is of Hispanic origin, and in Starr and Maverick counties that proportion is over 95 percent. In both counties, Spanish is the dominant language spoken at home and in coffee shops, retail stores, and community centers. Because of their huge populations of new immigrants from Mexico, documented and undocumented alike, and their famously "independent" local political cultures, Starr and Maverick are considered something akin to "outlaw" territories in the region and are respectively referred to as "the most Mexican place in the United States" and the "Free State of Maverick County."

It is difficult to convey the extent to which and the various ways in which Mexico and the United States come together in the Valley. Nestor Rodriguez and Jacqueline Hagen (2001) begin their discussion of U.S.-Mexican relations at the border by citing a Mexican official in Nuevo Laredo, who stated: "The border zone is a different world, apart from the rest of the two countries. The people of Laredo, Texas understand this, and we [in Nuevo Laredo] understand it" (88). This statement is even truer in the more isolated Starr and Maverick counties, where the political, economic, and social practices and the beliefs and conflicts of the past play a larger role in the present than they do in large urban areas that have diversified and moved on. As local leaders often told us, "You see the river as something that divides us, we see it as something that unites us."

The connection of past with present is mirrored in the connection between Mexico (past) and Texas (present) in the lives of Valley residents and is captured on the streets of Rio Grande City and Eagle Pass. The main street of Rio Grande City in Starr County is devoid of pedestrians and lined with eroding and faded nineteenth-century brick and adobe buildings from its riverboat heyday. These relics of the past contrast sharply with the steady stream of gleaming eighteen-wheelers, late-model pick-up trucks, and SUVs flowing back and forth between Laredo, northern Mexico, the Gulf Coast of Texas, and parts farther north. A similar juxtaposition obtains between the "old" downtown of Eagle Pass in Maverick, bustling with Mexican shoppers who cross the international bridge from Piedras Negras by foot, and a new commercial district which looks down upon the old from a perch on a high bluff overlooking the Rio Grande and offers more affluent shoppers—perhaps more Mexicans than Texans—access to major U.S.

franchises. In both places, the cultures, commerce, and people of Mexico and the United States are inextricably linked.

Although not immune to the colonizing effects of the "McCulture," Maverick and Starr exude a strong sense of place or "authenticity." For example, handmade Mexican pastries, tamales, and enchiladas, among many other things, are found at numerous family-operated bakeries and lunch stands. Local farmers in Rio Grande City sell fresh fruits and vegetables from the back of old trucks directly across the street from the Wal-Mart Super Center.

In sum, the Valley is the epitome of a hybrid social space, and this characteristic is also strongly manifest in local political institutions. A combination of Mexican political practices with U.S. machine politics largely defines the operation of public administration in the Valley. It is common knowledge that elections for local offices in these counties are still bought and that entrenched political bosses stand behind the candidate of the day. Public schools as well as the local workforce development boards that now manage TANF are not immune from the influence of bossism. In the context of weak private sector labor markets, control of these institutions equates to control over the distribution of the few good jobs in the area as well as funds for private construction contracts and other contracts for services.

It should also be noted here that, in terms of development, the Texas counties are outliers among our counties in a number of key respects. Their populations have exploded over the past thirty-five years. In recent years, the development of the *maquiladora* sector, the admission of Mexico into the General Agreement on Trade and Tariffs (GATT), and finally, the passage of the North American Free Trade Agreement (NAFTA) have contributed to solid economic growth. In short, they are well on their way to becoming metropolitan counties or to incorporation into expanding MSAs.

The Mississippi Delta is a vast alluvial plain that began to take form when the most recent glaciation receded and left behind land that includes portions of Arkansas, Louisiana, Mississippi, Missouri, and Tennessee. Since then, the annual flooding of the Mississippi River has deposited billions of tons of rich topsoil onto the bed of what once was a sea.

Beginning in the 1820s, settlement of the Mississippi Delta was left to wealthy pioneers who had the financial resources and sufficient slave labor to undertake the forbidding task of draining and clearing the virtually impenetrable jungle of brambles and swamps. Their reward was a land of endlessly deep and rich soil that could grow cotton for decades without "wearing out." Huge cotton plantations, worked by slave and then tenant labor, created great wealth for a handful of white planter families and deep and pervasive poverty for the mostly African American farmworkers.

Emancipation created a temporary crisis in agricultural labor relations. Former slaves were free to seek their economic fortunes, but lacked financial capital to establish their own farms or businesses. Moreover, the vast majority lacked the human capital necessary to seek employment in nonagricultural occupations. And in any case, that would have required migrating to communities outside the Mississippi Delta, an experience for which they were ill-prepared. At the same time, white planters still owned huge tracts of rich agricultural land, but did not have the capital to pay wages for the labor that slaves had provided to operate their plantations. Planters and freedmen experimented with a number of labor arrangements throughout the 1870s and 1880s. By the turn of the century sharecropping had gained widespread popularity among planters and ultimately became the dominant arrangement (Dollard 1957 [1936]; Powdermaker 1968).

In the sharecropping system, which lasted for nearly three-quarters of a century, the white planter typically provided the tenant with land, seed, tools, housing, a garden plot, and other "furnishes." The mostly African American tenants provided the labor. The planter also might provide the tenant farmers with advances against next year's crop for meager amounts of food, medical care, clothing, Christmas gifts, and family emergencies. At the end of the harvest season when the crop was sold, the tenant received a share of the sales revenue, usually 50 percent, from which the planter deducted the advances made to the tenant. On the face of it, the system seemed fair; however, since most tenants were illiterate, the planter kept all the records, a situation unscrupulous planters exploited to their economic advantage (Dollard 1957 [1936]). The system also demanded total dependence of farm tenants on the planter elite to provide for their needs.

One might reasonably argue that the institution of sharecropping created a culture in which dependency was deliberately constructed and relatively easy to transfer from the wealthy planter to minimal government-sponsored welfare programs. When welfare programs were established by the federal government, "they were tightly controlled and manipulated by the elite, who ensured that the benefits reinforced rather than undermined their absolute control over the livelihood of those who remained. . . . They were able to make federal assistance available to black families when there was no work in the field, and then have it withdrawn when they needed workers" (Duncan 1999, 92). James C. Cobb concludes, "Although the cumulative influences of the New Deal and World War II brought dramatic changes to the

Table 1   Demographic characteristics of the counties studied (2000)

	Total population	Area (in square miles)	Persons per square mile	Rural percentage of population
Kentucky	4,041,769	39,728	101.7	44.2
McCreary	17,080	428	39.9	100.0
Owsley	4,858	198	24.5	100.0
South Dakota	754,844	75,885	9.9	48.1
Shannon	12,466	2,094	6.0	75.9
Todd	9,050	1,388	6.5	100.0
Texas	20,851,820	261,797	79.6	17.5
Maverick	47,297	1,280	36.9	11.6
Starr	53,597	1,223	43.8	21.3
Mississippi	2,844,658	46,907	60.6	51.2
Holmes	21,609	756	28.6	72.1
Sunflower	34,369	694	49.5	36.3
United States	281,421,906	3,537,438	79.6	21.0

SOURCE: U.S. Bureau of the Census, 2000 census, Summary Tape File 1, table DP-1. Profile of General Demographic Characteristics: 2000; U.S. Bureau of the Census, State and County Quick Facts.

Delta's economy, the transformation of Delta agriculture left the region's planter-dominated social and political framework fundamentally intact" (Cobb 1992, 207). Welfare reform must be understood within this context.

Diversity in Demographics

The differences between these poor rural counties may be seen in statistical data. The Mississippi and Texas counties are significantly more populous than the others, while Owsley County is especially notable because of its small population. Population densities in all these counties are below their state averages and the national average (Table 1). Greater population density often translates into a greater density of demand for products and, thus, more businesses and employment (Mushinski and Weiler 2002, 79). While the Texas, Mississippi, and Kentucky counties are generally similar in their densities, the South Dakota counties stand out in that their population densities are less than one quarter of the population density in Owsley, the next most sparsely populated of our study counties.

The type of economic activity undertaken in the county is affected by the degree to which the population in a county is rural and the distribution of that population through the county. Towns can support specific retail activities only when their populations reach a certain size (see Deller and Harris 1993 and Mushinski and Weiler 2002). The greater the population in a town the greater the array of retail establishments the town can support and, consequently, the greater the number of retail jobs in the county. Looking within these counties, the concentration of populations in towns varies significantly (see Table 1). Using the census definition of an urban area as a place of more than 2,500 persons, McCreary, Owsley, and Todd counties have no urban centers. In contrast, the populations of Maverick and Starr are both heavily concentrated in urban centers. Indeed, Maverick County is notably less rural than either Texas or the United States as a whole.

Another way of identifying the economic potential of towns in these counties is to look at the largest cities in each county. The Kentucky and South Dakota counties have the smaller cities, while the Texas and Mississippi counties have the larger cities (Table 2). The size of Eagle Pass in Maverick County reflects its healthy array of retail activity, while the nominal size of Booneville in Owsley County indicates that Owsley has a limited level of overall retail economic activity. Furthermore, the statistic for Maverick County understates its potential for retail activity, because it does not include the approximately 130,000 people who live just across the bridge from Eagle Pass in Piedras Negras, Mexico.

The physical size and population of a county also affect the flow of market-related information among market participants. Information is important to the efficient functioning of markets. The efficient operation of labor markets requires that job applicants easily obtain information about job openings; the cost of a job search increases as it becomes more difficult to obtain information about openings. Similarly, in the face of limited information, employers often rely on informal networks to fill jobs (Weiler 1997; Mushinski and Pickering 2005). Generally, the costs associated with these informational limitations lead to economic inefficiencies, which may include unemployment. Market participants in rural areas tend to face marked informational limitations (Scorsone and Weiler 2004). Counties like Shannon and Todd, which are physically large but have low population densities and small towns, may face the greatest informational limitations.

Before and After Welfare Reform:
The National and Local Specifics of TANF

The Personal Responsibility and Work Opportunity Reconciliation Act of 1996 (PRWORA) consolidated three federal-state matching programs, Aid to

Table 2 · Largest cities in each county (2000)

	Largest city	Population
Kentucky		
McCreary	Pine Knot	1,680
Owsley	Booneville	111
South Dakota		
Shannon	Pine Ridge	3,171
Todd	Mission and Antelope	1,771
Texas		
Maverick	Eagle Pass	22,413
Starr	Rio Grande	11,923
Mississippi		
Holmes	Durant	2,932
Sunflower	Indianola	12,066

SOURCE: U.S. Bureau of the Census, 2000 census, Summary Tape File 1, table DP-1. Profile of General Demographic Characteristics: 2000.

Families with Dependent Children (AFDC), Emergency Assistance (EA), and the Job Opportunity and Basic Skills program (JOBS) into one block grant program called Temporary Assistance to Needy Families (TANF). The three major goals of the program were to "end the dependency of needy families on government benefits," "prevent and reduce the incidence of out of wedlock pregnancies," and "encourage the formation and maintenance of two-parent families" (Greenberg and Savner 1996). The most significant provision of PRWORA was its replacement of AFDC, a federal entitlement program established through the Social Security Act of 1935, with a block grant to the states. This meant that, one, families with children who once qualified for public assistance on the basis of income no longer had a federally protected "right" to it and, two, significant authority over program design and use of funds was devolved to the states. Adult recipients of TANF were mandated to perform various work activities in exchange for assistance, and their households were subject to five-year lifetime limits on benefits. Under the system, eligible children could be denied access to assistance in myriad ways, including time limits and full-family sanctions. Additionally, if a state were to expend all of its TANF funds, eligible families willing to participate in work requirements could be placed on waiting lists (Super et al. 1996). Moreover, it allowed states to deny additional benefits to welfare participants who had additional children (i.e., the "family cap") and any benefits to unmarried-teen parents not in school or not living with an adult guardian (Greenberg and Savner 1996). The law made its deepest cuts, however, by reducing the number of persons eligible for the Food Stamps Program and Supplemental Security Income, including legal resident aliens. While some of these cuts were restored in the Balanced Budget Act of 1997, they remain sharp.

Devolution granted states broad latitude in setting TANF eligibility criteria, benefit levels, administrative structure, participation requirements, time limits, and sanctions. This latitude was limited, however, by federal mandates. Perhaps most important, the federal law required that 25 percent of all state's caseloads participate in a "qualified work activity" during 1997. This rate increased by 5 percent annually to 50 percent of all family caseloads in 2002. The law also set work participation levels at 20 hours per week for single-headed families (increased to 30 hours per week in 2000) and 35 hours per week for two-parent families (increased to 55 hours). States were also required to engage all "nonexempt" TANF participants in work within 24 months of receiving assistance (U.S. DHHS 1997). All of the states examined here require participants to begin working immediately, a low-cost approach to reform known as "work-first" (see Peck 2001).

South Dakota's TANF Program

South Dakota was an early participant in work-oriented welfare reform, implementing its first waiver program in 1994. On July 1, 1997, the welfare waiver became the state TANF program. In light of a statewide unemployment rate of about 3 percent since 1996, some people have argued that employment is available to all who seek it (South Dakota Department of Labor 2003). However, the state has several pockets of chronic poverty, predominantly concentrated on and near Indian reservations, which bear no resemblance to the optimistic economic outlook of the rest of the state. Analysis of a cluster of seven persistently poor South Dakota reservation counties reveals significantly higher rates of unemployment, as well as poverty, and more extensive participation in welfare programs than statewide figures.

Under PRWORA, Native American tribes were given the option of participating in state TANF programs or running their own tribal programs. However, neither the Oglala Sioux Tribe nor the Rosebud Sioux Tribe chose to administer their own TANF grants, despite years of planning and efforts to identify the resources needed to run reservation TANF programs. The tribal decisions not to administer TANF turned in large part on the decision of the state of South Dakota not to provide tribes with the state's matching portion of welfare benefits, in contrast to states like Arizona where tribes received the matching portion from the state and are administering their own TANF programs.

The historic conditions on Pine Ridge and Rosebud, and their high rates of unemployment, led to some special provisions in the implementation of TANF. Foremost, in determining the number of months of assistance received, the South Dakota Department of Social Services (DSS) disregarded any months during which the parent participating in TANF lived on an Indian reservation if, during the month, at least 50 percent of the adults living on the reservation were unemployed (South Dakota DSS 1997). Because of the high unemployment rates, estimated by the Bureau of Indian Affairs at 74 percent for both Pine Ridge in 1998 and Rosebud in 1997, there were no lifetime limits imposed on either reservation at the time of our data collection.

South Dakota's TANF plan has been and still is a work-first program that states as a goal the movement of "applicants/recipients into whatever private sector job they are capable of handling as quickly as possible, while trying to empower them to support their own families." The plan places strong emphasis on immediate labor force participation, diversion of TANF applicants to other programs, and follow-up to prevent future welfare use (South Dakota DSS 2003). In general, everyone who received aid under TANF had to complete thirty work activity hours per week, twenty if they had children under six. Work activity could include a job search, volunteer or community service, or working for pay, depending on the person's skills, ability, and experience. Individuals had the option of finding their own jobs or being placed by the DSS. While satisfying the work requirements was not a problem in the non-native areas of the state, the requirements have been a problem on the reservations. As one South Dakota DSS employee explained, "The federal requirements are up to a 50 percent caseload reduction, but people have been hired that were put into placements, so we more than met that expectation. That's state-wide. It's been a struggle since the first year on the reservation to meet 50 percent. Most clients we have now are repeats, and they know a work site already they can use."

The state plan provides transitional support for cases closed for employment that "appear[s] to be permanent." This support includes a Transitional Employment Assistance Payment, which consists of an additional payment for one month. The South Dakota DSS may provide the following support services to assist applicants/recipients: minor auto repairs and car insurance, relocation, interview expenses, employment-related medical care, clothing related to training or employment, tools or equipment, job-related education, and diversion payments for unmet expenses (South Dakota DSS

2003). Furthermore, the state places strong emphasis on follow-up to help make permanent the transition from welfare to work. Follow-up is intended to help former participants find child care, transportation, housing, community resources, and secure new jobs if needed. Supportive service payments may also be used to help former participants remain employed and thus avoid reapplication for cash assistance. Finally, follow-up is intended to assist in the development of opportunities to upgrade employment through additional skills training (South Dakota DSS 2003).

Kentucky's TANF Program

Kentucky's welfare reform policies were by far the most progressive of the four states included in this study. Kentucky's TANF program, called the "Kentucky Transitional Assistance Program," or K-TAP, was certified by the U.S. Department of Health and Human Services on November 18, 1996. Because Kentucky was one of only a handful of states that did not implement a waiver prior to federal welfare reform, the implementation of K-TAP represented the first significant transformation of the public safety net in the state. The goal of the welfare aspect of the K-TAP program was to ensure that participants who were "work ready" obtained unsubsidized employment and that those not ready for work developed skills to enable them to work "as soon as possible" (Kentucky Cabinet for Families and Children 1997; Jenkins and Miller 1999, 3).

The Kentucky Cabinet for Families and Children (CFC) is the sole government agency responsible for the state's TANF block grant. Administration of K-TAP is the responsibility of the Department for Community Based Services (DCBS), a department within the CFC. DCBS offices are located in every county in Kentucky with case managers available to help K-TAP families reach self-sufficiency. Within the DCBS, the Division of Service Regions determines eligibility and strives to protect children and adults and create self-sustaining, self-sufficient families. The CFC also contracts with the Workforce Development Cabinet "to provide employment services to Kentucky Works participants" (Kentucky CFC 2003).

Adult applicants for K-TAP, except teens enrolled full-time in school, are required to register for work with the Kentucky Works Program and complete a "Transitional Assistance Agreement" or "self-sufficiency plan." The Transitional Assistance Agreement identifies an employment goal, the employment services to be accessed, and work activities required. Regional variances across the state, such as rates of unemployment and poverty, figure in the development of the self-sufficiency plan. Individuals assessed as work-ready are referred to the Department of Employment Services, which either places them with an employer as an unsubsidized worker or in a qualified work activity such as the Other Work Employment Program (OWEP) or community service. All work-ready participants are to immediately begin at least twenty hours per week of participation in job search activities and are expected to secure unsubsidized work within six months. Applicants are deemed work ready if they live in an area where jobs are available and meet the following criteria: have a high school diploma or GED, know a skilled trade or have prior successful work experience, and are not incapacitated or caring for a severely disabled child (Kentucky CFC 1997). Supportive services provided through K-TAP are limited "to the extent that funds are available" (Kentucky CFC 1997).

Two types of sanctions are employed under K-TAP, those that remove only a portion of a family's K-TAP check and a "discontinuance," which cuts all of a family's cash assistance. Discontinuances are applied when a family has been previously sanctioned for at least six months and has received assistance for at least twenty-four cumulative months. Benefits are reinstated upon compliance with requirements. The CFC monitors sanctioned families to determine if the sanctions have a detrimental effect on well-being. In cases where family members, particularly children, might be harmed by the loss of benefits, the CFC designates a "protective payee" (Jenkins and Miller 1999), someone outside the household to receive the benefits and pay for the children's needs.

Texas's TANF Program

In 1995, the Texas legislature initiated welfare reform by passing House Bill 1863, which directed the Texas Department of Human Services (TDHS) to restructure the state's welfare system and apply for a federal waiver to implement a state welfare-to-work program. Administratively, the law created the Texas Workforce Commission (TWC) to oversee all workforce development programs and coadminister AFDC with the TDHS. Under the TWC, the state was divided into twenty-eight administrative regions called "Local Workforce Development Areas," and all workforce-related programs in each area were placed under the control of the "Local Workforce Development Board." The intent of the new administrative structure was to meet the private sector demand for labor, and the law mandated that boards be comprised of at least 51 percent business leaders (Pindus et al. 1998).

The law led to the statewide implementation in 1997 of "Achieving Change for Texans" (ACT), the state's work-first waiver program. The main provision of the waiver was the "Choices" program, which emphasizes "immediate labor force participation" over education and training. Under Choices, every nonexempt TANF participant was required to begin participation in work activities prior to being certified to receive assistance. The ACT program also created a system of "tiered" time limits such that adult TANF participants deemed work ready were eligible for only twelve months of assistance, while those in need of some remedial assistance were given twenty-four months. Those in need of significant assistance, the "hard to serve," were given thirty-six months of eligibility. These time limits applied only to the eligibility of household heads. Thus, children in Texas can continue to receive TANF once their parent(s) have exhausted their time. This means that households can continue to receive their TANF grants less the adult portion of $78 per month after having timed-out. Additionally, parents can return to the program after a five-year "freeze-out" period (Cherlin et al. 2001, 7).

Applicants were required to sign a "personal responsibility agreement" with the state in which they agree to fulfill the work requirements and cooperate with state efforts to obtain child support, among other things. Sanctions were also limited to the noncompliant adult's portion of the TANF grant ($78), and failure to comply with any of the above conditions was cause for sanction (Pindus et al. 1998). In addition, the state allowed the twenty-eight local workforce development boards some latitude to decide which counties in their regions would be subject to work participation requirements (see Chapter 7 for a detailed description of Texas TANF policy).

Mississippi's TANF Program

Historically, Mississippi made minimal investments in human services and relied heavily on federal funding, private charities, particularly faith-based groups, and district or local organizations to provide human services (Kirby et al. 1998, 6–8). The state's lack of commitment to helping TANF participants make the transition from welfare to work is highlighted by the fact that it was among a handful of states that failed to apply for the U.S. Department of Labor's "Welfare to Work" grants program. This program, established in the wake of welfare reform, made $3 billion available to the states to provide additional resources above and beyond TANF block grants to help the hard-to-serve into the workforce. By failing to put up the matching funds required to participate in the program, Mississippi left $12,990,000 on the table in Washington, D.C., for fiscal year 1998 alone (Nightingale and Brennan 1998).

Mississippi's AFDC program offered the lowest cash benefit in the nation, $120 a month for a single parent with two children. Such low benefits contributed to low rates of participation; only 30 percent of families eligible for the program in 1995 received it compared to 47 percent nationwide (Kirby et al. 1998, 5). According to the Urban Institute, the Food Stamps Program, Supplemental Security Income (SSI), and emergency food and utilities were much more important forms of assistance in Mississippi than welfare (Kirby et al. 1998, 9).

As in Texas, underdevelopment of welfare-to-work services in Mississippi prior to welfare reform led to administrative chaos after welfare reform (Mead 2004; Breaux et al. 2000). Prior to the enactment of PRWORA, the Mississippi Department of Human Services (MDHS) determined eligibility for AFDC, food stamps, and Medicaid and referred a small percentage of participants to the State Department of Economic and Community Development (MDECD) for Job Opportunities and Basic Skills program (JOBS) services. The case management of JOBS participants was performed by the state's Planning and Development Districts or PDDs. These multicounty entities are regional "intergovernmental bodies," which were created in the late 1960s to implement regional economic development plans and help diversify employment and build skilled workforces within each region. The PDDs contracted the actual delivery of job readiness services to the Mississippi Employment Security Commission (MESC). Yet another set of nongovernmental agencies, Community Action Agencies (CAAs), managed the Child Care Development Block Grant (CCDBG) (Kirby et al. 1998, 14).

According to the Brookings Institution and the Urban Institute, coordination between the state MDHS and the PDDs was weak (Breaux et al. 2000; Kirby et al. 1998). Reliance upon the PDDs and CAAs to manage programs meant that services were provided by organizations with funds administered by state agencies but not directly managed by them (Kirby et al. 1998, 15). According to the Urban Institute, in the areas of "employment and training, child care, and emergency services, there [was] little but a policy role for the state's [MDHS] and [MDECD]" (Kirby et al. 1998, 5).

The roots of welfare reform in Mississippi date to 1992, when Republican gubernatorial candidate Kirk Fordice made welfare reform a top issue. In 1993, the Mississippi legislature passed the Mississippi Welfare Restructuring Program Act, mandating the MDHS to seek waivers from the federal government to alter the state's AFDC program. On December 22, 1994, Mississippi's New Direction Demonstration Program was approved by the U.S. Department of Health and Human Services. The waiver was implemented between October 1995 and January 1996 and became the model for the state's TANF plan, approved in October 1996. The New Directions demonstration was also a work-first program, and all non-exempt AFDC and Food Stamp Program participants who failed to find immediate private sector employment were placed in subsidized work. A participant's AFDC and Food Stamp grants were used to cover all but $1.00 per hour of the minimum wage, which was paid by the employer (Kirby et al. 1998, 5).

The program also reorganized the delivery of services through the creation of "One Stop Shops," which put MDHS eligibility workers, JOBS case managers (from the PDDs), and job readiness providers (from the MESC) under one roof so that applicants met with all three upon applying for assistance (Kirby et al. 1998, 19). Similar to the Texas program, participants who were not immediately employable or could not find work were required to complete up to twenty hours of Basic Job Readiness / Life Skills training during the first week of a four-week training program designed to help them gain and retain employment. Assessments were made of those who did not find work. They could then be referred to additional job search or placed in remedial services, community service, or vocational education (Brister, Beeler, and Chambry 1997, 15). The maximum number of work hours required of participants was equal to their combined TANF and Food Stamps benefits divided by the federal minimum wage (Mississippi Department of Human Services 2003).

Theoretical Frames

Devolution, State Policy, and Local Administration

A central debate in the welfare reform literature focuses on whether welfare reform or strong labor demand caused the marked decline in welfare caseloads in the late 1990s. This debate remains unresolved, in part, because it attempts to uncover relationships of cause and effect using units of analysis (states) that are not homogeneous across regions in terms of the implementation of welfare reform, labor market conditions, and service delivery capacity. Bradley R. Schiller (1999) attributes the ambiguity of the findings to researcher's failure to account for intrastate variation in welfare reform, that is, the jurisdictional differences in the content, timing, and enforcement of welfare regulations *within* states. By incorporating such variation into his model, he finds that state welfare reform initiatives were the key factor that drove caseload declines. Moreover, he attributes all of the aggregate impact of these programs to a few "tough" provisions that limited access to cash benefits. This study lends ethnographic support to Schiller's argument.

In the counties studied here, caseload declines occurred more as a result of local welfare administration and policy than transitions to employment. Welfare offices across the nation have struggled with the transition to TANF as their historical role of determining eligibility and administering benefits has been extended to include assisting participants in finding work (Gais et al. 2001). Because TANF agencies are now more likely to be involved in a broad array of formal and informal relationships with public, nonprofit, and for-profit service providers, staff work loads and training needs are quite different than they were under AFDC (Burt 2002, 172–74; Gais et al. 2001). None was less prepared to provide supportive services and find jobs for TANF participants than those analyzed here. In general, states included in this study made few investments in pre-reform work programs such as JOBS. As a result, they were ill-prepared for the sweeping and potentially costly changes mandated by PRWORA. In South Dakota, Mississippi, and Texas underdeveloped administrative capacity and conflict resulted in serious failures and regional inequities (see also Besharov 2003, 17; Bradshaw 2003; East 1999, 301; Winston 2002; Mead 2004; and Capps et al. 2001).

Welfare reform greatly increased the discretion exercised by local case-workers and thus increased the potential for inequitable treatment. The combination of local control and mandatory work requirements allowed the individual characteristics of caseworkers and the culture of local county welfare offices into the eligibility determination and job-placement process. It also affected the distribution of other support services. These "street corner bureaucrats" became extremely important in determining the individual outcomes of TANF participants. Understanding their role is crucial to understanding the real impacts of reform (Foster and Julnes 2001, 130; Reisch and Sommerfeld 2003, 317).

The literature shows that race, class, and social networks play key roles in the distribution of jobs and public benefits in high-poverty rural areas. Cynthia Duncan (1999) found that blacks in the Mississippi Delta and poor whites from "bad" families in Appalachia were discriminated against in local welfare offices in access to jobs and services. Kenneth Finegold and Sarah Staveteig (2002) found that upon their departure from welfare to work, whites were more likely to receive discretionary support from their caseworkers, such as health insurance, job training, or help with expenses (207). Susan T. Gooden (2000) found that African American welfare participants were interviewed five minutes or less, while their white counterparts were interviewed at least ten minutes, even when they had less education or experience. Yet another finding showed that African Americans were more likely to have left welfare because of administrative problems, time limits, or a determination by their social workers that they were not following rules than were whites or all races combined (Finegold and Staveteig 2002, 207–8; see also Littrell and Diwan 1998). When combined with the subjective perceptions of employers that white employees have better "soft skills," like getting along with coworkers, the probabilities for successful transition to work take on distinctly racial dimensions (Finegold and Staveteig 2002, 212; Holzer, Stoll, and Wissoker 2001, 38).

Racial issues also arise in voluntary exits from welfare and exits forced by the imposition of sanctions or time limits. While African Americans and other "less desirable" clients are less likely to be offered positive incentives, such as opportunities to obtain good jobs and support services, they are also more likely to receive negative incentives to quit the program. A major qualitative study of welfare reform conducted in Boston, Chicago, and San Antonio (the "Three Cities" study) found that three times as many families lost TANF because of sanctions than because of time limits, that most sanctions were for missed appointments or failures to meet with caseworkers rather than for work-placement problems, and that 17 percent of the sample had their benefits terminated or reduced for not following administrative rules (Cherlin et al. 2001, 2, 4, 6). A particularly worrisome finding is that those most likely to be sanctioned may be those most in need of support or most subject to other forms of discrimination. The Three Cities study found that households receiving sanctions tended to be the more vulnerable; that is, headed by individuals with lower levels of education and poorer health. Those households had lower monthly incomes, suffered more hunger, lived in poorer housing, and had fewer necessities, including telephones and cars (Cherlin et al. 2001, 5). A study of welfare leavers in rural areas by Bruce Weber, Mark Edwards, and Greg Duncan (2003) also found that the positive benefits of welfare reform tended to be captured by those who were best off to begin with, whereas sanctions tended to be concentrated among those worst off.

Caseload declines also fail to reveal the importance of local political dynamics under reform and the potential for TANF to reinforce the position of local elites and further social exclusion. Good government is key in making policy initiatives successful. Lawrence Mead (2004) argues that since states with histories of strong administrations and good government are more effective at implementing social policy, measures are needed that improve the quality of government itself. As devolution provides more authority to local governments, more attention should be paid to their capacity for handling these new burdens, particularly since greater variability is likely to emerge and local implementation may differ widely from formal descriptions of state programs (Blank 2002, 1121; Lobao and Kraybill 2003).

In short, the substandard local labor market conditions found in persistently high-poverty rural areas tend to be accompanied by substandard social service systems and ineffective political leadership. Given these deficits, some authors have argued that key universal elements of PRWORA, particularly its maximum lifetime limit of sixty months and mandatory participation rates should be amended to account for such variation (Weber and Duncan 2001).

An important characteristic of many persistently poor rural areas is that not all residents are poor. Indeed, such regions tend to exhibit extreme income inequality grounded in class differences. Rural communities represent a type of "micro social system," with the entire class structure of power and domination, inequality and stratification, social networks and social exclusion, located within the boundaries of a single place (Duncan 1996, 105). In poor rural places, a political economy that relies on low wages and extreme control over labor generates a two-class system of haves and have-nots. Patron-client relationships undermine trust in both social institutions and personal social relationships (Duncan 1996, 119). To understand persistent poverty, it is therefore imperative to study the social class context and the way the class structure in a community shapes opportunities for mobility and prospects for community development (Duncan 1996, 103, 119).

In local rural contexts, class is closely associated with race within "social relations that are institutionalized in the rural political economy—slavery, sharecropping, migrant labor pools, and reservations—that perpetuate poverty for African Americans, Native Americans, and many Hispanic Americans" (Duncan 1996, 109–10). For example, in the Mississippi Delta, census data on poverty show that white Delta residents are not only much better off than their black neighbors, but equal to or better off than the national population. African American residents in parts of the Delta experience poverty at a rate three to five times that of the nation and are similarly disadvantaged in terms of income and education (U.S. Bureau of the Census 1999).

Some would argue that "no social issue in the United States can be discussed without talking about race" (Levine 2001, 737). Because PRWORA does not explicitly address racial and ethnic disadvantages, its implementation is likely to aggravate them (Finegold and Staveteig 2002, 217). The process of welfare reform at the state level reveals dimensions of racial politics. Those states with poor incorporation of African Americans and other minority groups into the workforce, like Mississippi, Texas, and South Dakota, were at the forefront of adopting punitive welfare reform through state waivers (Zylan and Soule 2000, 624–25) and historically insisted on local-level administrative flexibility to ensure the continued supply of low-wage laborers (Breaux et al. 1998; Quadagno 1994). Racial composition had a strong and significant effect on whether restrictive welfare policies were enacted or not, with higher concentrations of minorities correlating with more restrictive policies (Zylan and Soule 2000, 625, 639; Soss et al. 2001, 384, 389–90).

Reliance on Social Networks and the "Everyday Economy"

The myriad disadvantages encountered by rural minorities in pockets of persistent poverty in negotiating locally controlled, work-mandated, and time-limited welfare reform raise serious concerns about family well-being. While some commentators cite caseload declines as indicating the success of welfare reform (Rector and Fagan 2001; Haskins 2001), the phenomenon of families returning to welfare raises questions about the ability of TANF leavers to sustain employment.

An estimated 15 to 30 percent of the families on the TANF caseloads cycle off and onto TANF, generally because they have low total household incomes and no other sources of support when they suffer setbacks. There are limited data about this group, and yet they are the one category of participant which appears to have experienced a substantial increase in hardship because of welfare reform (Besharov 2003, 12). Scholars and policymakers acknowledge how little is understood about low-income life and the social supports that are strained when one leaves TANF without regular work (Besharov 2003, 11–12; Cherlin et al. 2001, 6; Julnes, Hayashi, and Anderson 2001, 83; Walsh and Duncan 2001, 119). This study attempts to shed light on the choices available to participants who leave TANF without jobs.

For extremely poor families, the cost of participating in TANF may be dear. Not only must they find transportation and child care but they also face lost or reduced access to supports from nonmarket systems of economic activity. Several studies have identified various forms of informal earnings as critical to the survival of welfare participants, because of the inadequacy of the support provided by state welfare benefits packages (Edin and Lein 1997; Pickering 2000b; Seccombe 1999). Some of this activity is defined by the strength and resourcefulness African Americans, Native Americans, and Hispanics have developed to compensate for their deliberate exclusion from mainstream economic, political, and social institutions (Jones 1998, 700; Ownby 1999; Wagoner 2002; Vila 2000). With limited access to activities within formal markets, alternative activities defined by social relationships, culturally defined obligations, and sporadic opportunities come to dominate economic life for these marginalized communities.

The "everyday economy" is not limited, however, to the informal exchanges which occur outside formal state regulation. Rather, it represents the totality of economic activities in which low-income families engage to make ends meet, including how they merge participation in formal and informal sectors and how participation in one is often contingent upon participation in the other. For example, state assistance programs, such as food stamps, are often key resources in the everyday economy.

Community and Family Well-Being: TANF and the Role of Women

One cannot assess the group impacts of individuals exiting from TANF by measuring caseload declines. Communities may be at the limits of their abilities to absorb those displaced from welfare without any real job prospects. Family and community well-being depends in large part on the well-being of women. Yet within the massive volumes discussing welfare reform, few explicitly pursue the implications of the fact that the policy change is primarily affecting women (Gault and Um'rani 2001, 102). Poor single-mothers made the smallest gains of any demographic group over the economically strong 1990s, with some at the very bottom actually losing ground (Blank 2002, 1119).

In addition to the well-documented disparities in labor market outcomes that continue to affect women's earnings and occupational status, social disparities also plague the efforts of women to leave poverty through work. The role of women in the workforce and in the home has been heavily contested and revised over the last forty years. It is interesting to keep in mind that in 1960, only 28 percent of married women with children were in the workforce, whereas by 1992, that number had increased to 68 percent (Hochschild 1998, 530). On the one hand, women are said to want to work outside the home to increase their incomes, provide security from a divorce rate of more than 50 percent, engage in the challenges and community of work, and acquire the identity provided by a job (Hochschild 1998, 529, 532; Seccombe, Walters, and James 1999, 201–2). At the same time, there has been a "stalled gender revolution," in which the social norm of women as caregivers has not changed significantly, so while women are more involved in the workforce, men receive no recognition for engaging in housework and child care or taking on the emotional labor of women (Hochschild 1998, 529–31; La Rossa 1998, 377–78, 383). Poor and less educated women who resist the notion that mothers of young children should work outside the home end up even more vulnerable in the event of divorce or abandonment (Finegold and Staveteig 2001, 217; Hansen and Garey 1998, 672; Smith 2002, 135).

In addition to increasing the burdens on women, this stalled revolution has also produced a "care gap," in which the needs of children and families are simply not being met to the same extent they were forty years ago (Hochschild 1998, 528; Myles and Quadagno 2000, 160; White 2001, 136). The TANF perspective on women as, first and foremost, members of the official workforce and its policy prescription of mandatory work addresses neither the stalled gender revolution nor the care gap. Indeed, it represents a new social contract in which care work not provided through the market is assigned no value at all (Myles and Quadagno 2000, 160; White 2001, 135).

A largely overlooked contradiction in the TANF work requirements is the fact that participants are by definition raising children who need time, care, and affection. Mandating work in low-skilled, inflexible work placements interferes with the care and nurturing of the participants' children (Beck 2000, 42). This group of impoverished parents is expected to manage their own transition to work and the inevitable illnesses of their children without accumulating sick leave, vacation days, compensation or flex time, or the financial bonuses that allow affluent parents to cope with the conflicts between parenting and work.

To understand the impacts of TANF work requirements and how the children of women who leave welfare are doing, research must address the broader context in which poor mothers live and the challenges they continue to face once they are in the workforce. Those challenges include depression, illness, childcare problems, and problems with male partners who hold traditional views of the role of women and mothers (Foster and Julnes 2001, 128). Between 34 and 64 percent of welfare-to-work participants are estimated to be former domestic violence victims, and 15 to 32 percent current victims (East 1999, 297; Lawrence 2002, 2; see also Smith 2002, 154). And while all social classes of men include batterers, poor women are more likely to be trapped in a violent situation because of their economic vulnerability (Ptacek 1998, 620; Smith 2002, 141). While PRWORA allows states to provide some temporary relief for victims of domestic violence and most states have created such legislative or regulatory exemptions, eighteen states provide no exemptions at all (Smith 2002, 161), and many states with exemptions provide only weak protection for women. In Texas, for example, the exemption from paternity identification expires after one year, after which time participants must identify the fathers of their children or lose TANF benefits (Smith 2002, 159).

A major problem with PRWORA is that, from the perspective of participants, the new system is more rigid than AFDC and allows women less flexibility in dealing with such complex realities than AFDC did. Welfare caseworkers who are now under pressure to meet participation rates are often more rigid than private sector employers in demanding that TANF participants place every aspect of family life below their obligation to appear at the work site. For those with jobs, low wages and limited hours of work are exacerbated by the costs of going to work in the first instance. The biggest market costs of being in the workforce are child care and transportation. One of the unstated outcomes of welfare reform is an increase in the amount of time, for both men and women, that lies within the cash economy, especially child care (Hochschild 1998, 534).

Therefore, if the measure of welfare reform's success is stronger families and children, the jury is still out (Besharov 2003, 14). The information on how children are faring under TANF remains limited, especially given the heterogeneity of the population of persons who ever use TANF (Rickman and Foster 2001, 60–61). Nationally, objective measures indicate little improvement in poor children's well-being. Child poverty rates in 1998 were 18.9 percent nationally, but 36.7 percent for African American children (Bernstein 2001, 92). According to Kids Count, children living in working-poor families increased from 4.3 million in 1989 to 6.9 million in 2001 (Kids Count 2003; Robinson and Nackerud 2000, 196). Hispanic children covered by health insurance dropped by 5 percent since welfare reform (Finegold and Stavetieg 2002, 210). And while parental involvement has been shown to offset some of the disadvantage of poverty, the work requirements of TANF directly conflict with the time participants need for parenting (Beck 2000, 38–39, 42). Certainly, children are the victims of the care gap (White 2001; Hochschild 1998). In all, better measures of well-being are needed to test the premise that work makes single-parent households better off, and a more complete picture is needed of the changes in the actual economic well-being of less-skilled single-mother families and their children.

The Personal Responsibility and Work Opportunity Reconciliation Act of 1996 is blind to how issues of race, ethnicity, class, and gender are intricately tangled with politics and economics. The case studies in this monograph will demonstrate that these issues are critical in determining whether or not welfare reform has been a success. The rhetorical promise of devolution is governmental decision-making situated at the local level so that the "true" needs and priorities of coherent communities are realized. The nightmare of devolution is the transfer of governmental funds to local elites to reinforce and enhance power differentials and economic inequalities that have selectively

included the favored and excluded the disfavored from civil society for generations (Duncan 1996; Finegold and Staveteig 2002, 204; Soss et al. 2001).
The political question for welfare reform is whether TANF has achieved
its promise or whether it has been a nightmare.

PART ONE

What the Numbers Tell Us

TWO

Welfare Caseloads:
Changes in Public Assistance Program Use

The implicit goal of ending welfare as we "knew" it was the elimination of the federal entitlement to cash assistance benefits for working-age adults with children. From this perspective, reductions in the number of TANF cases are the ultimate measure of welfare reform success. Since passage of PRWORA in 1996, nationally there has been a 60 percent decline in the TANF caseload (Besharov 2003, 5–6). One avenue of research has explored whether or not these declines can be attributed to changes in welfare policy, and whether those who leave TANF end up in the workforce, as policymakers assume, or somewhere else.

If success for welfare reform is equated with caseload declines, then the success is dramatic, not only for the nation as a whole, but even in these pockets of persistent rural poverty. The economy of the United States from 1996 to 2000 was a best-case scenario for the implementation of welfare reform, given the strong demand for workers and other favorable macroeconomic conditions (Finegold and Staveteig 2002, 213). Looking at the pre-TANF state waivers under AFDC, James P. Ziliak and his colleagues conclude that caseload declines between 1993 and 1996 were largely caused by robust state economic activity, not federal welfare policy waivers (2000, 583). According to Douglas J. Besharov, welfare reform can account for about 25 to 35 percent of the caseload decline, the national economy for a more important 35 to 45 percent, and expanded aid to low-income working families, like the Earned Income Tax Credit, for another 20 to 30 percent (2003, 9). Rebecca Blank concurs that virtually all research agrees that state economies had a significant effect on caseloads, but that economic changes alone cannot explain the majority of caseload movements over the 1990s, indicating that policy variables also matter (Blank 2002, 1134–35). For the

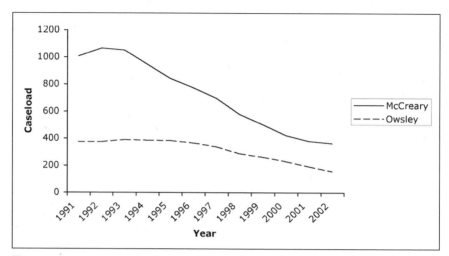

Fig. 1   TANF/AFDC cases, Kentucky

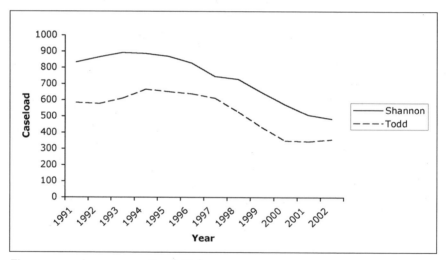

Fig. 2   TANF/AFDC cases, South Dakota

eight counties in this study, there were substantial drops in TANF/AFDC caseloads after welfare reform, the number of food stamp recipients generally fell over the 1992–2002 period, and the number of SSI recipients generally increased between 1992 and 1996 and leveled off or fell thereafter (Figures 1 through 4). With the exception of Starr County, caseloads fell after peaking between 1993 and 1994. The rate of decrease generally accelerated after 1996, likely reflecting implementation of TANF. The percentage changes

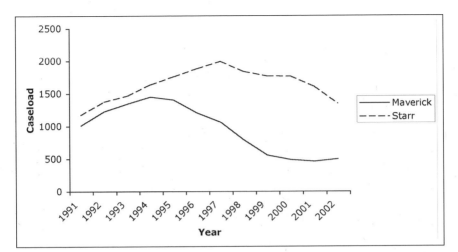

Fig. 3   TANF/AFDC cases, Texas

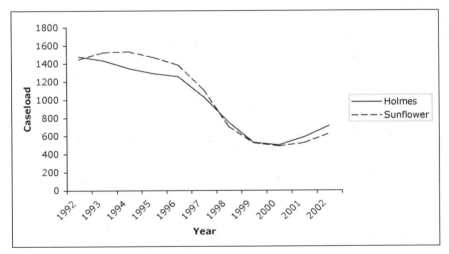

Fig. 4   TANF/AFDC cases, Mississippi

in caseloads in the Kentucky and South Dakota counties did not differ notably from the changes in their respective states. State-level data for Mississippi and Texas were not available for 1996 to 2002. In several counties, caseloads increased nominally in the early 2000s, likely reflecting the weaker national economy.

Table 3 shows the change in caseloads before and after implementation of welfare reform. After welfare reform caseloads fell dramatically. Between 1992 and 1996 caseloads fell in six of the eight counties. The largest decrease

Table 3   Changes in AFDC/TANF caseloads

	Before welfare reform			After welfare reform		
	Caseload (1992)	Caseload (1996)	Change (%)	Caseload (1996)	Caseload (2002)	Change (%)
Kentucky	82,517	71,978	−13	71,978	32,125	−55
McCreary	1.064	771	−28	771	362	−53
Owsley	372	364	−2	364	156	−57
South Dakota	7,208	6,056	−16	6,056	2,869	−53
Shannon	863	825	−4	825	482	−42
Todd	576	636	10	636	355	−44
Texas	263,632	226,816	−14	226,816		NA
Maverick	1,225	1,202	−2	1,202	488	−59
Starr	1,371	1,879	37	1,879	1,343	−29
Mississippi	60,396	47,581	−21	47,581		NA
Holmes	1,474	1,253	−15	1,253	707	−44
Sunflower	1,442	1,378	−4	1,378	622	−55

SOURCE: Data obtained in 2003 from the Kentucky Cabinet for Families and Children, the Mississippi Department of Human Services, the South Dakota Department of Social Services, and the Texas Department of Human Services.

was in McCreary County with 28 percent, while most declines were between zero and ten percent. Between 1996 and 2002 caseloads fell in all counties. The smallest decrease was in Starr County with 29 percent, while fully one-half of the counties had declines greater than 50 percent.

Prior to implementation of welfare reform, observers were concerned that people who were removed from federal welfare rolls would believe that they had also lost their eligibility for food stamps. The result would be a drop in the number of food stamp recipients that was greater than any decrease in food stamp eligibility. The number of food stamp recipients in the eight counties generally fell between 1992 and 2002, with the greatest decreases between 1996 and 2000. Figure 5 provides insights into changes in the number of food stamp recipients across the states. Because the movements of changes in recipients tended to be the same for the pairs of counties in each state, while differing across the states, Figure 5 identifies the changes in recipients for one county in each state. The changes in food stamp recipients in the Kentucky and South Dakota counties tended to be nominal. The number of recipients generally fell between 1992 and 2000 and then increased slightly between 2000 and 2002, potentially reflecting the strength of the national economy. Shannon County differed somewhat in that food stamp use increased nominally between 1997 and 2000 and leveled off thereafter.

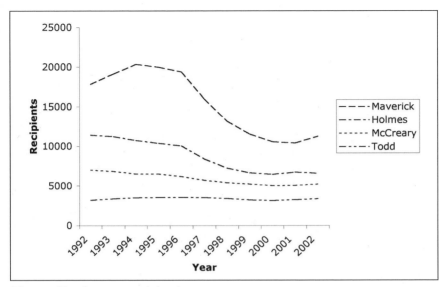

Fig. 5   Food stamp recipients

Texas and Mississippi were similar in that they experienced more noticeable decreases in food stamp recipients after 1996. Three of the counties studied in those states also experienced slight increases in food stamp recipients between 2000 and 2002.

Table 4 provides some insights into the magnitudes of changes in food stamp recipients for the eight counties from 1992 to 2002. The table indicates that during both periods the number of food stamp recipients across the counties generally fell. The Mississippi counties experienced the greatest percentage drops in both periods, while the South Dakota counties experienced nominal changes in those periods. Todd county and the Texas counties were exceptions during the 1992 to 1996 period in that they experienced increases in the number of recipients. On the other hand, the Texas counties had the largest drops in recipients between 1996 and 2002. The declines in the Texas Food Stamps caseload are directly related to provisions of PRWORA that eliminated access to food stamps for legal immigrants. The nominal nature of changes in the South Dakota counties may be due to reservation residents' greater familiarity with food-based, in-kind federal programs. Since treaties signed between Lakota tribes and the U.S. government in the nineteenth century, tribal members have had access to commodities from the federal government and have come to expect such food-based programs to be available regardless of their eligibility for other federal programs such as AFDC or TANF.

Table 4   Changes in food stamp recipients

	Before welfare reform			After welfare reform		
	Recipients (1992)	Recipients (1996)	Change (%)	Recipients (1996)	Recipients (2002)	Change (%)
Kentucky						
McCreary	6,980	6,176	–12	6,176	5,236	–15
Owsley	2,482	2,422	–2	2,422	2,035	–16
South Dakota						
Shannon	4,925	4,654	–6	4,654	4,727	2
Todd	3,186	3,541	11	3,541	3,373	–5
Texas						
Maverick	17,806	19,378	9	19,378	11,236	–42
Starr	21,305	25,858	21	25,858	17,561	–32
Mississippi						
Holmes	11,385	10,031	–12	10,031	6,583	–34
Sunflower	11,232	10,641	–5	10,641	7,382	–31

SOURCE: Data obtained in 2003 from the Kentucky Cabinet for Families and Children, the Mississippi Department of Human Services, the South Dakota Department of Social Services, and the Texas Department of Human Services.

At present, tribal members can choose between food stamps and commodities available through the Food Distribution Program on Indian Reservations (see *Code of Federal Regulations,* title 7, secs. 250, 253 and 254). Comparing the changes in food stamp recipients with welfare caseloads, we see that the decline in food stamp recipients was not as great as the drop in welfare caseloads.

We also consider changes in the number of recipients of SSI for the 1992 to 1996 and the 1996 to 2002 periods. Some observers believed that implementation of welfare reform would result in people moving from TANF/AFDC to SSI. The statistics in Table 5 do not support this hypothesis. With the exception of McCreary and Starr counties, the number of people on SSI increased between 1992 and 1996 and then leveled off or fell somewhat.

As a final matter, we turn to the sources of household income to examine the relative rates of participation in TANF relative to other programs and relative to wage work (Table 6). Most of the counties are close to the state and national averages for households with earned income, demonstrating that people in these counties do work. It is important to note that people in the Texas counties receive income from relatives who undertake migrant work in other states. The percentages of households with earnings in the Kentucky counties and Holmes County are notably below the state and

Table 5   Changes in SSI recipients

	Before welfare reform			After welfare reform		
	Recipients (1992)	Recipients (1996)	Change (%)	Recipients (1996)	Recipients (2002)	Change (%)
Kentucky						
McCreary	1,165	1,642	41	1,642	1,788	9
Owsley	667	791	19	791	777	−2
South Dakota						
Shannon	572	818	43	818	776	−5
Todd	471	486	3	486	389	−20
Texas						
Maverick	968	1,248	30	1,248	1,273	2
Starr	756	1,041	38	1,041	1,338	29
Mississippi						
Holmes	1,350	1,626	20	1,626	1,458	−10
Sunflower	1,207	1,628	35	1,628	1,422	−13

SOURCE: Data obtained in 2003 from the Social Security Administration, *SSI for States and Counties.*

Table 6   Sources of household income (in percentage of households with a given source of income)

	Types of income				
	Earnings	Public assistance	SSI	Social Security	Retirement income
Kentucky	77	4	7	29	18
McCreary	65	12	19	30	13
Owsley	59	17	27	35	17
South Dakota	81	3	3	28	13
Shannon	77	17	13	20	7
Todd	80	18	10	16	8
Texas	84	3	4	22	13
Maverick	79	9	13	29	8
Starr	77	16	13	24	9
Mississippi	77	4	8	28	16
Holmes	65	10	17	31	13
Sunflower	78	6	13	28	13
United States	81	3	4	26	17

SOURCE: U.S. Bureau of the Census, 2000 Census, Summary Tape File 3, Table DP-3. Profile of selected economic characteristics: 2000.

Table 7   Age distributions (2000) (expressed as percentages of the total population)

	0–18	19–64	65 or older	Median age
Kentucky	24.6	62.9	12.5	35.9
McCreary	27.7	61.7	10.6	34.2
Owsley	24.6	60.4	15.0	38.2
South Dakota	26.8	58.9	14.3	35.6
Shannon	45.3	49.9	4.8	20.6
Todd	44.0	50.2	5.8	21.7
Texas	28.2	61.9	9.9	32.3
Maverick	36.9	53.6	9.5	27.8
Starr	37.4	54.4	8.2	26.1
Mississippi	27.3	60.6	12.1	33.8
Holmes	32.1	55.5	12.4	29.7
Sunflower	27.9	62.4	9.7	30.2
United States	25.7	61.9	12.4	35.3

SOURCE: U.S. Bureau of the Census, 2000 Census, Summary Tape File 1, Table DP-1. Profile of general demographic characteristics: 2000.

national averages, suggesting that fewer households are engaged in their local economies.

As would be expected, the county percentages for public assistance income are all higher than their respective state and the national percentages (see Table 6). However, relative to the other counties, a smaller percentage of households in Sunflower County receive public assistance. This result is consistent with the higher income levels and lower poverty rates in this county. The Kentucky counties and Holmes County have the highest percentages of households receiving ssi or Social Security disability and old age income, consistent with the higher percentage of older people in Owsley County (Table 7).

The South Dakota counties have the lowest percentages of households receiving retirement income. This finding reflects the very low percentage of elderly people in those counties and their receipt of virtually no export income from retirees (Table 7). The percentage of households in the Kentucky and Mississippi counties receiving Social Security income is higher than the national average, reflecting the older populations in these counties. All of the statistics for the Kentucky counties and Holmes County suggest that they have fewer people in the workforce because they have more retired and disabled persons.

In conclusion, TANF caseload declines not only followed but preceded the implementation of welfare reform. At least some evidence points to a strong economy as part of the explanation. The question of why caseloads declined even in severe pockets of persistent poverty is not answered by the statistics alone, however. To determine whether participants left for wage work, we need to examine labor force statistics, which is the focus of the next chapter.

THREE

Labor Markets:
From TANF to Low-Wage Part-Time Jobs

The work orientation of welfare reform necessarily makes labor markets an integral part of any discussion of its impacts. The labor market conditions in persistently poor rural areas are marked by unique characteristics that make the implementation of successful workfare as put forth in PRWORA highly unlikely.

Job Opportunities

First, a decline in good jobs for low-skilled workers is deteriorating job security and economic stability across the nation. The United States is confronting postindustrial economic conditions, including a flight of capital to cheap labor pools in developing countries. This is accompanied by the disappearance of well-paid industrial jobs, the rise of poorly paid low-skilled service jobs, the weakening of labor unions, and an influx of migrant workers (Hochschild 1998, 529). Manufacturing jobs, the most likely to pay living wages and the least likely for underemployment, are declining nationally, with no counterbalancing increases of well-paying jobs in other sectors for unskilled workers (Beck 2000, 36; Jensen et al. 1999, 427). Instead, a rigid, multitiered service economy has developed in which people no longer move from entry-level, low-paying jobs to higher-paying jobs in the same firm but rather remain trapped in low-level, low-skill, low-paying jobs as they shuffle between industries and firms (Landale and Lichter 1997, 877). Among the "postindustrial" jobs that have been created, more than 50 percent are part time, so that by 1995, one-fifth of all jobs in the U.S. economy had been reengineered into part-time employment (Beck 2000, 37–38). This "deindustrialization" has left TANF participants in many regions competing with laid-off manufacturing workers for these "bad" jobs (Beck 2000, 38; see Nelson and Smith 1999).

Looking specifically at rural labor markets, the literature indicates major structural change since the 1970s as the rural industrial base has been transformed from agriculture, natural resource extraction, and manufacturing to services (Duncan and Sweet 1992, xxii; Nelson 1999, 22–23). In contrast to major metropolitan areas, the service sector employment that has emerged is predominantly labor-oriented and concentrated in the janitorial, fast food, hotel, and home healthcare sectors (Gorham 1992, 24; Nelson 1999; Nelson and Smith 1999). The rural areas included in this study have participated fully in these developments.

TANF precipitated over one million women moving into the less-skilled and low-wage labor market between 1996 and 2002 (La Rossa 1998, 384; Pleck 1998, 354).

While the labor markets have changed, the preconceptions of a male breadwinner in the household have not (La Rossa 1998, 384; Pleck 1998, 354). Inflexible, highly demanding jobs that assume the complete separation of market and family obligations were born of an early industrial period in which men were expected to work outside the home and women were expected to nurture the family. With deteriorating wage rates and a dramatic increase in dual-earner households, family consumption and security are even less possible for single-parent families trying to escape poverty (La Rossa 1998, 384; Myles and Quadagno 2000, 159; Pleck 1998, 354).

Women in rural labor markets face even greater discrimination than their sisters in urban areas (Lichter 1989, 200). Sex differences in rural employment-related hardship may actually have become more pronounced over the last decades, as male-female earnings inequalities are greatest in the peripheral sector of manufacturing jobs, where low-skilled laborers perform rote production processes (Jensen et al. 1999, 435; Lichter 1989, 201).

Racial dynamics also affect job prospects, both at the individual level and through the spatial segregation that is constitutive of pockets of both rural and urban poverty. Because different occupations are less accepting of nonwhite workers, a wage gap based on race alone exists for TANF participants exiting for work. White post-TANF workers earn $7.31 per hour while their African American counterparts are earning $6.88 per hour and their Hispanic counterparts are earning $6.71 per hour (Finegold and Staveteig 2002, 207–9). Among women, African Americans earn $ 0.65 and Hispanics $ 0.56 to every $1.00 earned by whites (Beck 2000, 38). In rural areas, those who are adequately employed are more likely to be white and married than in central cities, and employed rural nonwhites are 20 percent more likely to slide into underemployment than whites (Jensen et al. 1999, 425, 427).

While racial and ethnic minorities generally have been especially hard hit by the transition to a service economy (Landale and Lichter 1997, 877), racial dynamics have an even greater impact in the context of "hypersegregated" residential patterns, such as those in many persistently poor rural areas (Finegold and Staveteig 2002, 213; Hartman 2001, 91). Beginning in the 1960s, many U.S. manufacturing firms began to move basic, low-skill operations to rural Southern states where unions were absent and wages were low. During the 1980s a disproportionate share of industrial growth in rural areas was concentrated in these "bottom of the cycle" manufacturing industries, with routinized processes of production and low demand for highly skilled labor (Lichter 1989, 201). Rather than leading to diversification in these areas, the process merely continued the historical trend of rural economies concentrated in a few sectors (Latimer 1998, 71; Mencken 1997, 82). About half of the counties examined in this study, specifically the Mississippi counties and Maverick County, Texas, participated in this trend. However, with the passage of NAFTA and the rise of China in globalized production chains, these firms quickly began to disappear, leaving TANF participants in competition with displaced workers not only for jobs but also for highly limited workforce development services and opportunities.

Unemployment and Underemployment

If unemployment rates generally reflect the health of a local labor market, then all the counties in this study have labor markets in poor to critical condition. Low unemployment rates suggest that the number of people who want employment but do not have it is low. The "labor force" includes those people with jobs and those people without jobs who are actively searching for a job. The latter group constitutes the officially unemployed reflected in unemployment rates. These rates do not capture people who want jobs but who are not actively searching for them through their local unemployment offices. These people are called "discouraged" workers; and since unemployment rates do not include these workers, some argue that unemployment statistics can be misleading (Buss and Redburn 1988, 5; Lichter and Costanzo 1987).

The numbers of discouraged workers in the counties in this study are probably significant, since when there are few jobs available, employers tend to hire through the use of personal networks, and an active job search is

Table 8   Labor force involvement of persons sixteen to sixty-four

	All persons		Females	
	Not employed	In civilian labor force	Not employed	In civilian labor force
Kentucky	34.5	69.5	39.1	64.6
McCreary	52.5	53.7	55.2	50.0
Owsley	52.5	53.7	55.2	50.0
South Dakota	24.2	79.4	26.0	77.2
Shannon	63.4	55.4	62.3	54.0
Todd	49.7	61.9	47.1	62.3
Texas	34.0	70.3	40.0	64.2
Maverick	52.1	58.1	61.9	47.6
Starr	58.5	52.7	64.3	44.5
Mississippi	37.6	67.5	41.9	63.3
Holmes	53.0	57.1	53.5	53.7
Sunflower	56.0	50.5	47.3	60.5
United States	31.2	73.0	35.8	68.1

SOURCE: U.S. Bureau of the Census, 2000 Census, Summary Tape File 3, Table QT-P24. Employment status by sex: 2000.
NOTE: Entries are percentages of the population between the ages of sixteen and sixty-four.

not likely to lead to a job. A statistic that could account for discouraged workers would lie between the percentages of people not employed and the official unemployment rate.

These data refer to a person's labor force status at the time of the 2000 census. The "not employed" is the total number of people between sixteen and sixty-four who were not employed divided by the total number of people in that age group. "Percent in civilian labor force" is the number of people in the labor force in the age group divided by the total number of people in the age group.

For the places in this study, the high percentage of not employed persons indicates that a substantial percentage of the human resources in these counties are not utilized (Table 8). The national average for not employed persons is 31 percent for all people and 36 percent for females. With the exception of Todd County and Sunflower County for females, all percentages are above 50 percent, reaching a high for all persons of approximately 63 percent in Shannon County and for females of 64 percent in Starr County. The contrast in South Dakota between Shannon and Todd counties is especially notable, since Todd had the lowest percentage of not employed persons,

Table 9   Unemployment rates of persons sixteen and older

	All persons		Females	
	1990	2000	1990	2000
Kentucky	7.4	5.7	7.2	5.5
McCreary	20.4	11.3	20.3	9.5
Owsley	17.2	8.8	7.9	5.4
South Dakota	4.2	4.4	4.0	4.0
Shannon	30.5	33.0	26.3	29.7
Todd	20.6	18.4	16.5	15.1
Texas	7.1	6.1	7.2	6.1
Maverick	21.1	17.6	22.5	19.8
Starr	18.8	20.9	17.6	19.4
Mississippi	8.4	7.4	9.6	7.4
Holmes	15.8	17.3	16.1	13.3
Sunflower	10.8	12.9	13.3	13.1
United States	6.3	5.8	6.2	5.8

SOURCE: U.S. Bureau of Census, Census 1990, Summary Tape File 3, Table PO70. Sex by Employment Status: Persons 16 years and over; U.S. Bureau of Census, 2000 Census, Summary Tape File 3, Table P43. Sex by Employment Status: Persons 16 years and over.

NOTE: Entries are percentages of the population sixteen and older. The "unemployment rate" is the percentage of people in that age group in the labor force who do not have a job.

while Shannon had the highest, suggesting that Todd has a stronger labor market than Shannon.

For most of the counties in this study, females are more likely to be not employed than the general population. However, Todd, Shannon, and Sunflower counties are notable in that a smaller percentage of females in those counties are not employed compared with the population as a whole. In contrast, Starr County has the largest percentage of females not employed. Women appear to be more involved in labor markets in the South Dakota counties than in the Texas counties, as is reflected in the percentage in the civilian labor force in those counties. In South Dakota, women are in the labor force in percentages that about equal the population as a whole, whereas Texas has the greatest difference between female labor force participation and the general population. These differences reflect deep-rooted cultural differences in the role of women in these communities. The unemployment rates in all counties were above the national and their respective state averages in the last two censuses (Table 9).

With the exception of Owsley County in 2000, all counties have double-digit unemployment rates for all persons across both censuses, reaching a high of 33 percent for Shannon in 2000. With the exception of the Kentucky counties, similar results hold for females. To get a feel for the magnitude of these unemployment rates, we note that national unemployment rates never exceeded 25 percent during the Great Depression (Walton and Rockoff 1998, 517).

The statistics indicate that even if we assume that no discouraged workers exist, the human resources in these counties are significantly underutilized. The persistent magnitude of unemployment in Shannon County is especially notable. The low unemployment rates for all persons and females in Owsley County, combined with the lowest labor force participation rates, suggest that people in Owsley are not as involved in labor markets, most likely because of a generally older population. For most persons who ever use TANF in the counties in this study, chronic underemployment is as much of a problem as unemployment. The counties share a similar profile in relation to a lack of full-time, year-round work (Table 10). Full-time jobs typically involve working more than thirty-five hours a week and year-round jobs are those held for fifty or more weeks a year. All counties in the study have lower percentages of year-round, full-time jobs than the state and national averages of around 58 percent for all persons and 50 percent for females. The Texas counties, with significant populations of migrant and seasonal farmworkers, and Shannon County have substantially lower percentages of year-round, full-time jobs for both groups, with Starr County having 25 percent or fewer people in the two groups holding such jobs. These statistics, combined with the high unemployment rates, indicate that these counties have few steady jobs necessary for an effective transition from welfare to work.

The percentages of employed people who had full-time jobs provide an interesting contrast (Table 10). The percentage of people in the counties with full-time jobs was generally similar to their respective state and national averages. For all persons, Owsley and Starr counties were the only two counties below the national average for full-time work, and for females Starr was the only county below the national average. This demonstrates that people in these counties generally do work, they just do not work year-round. The percentage of people in the South Dakota counties who worked full time are interesting in that they are notably higher than the South Dakota state averages. Fourteen percent more females in the labor force in Shannon County worked full time compared with the state average. On the other hand, Shannon County had one of the lowest percentages of females

Table 10   Work status of employed persons sixteen and older

	All persons		Females	
	Year-round full time[a]	Full time[b]	Year-round full time	Full time
Kentucky	58.7	79.4	50.3	72.0
McCreary	49.4	79.8	42.0	72.0
Owsley	48.2	75.1	43.9	73.2
South Dakota	57.5	76.6	49.3	68.6
Shannon	40.9	84.7	37.8	82.7
Todd	49.8	84.5	48.8	81.3
Texas	58.8	82.1	51.4	75.7
Maverick	39.3	80.7	32.3	71.2
Starr	25.1	75.8	20.8	65.9
Mississippi	57.5	81.5	50.2	75.8
Holmes	46.2	80.6	44.6	79.7
Sunflower	51.1	82.9	45.1	77.1
United States	58.3	79.0	50.2	71.0

SOURCE: U.S. Bureau of the Census, 2000 Census, Summary Tape File 3, Table QT-P31. Work status in 1999 and earnings in 1999 of full-time, year-round workers, by sex: 2000.
NOTE: Entries are percentages of the population sixteen and older.
[a] "Year round" work involves working fifty or more weeks in a year.
[b] "Full time" work involves usually working thirty-five or more hours a week.

in year-round, full-time jobs. Again, while people in Shannon work, they do not have year-round jobs.

One hypothesis regarding the lower percentages of year-round, full-time workers may be that federal and state public assistance laws, rather than employer preferences, discourage work. Reductions in TANF benefits, the Earned Income Tax Credit, food stamps, and housing assistance may significantly influence the decision to work and how much to work. Indeed, it is well documented that such work penalties, particularly the loss of Medicaid, functioned as a strong incentive to prefer welfare over work. Indeed, under some circumstances one might lose more than $1 in benefits for every dollar earned (Nelson 2004, 14). It is not surprising that these laws create disincentives for work above a certain amount (Wolfe 2002). Ultimately, these disincentives hinder the transition from welfare to work.

The structural underemployment that obtains in these places cannot, however, be reduced to the rational calculations of persons seeking to maximize income available by combining some amount of work activity with welfare benefits. As the data show, disproportionately large percentages of persons

Table 11   Percent of employed civilian population sixteen and older in industries which produce for local consumption (2000)

	Construction	Retail	Education, health, and social services	Arts, entertainment, recreation, and food services	Public administration	Total employed in local consumption industries
Kentucky						
McCreary	7.2	12.1	20.3	7.2	4.3	51.1
Owsley	7.4	10.8	23.5	6.4	2.5	50.6
	9.4	9.3	35.5	3.9	6.5	64.6
South Dakota						
Shannon	6.3	12.0	22.0	8.3	4.8	53.4
Todd	5.8	5.8	40.6	9.8	20.3	82.3
	5.8	6.7	42.7	8.2	11.3	74.7
Texas						
Maverick	8.1	12.0	19.3	7.3	4.5	51.2
Starr	6.8	14.7	26.7	5.8	7.6	61.6
	10.7	11.7	33.7	5.6	4.0	65.7
Mississippi						
Holmes	7.6	11.8	20.1	8.3	5.1	52.9
Sunflower	5.9	11.1	22.9	4.1	5.8	49.8
	4.7	10.1	21.7	4.8	9.1	50.4
United States	6.8	11.7	19.9	7.9	4.8	51.1

SOURCE: U.S. Bureau of the Census, 2000 Census, Summary Tape File 3, Table QT-P30. Industry by sex-percent distribution: 2000.

in these counties are employed in the public sector (see Table 11). Thus, political changes and program funding uncertainties exert a large impact on work opportunity. Additionally, the prevalence of seasonal and informal work also affects work activity through no intent of individual workers. Finally, responsibilities toward children and families, including elderly relatives, often pull women out of the workforce through no fault of their own. The types of jobs available to TANF participants affect not only individual opportunities but the economic opportunities of the region as well. In analyzing the distribution of employment across industries for a region, economists distinguish between industries that are the engines of growth, in that they produce for export to other regions, and industries that produce for local consumption (see, e.g., Isserman 1980, Krikelas 1992, and Shaffer 1989). Automobile manufacturing and grocery stores make the distinction apparent. Automobiles are manufactured for export to consumers outside the area where they are produced. Grocery stores produce for and depend on consumption from local residents. Export industries like automobile manufacturing are viewed as the engines of local economies because income received by employees does not depend on the presence of local consumers. Employees in export industries will receive their income and spend most of it on local goods and services like the commodities in grocery stores. In contrast, the income received by employees in grocery stores is dependent on the presence of people who receive income from outside sources. Without people with income from outside sources, the grocery store could not exist.[1]

The census parses industries into several groups. Some groups are composed primarily of export industries, whereas other groups include local industries for the most part. Because the census asks individuals to identify the industry in which they are employed, the jobs do not necessarily have to be held in the county in which the individuals reside, but still reflect the types of jobs that are within commuting distance.

Impoverished rural communities historically have tried to attract manufacturing plants, and the experience with manufacturing is diverse across the study counties. The Mississippi counties and McCreary County have percentages of employment in manufacturing substantially higher than the national average and their respective state averages (Table 12). Since they have stronger bases in export employment, they have stronger sources of export income. At the other extreme, manufacturing activity is effectively

---

1. Some industries are hybrid in the sense that they have both local and export characteristics. For example, automobile wholesalers sell to both local residents and people outside local areas. See Nichols and Mushinski 2003.

Table 12   Percent of employed civilian population sixteen and older in industries which produce for export (2000)

	Agriculture, forestry, fishing, etc.	Manufacturing	Professional scientific, managerial	Total employed in export industries
Kentucky	3.3	17.6	6.2	27.1
McCreary	4.2	29.6	2.1	35.9
Owsley	5.2	11.9	4.4	21.5
South Dakota	8.1	11.1	5.0	24.2
Shannon	2.0	0.8	2.9	5.7
Todd	8.3	1.8	3.8	13.9
Texas	2.7	11.8	9.5	24.0
Maverick	3.8	10.1	3.3	17.2
Starr	11.5	3.0	3.6	18.1
Mississippi	3.4	18.3	5.2	26.9
Holmes	5.5	24.6	3.8	33.9
Sunflower	8.7	20.4	3.0	32.1
United States	1.9	14.1	9.3	25.3

SOURCE: U.S. Bureau of the Census, 2000 Census, Summary Tape File 3, Table QT-P30. Industry by sex-percent distribution: 2000.

absent in the South Dakota counties and in Starr County. To the extent that employment in these types of industries is important for permanent exits from welfare, then these latter counties are at a distinct disadvantage. On the other hand, in McCreary and the Mississippi counties, greater reductions in poverty rates of single-mother families with children coincided with increases in the percentage of the labor force employed in manufacturing between the 1990 and 2000 censuses.[2] Greater job opportunities in manufacturing appear to redound generally to the benefit of these families.

Agriculture, forestry, fishing, hunting, and mining depend on the natural resource base in the locality. Even though these counties are rural, percentages of employment in these industries are generally not notably higher than their state percentages (Table 12). The statistics indicate that none of these counties are natural resource dependent.

One may get a feel for the extent of export production in these geographic areas from Table 12. High percentages of employment in these industries suggest greater economic strength, relative to the other counties.

2. We compare the percentages in table 12 with data obtained from Tables P070 and P077 of the 1990 census, Symmary Tape File 3.

At the state and national levels, employment in these industries ranges between 24 percent and 27 percent. At one extreme, McCreary and the Mississippi counties have a notably larger percentage of people employed in export industries; reaching a high of 35.9 percent for McCreary County. At the other extreme, Shannon County has only 5.7 percent of its employment in these industries, which is less than one-quarter of the state and national percentages. Todd County has the second-lowest percentage of jobs in export industries. As a final matter, it is important to remember that the statistics in Table 12 do not include employment in informal and illegal export industries. This observation may be important for all of the counties but is especially true for the border counties of Starr and Maverick, both of which are alleged to function as major points of entry for illicit drugs.

All of the study counties have high percentages of the labor force employed in local consumption industries. State and national percentages for these industries are slightly above 50 percent (see Table 11). With the exception of the Mississippi counties, all of the counties in this study have percentages of employment above 50 percent in these industries, reflecting weaker employment in export production. For example, fully 82 percent of working people in Shannon County and 75 percent of working people in Todd County are employed in production for local consumption.

Not surprisingly, employment in government administration and government-funded industries, such as education, health, and social services, is also higher in all these counties than the state and national percentages. In the extreme case, over 60 percent of employment in Shannon County is in these government-provided services. A similar story holds for Todd County, where over 50 percent of employment is in these industries and, to a lesser extent, Owsley and Starr counties.

The lower percentage of employment in retail trade in Shannon and Todd counties is also notable. Not only do these counties lack export employment, but they also lack employment in the types of businesses one tends to see everywhere. To some extent, the absence of retail trade employment in the South Dakota counties may be due to their smaller populations (see Tables 1 and 2). These counties lack towns with the critical masses of people necessary to attract retail establishments and establishments which provide food and services. In any event, all of the industry statistics for Shannon and Todd counties suggest that, with the exception of resource-based industries in Todd County, there is not much economic activity and that the primary type of employment available is government-related. As a final matter, the higher level of retail trade in Maverick County, when considered in light of the concentration of people in Eagle Pass and the more than 200,000 people in nearby towns in Mexico (see Table 2), suggests that retail trade is a significant source of export employment for the county. There have also been significant changes in several of these counties since TANF was implemented (Table 13). The Kentucky and Mississippi counties generally have lower growth rates than do the South Dakota and Texas counties. Shannon and Todd counties, which had generally weak economies, experienced the largest increases in employment. Of course, these larger increases may reflect the extremely low base from which the change arose. However, the 16.7 percent drop in employment in Holmes County is especially notable. At the time welfare reform was implemented jobs were emerging in Shannon and Todd counties but leaving Holmes County.

Consistent with national trends in labor markets, manufacturing employment declined between 1996 and 2000 in many of the study counties.[3] Indeed, although manufacturing is relatively strong in McCreary, Holmes, and Sunflower counties, they each suffered losses in manufacturing employment. The 53 percent drop in manufacturing employment in Holmes is especially remarkable. All of the loss of employment in manufacturing in the county occurred between 1998, when manufacturing employment hit a high of 1,749 employees, and 2000, when that employment was 780 people.

The fall in manufacturing employment in McCreary, Holmes, and Sunflower counties may in part explain the nominal increases or decreases in population in these counties; people who lived in the counties because of those jobs migrated elsewhere (see Table 1). The drop in manufacturing employment in Holmes and Sunflower counties also likely explains the fall in per capita income in Holmes, the virtual absence of growth in per capita income in Sunflower, and the higher unemployment rates in those counties between the 1990 and 2000 censuses (see Table 10).

The contrast between the drop in manufacturing employment in Maverick County and its increase in total employment is also notable. It appears that Maverick's economy has moved from manufacturing to other export and local industries. Between 1996 and 2000, Maverick experienced a 55 percent increase in employment in services; a 30 percent increase in employment in finance, insurance, and real estate; and a 15 percent increase in retail trade. As we have seen, it also experienced a decrease in unemployment between the 1990 and 2000 censuses (see Table 10). Again, this is likely related to the large and rapidly growing population of the county, Eagle Pass, and

3. The reported manufacturing employment data uses Standard Industrial Classification (SIC) definitions. BEA manufacturing employment data for 2001 uses different, North American Industrial Classification System (NAICS), definitions. Since the SIC and NAICS data are not directly comparable, we did not report 2001 data.

Table 13   Changes in employment between 1996 and 2000

	Wage and salary employment		Manufacturing employment	
	1996 level	Change 1996–2000 (%)	1996 level	Change 1996–2000 (%)
Kentucky	1,781,551	8.7	321,386	2.8
McCreary	3,304	6.9	1,129	−5.7
Owsley	706	16.7	28	10.7
South Dakota	368,349	8.8	49,699	4.7
Shannon	2,828	37.9	0	Not available
Todd	2,592	22.3	18	Not available
Texas	8,780,039	13.9	1,100,079	3.0
Maverick	10,233	23.9	1,222	−17.1
Starr	9,970	12.6	142	7.7
Mississippi	1,182,184	6.0	253,383	−5.4
Holmes	5,880	−19.2	1,660	−53.0
Sunflower	13,525	2.6	2,984	−16.3
United States	127,264,000	9.4	19,186,900	−0.4

SOURCE: Bureau of Economic Analysis, Regional Accounts Data, Table CA25. Total full-time and part-time employment by industry.

NOTE: The manufacturing percentages use Standard Industrial Classification (SIC) definitions.

the towns located across the Mexico border; the admission of Mexico to the GATT and the growth of the *maquiladora* sector; and the explosion of trade following the passage of the North American Free Trade Agreement (NAFTA).

Jobs and Education

Access to education and training combined with some participation requirements have been shown to make transitions off welfare both remunerative and permanent (Harris 1996; Gueron 1995; see also Mazzeo, Rab, and Eachus 2003). However, in an average month in 2000, only 5 percent of TANF families had an adult receiving education or training (Besharov 2003, 7).

The federal regulations enacted under PRWORA contained strong disincentives for states to support the pursuit of education among TANF participants. Moreover, it created strong incentives for low-benefit states like Mississippi and Texas with very weak institutional bases for workforce development services to pursue low-road approaches to reform, the success of which relied on rapid caseload reductions. For example, PRWORA does not allow states to count college attendance as fulfilling mandatory work hours. To the extent that the law allows states to count participation in remedial education, such as GED, and job-targeted vocational education, such as cosmetology, it places severe restrictions on these activities. First, no more than 30 percent of a state's caseload may receive work hour credit for participation in such educational activities (including persons under the age of twenty attending high school). Second, job-targeted training programs are limited to twelve months or less. Third, in order to participate in such activities, participants must first perform at least twenty hours per week in community service or other work activity (Gault and Um'rani 2001, 104). Nationally, many welfare participants were forced to drop out of school to fulfill TANF requirements while those with the means dropped out of TANF to finish school (Gault and Um'rani 2001, 104).

Thus, the number of welfare participants in postsecondary education decreased dramatically over the period of TANF implementation (Mazzeo, Rab, and Eachus 2003, 145). Ironically, less education increases the probability of being poor, decreases labor force participation rates for both men and women, and increases the likelihood that a leaver will return to welfare, whereas postsecondary education leads to long-term employment stability and economic self-sufficiency (Harris 1996; Latimer 1998, 69; Mazzeo, Rab, and Eachus 2003, 145). Those who leave welfare without high school diplomas have greater difficulties with performance and retention in the workplace (Holzer, Stoll, and Wissoker 2001, 38).

PRWORA's restrictions on education do not, of course, apply to how states spend their own monies, and states may ignore the restrictions if they target their own funds toward such activities. Kentucky is exceptional for doing just that. Also, states that had waivers from federal law could maintain the education policies for the life of the waiver. Thus, Texas TANF administrators and participants were also able to get around these restrictions until its waiver expired in 2002 because it allowed college credit hours to count toward participation.

Rural areas are especially adversely affected by policies that disallow education, since they start from a position of disadvantage in relation to completed education (Jensen et al. 1999, 418). This rural disadvantage is readily apparent in most of the study counties. For the most part, levels of education in these counties are lower than the national level and their respective state levels, with the exception of South Dakota (Table 14). Generally, the education statistics in these counties are the inverse of their respective states as a whole, with the proportion in these counties with less

Table 14   Educational levels of persons twenty-five and older (2000)

	Fewer than nine years	Nine to twelve years, no diploma	High school diploma (or equivalent)	Some college, associate's degree	Bachelor's degree or higher
Kentucky	11.7	14.2	33.6	23.4	17.2
McCreary	26.6	20.8	31.0	14.8	6.7
Owsley	33.8	16.9	28.0	13.5	7.7
South Dakota	7.5	8.0	32.9	30.1	21.5
Shannon	9.3	20.7	26.4	31.4	12.1
Todd	6.5	19.4	31.3	30.7	12.1
Texas	11.5	12.9	24.8	27.6	23.2
Maverick	40.2	17.7	18.8	14.2	9.1
Starr	46.3	19.0	16.9	10.9	6.9
Mississippi	9.6	17.5	29.4	26.6	16.9
Holmes	17.2	23.1	26.7	21.8	11.1
Sunflower	17.0	23.7	25.6	21.7	12.0
United States	7.5	12.1	28.6	27.3	24.4

SOURCE: U.S. Bureau of the Census, 2000 Census, Summary Tape File 3, Table DP-2. Profile of selected social characteristics: 2000.

than a high school diploma mirroring the proportion in the states with postsecondary education.

All the counties in this study have educational deficiencies. The Texas counties in particular have an especially large percentage of people without much formal education; over 40 percent of persons age twenty-five and older had less than nine years of education and over 50 percent had less than a high school education. These figures reflect the high percentages of residents born in Mexico, a legacy of discrimination against Hispanics in Texas schools, and the politicization that pervades the hiring of teachers and administrators in border school districts resulting in unaccountability accompanying ineffectiveness. Generally, the levels of education in these counties undercut the prospects for these counties to attract employers with good jobs to offer to skilled employees.

Low Wage Rates

The trend away from livable wages in the growing low-skilled labor market means that in many places the problem is not finding a job but finding one that pays a living wage (Weber and Duncan 2001, 5). Deteriorating economic conditions and low wages for less-skilled workers means finding employment is no guarantee of escaping poverty (Blank 1997; Bradshaw 2003). The hours of work available in this "new economy" tend to be less than what many workers would prefer, and the problem of underemployment is expanding. In rural areas, 18 to 29 percent of all workers are underemployed, with even greater rates for women, African Americans, and Hispanics (Jensen et al. 1999, 420, 427). A full 70 percent of all the working poor are part-time workers (Beck 2000, 38).

The literature finds that most TANF leavers at the national and state levels secured employment after leaving TANF (see Loprest 2001). The share of poor families who did not work declined from 41 percent in 1989 to 34 percent in 1998 (Bernstein 2001, 95). Poor, female household heads who worked increased from 43 percent in 1993 to 60 percent in 1999 (Mead 2003, 164). On the other hand, it is also clear that most people who left TANF did not find full-time, year-round work, and some studies estimate that between 50 and 60 percent of them are not working regularly (Besharov 2003, 11; Holzer, Stoll, and Wissoker 2001, 3).

The "success story" of welfare reform is that people have left TANF to work at jobs offering an average of $6.06 per hour and $8,754 per year (Brustin 2003, 623 n. 16). Most studies have found earnings between $6.50 and $7.50 per hour for the two-thirds of former TANF participants who find work within the first year after exiting welfare (Loprest 2001). One study found that the net income of post-TANF households in Wisconsin was *lower* in the year after their exit from welfare, and a full 50 percent of former TANF households were in poverty within the first year after exit (Cancian et al. 2002, 3). This agrees with Edin and Lein's (1997) pre–welfare reform findings that women who left AFDC were worse off in terms of material well-being than those on the program. The evidence also indicates that for most people who leave TANF, keeping a job is far more difficult than finding one (Marshall and Kim 2002, 7). Many leave their jobs within three to six months after exiting welfare, and most leave within one year (Holzer, Stoll, and Wissoker 2001, 3 n. 2).

For the counties in this study, wage rates may be inferred in part from various income measures. To a large extent, the income statistics are a product of the demographic and labor market statistics we have reviewed. Individual wages will depend, in part, on one's age and level of education, in addition to the types of industries within commuting distance. Thus, these statistics reveal new aspects of the economies of these counties.

At the state level, median family incomes for families with children under eighteen in our case study states are below the national average (Table 15). Even with their low state-level figures, median family income figures for all counties in this study are well below their respective state medians. The state of Mississippi is well below the national median, and the median income for Mississippi families with children under eighteen as a whole is over 25 percent below the national median. The median family income in Sunflower County, which has the highest median income of the counties in our study and is the best off relative to its state, is still 19 percent below the Mississippi state median. Despite Mississippi's low standing among the states in this study, the Mississippi counties do not have the lowest median incomes. This distinction is held by Owsley County, with a median family income that falls fully 39 percent below that of Sunflower.

Single-mother families with own children under eighteen comprise the population most affected by welfare reform. At the national level, these families are not well off, and in these impoverished counties, they are the worst off. They are especially bad off in the Kentucky counties and, relative to these families in other counties, are better off in Shannon and Todd. The relatively superior condition of single-mother families in Shannon and Todd counties is likely due, again, to the prevalence of tribal government–related employment in those counties, which tends to be inclusive of women and related to historically unique gender roles.

Per capita income not only provides insight into the funds available, on average, to individuals in a given area, it also provides some insight into the level of economic activity in the area of interest. The statistics are consistent with our earlier discussion of labor markets in these counties. As would be expected, per capita income in all eight counties is lower than per capita income in their respective states (Table 15). The Mississippi and Kentucky counties exhibit the highest per capita incomes. These statistics likely reflect, in part, the higher percentages of employment in manufacturing in McCreary, Holmes, and Sunflower counties. The statistic for Owsley may arise from its having a higher percentage of people receiving retirement income.

Shannon, Todd, and Starr counties show the lowest incomes per capita. The results for Shannon County likely reflect the fact that it has the largest percentage of children under 18 (see Table 7), the lowest percentage of people age 65 and older (who bring in retirement monies), the lowest percentage of people between 16 and 64 who are employed, virtually no employment in export industries or, for that matter, any part of the private sector, and low percentages of year-round, full-time employment.

Table 15   Income measures (2000)

	Median family income (families with own children under eighteen)		
	All families	Single-mother families	Income per capita (all families)
Kentucky	$39,879	$15,713	$18,093
McCreary	20,651	9,924	9,896
Owsley	16,464	9,514	10,742
South Dakota	43,314	17,977	17,562
Shannon	19,709	13,390	6,286
Todd	18,211	14,022	7,714
Texas	42,549	19,769	19,617
Maverick	23,639	9,403	8,758
Starr	17,101	10,324	7,069
Mississippi	35,342	14,655	15,853
Holmes	19,314	10,318	10,683
Sunflower	25,212	13,750	11,365
United States	48,196	20,284	21,587

SOURCE: Kids Count Census Online, Table 19. Median family income for families with own children by family type in the 2000 census; U.S. Bureau of the Census, 2000 Census, Summary Tape File 3, Table DP-3. Profile of selected economic characteristics: 2000.

A similar story holds for Todd County with the exception of the percentage of people sixteen and older who are employed and the percentage of people in year-round, full-time jobs. A somewhat different story is true for Starr County. While Starr has a young population, although not as young as the South Dakota counties, it also has a high percentage of retirees. On the other hand, its population has notably lower levels of education than the populations in the South Dakota counties, indicating less human capital than the South Dakota counties. Starr has a low percentage of people employed, although not as low as Shannon County. On the other hand, it has the lowest percentage of year-round, full-time jobs. Further, it has little manufacturing. Again, Starr's border location supports high levels of seasonal and informal work as well as access to monies stemming from the cross border drug trade.

The differences in per capita income across these counties are also wide. At the extreme, Sunflower County has 80 percent more per capita income than Shannon County. These numbers suggest that Sunflower has more resources in its local economy. In general, the Kentucky and Mississippi counties have more resources available than do the South Dakota and Texas counties.

McCreary and the Mississippi counties stood out in our discussion of labor market and demographic statistics in several ways. On the positive side, they tended to have more year-round, full-time employment, more of that employment was in export industries, and manufacturing was notable among the export industries. On the negative side, their populations tended to have less education.

In addition, the retirement income received by older people may be important because, like manufacturing, it represents income received from what might be called outside (or export) sources (Hirschl and Summers 1982; Fagan and Longino 1993). That outside income may be spent in the local area and produce further employment and economic activity within the area.

With the exception of Owsley County, these counties have more young people than most counties (see Table 7). The median ages of persons in these counties are below their respective state averages and the national average. Owsley County has the oldest population, thus, it has fewer dependents and receives more outside income through retirees.

In contrast, the South Dakota and Texas counties are notable in that they have higher percentages of young people and lower percentages of people sixty-five and older than the other counties in this study. These percentages of younger and older people in the South Dakota and Texas counties have negative implications for their local economies because they have high numbers of people dependent on others and capture lower amounts of retirement monies.

Helping the Working Poor

With weak labor markets and stagnant or declining economic bases, the prospects for TANF leavers finding work that will permanently remove them from reliance upon the welfare system appear dim. One justification for eliminating AFDC was that it functioned to ghettoize or label participants as undeserving members of a deviant subgroup (Murray 1984). Over time, conservatives and liberal reformers came to agree that the best way to address this problem was to move participants, with coercion if need be, into the ranks of the working poor, a group that opinion surveys indicated the general population was willing to support (Ellwood 1988).

Welfare reform has been accompanied by a marked increase in spending on the working poor. From 1993 to 1997, federal spending on low-income working families increased by $74 billion, primarily through expansion of the Earned Income Tax Credit (EITC) (Marshall and Kim 2002, 2). Nevertheless, funding for education and training as well as childcare subsidies remained inadequate. One common conclusion in the evaluation literature is that more and better support services are needed to help low-income wage workers stay employed (Anderson, Halter, and Schuldt 2001, 87; Robinson and Nackerud 2000, 198).

Additionally, although limits on assets and earnings were relaxed under PRWORA, the legislation did not go far enough. It is still the case that as income increases, eligibility and benefit amounts eventually decline for crucial work-support programs, including the EITC, the Food Stamps Program, Housing Assistance, Medicaid, and child care (Hu 1999, 72). In Wisconsin, for example, a 95 percent marginal tax rate for certain wage levels and increased costs associated with work, like childcare costs and transportation, erased the benefits of receiving wages (Wolfe 2002). Only expanded aid, especially in child care, EITC, and health care, makes it worthwhile for low-income working families to leave welfare (Besharov 2003, 13). Among the recommended supports in the literature are an even broader EITC, an increase in the minimum wage to equal the actual cost of living, substantial healthcare coverage, and changes in eligibility for unemployment insurance coverage (Beck 2000, 41; Weber and Duncan 2001, 7–8).

Again, the distribution of supports for low-income working families is not uniform across all working poor. For example, low-income Hispanics are less likely to report having received EITC or to have health insurance coverage than non-Hispanics (Finegold and Staveteig 2002, 210). Similarly, policies that make work pay, like the EITC or minimum wage, appear to provide the greatest benefit to groups with historically strong attachment to the labor force (Landale and Lichter 1997, 891) rather than those with a community history of deep, persistent poverty. Steven G. Anderson, Anthony P. Halter, and Richard Schuldt conclude that those leaving welfare rarely package support services, such as childcare services, food stamps, healthcare programs, or the EITC, in the manner envisioned by public policy discussions about transitional supports after welfare (2001, 96).

FOUR

Poverty:
Family and Community Well-Being

If successful welfare reform is defined merely by caseload declines, then PRWORA was a grand slam. However, if the measure of welfare reform is the economic well-being of families, then success is harder to declare (Besharov 2003, 14). Despite the renowned strength of the U.S. economy in the 1990s, the 12.7 percent national poverty rate in 1998 was virtually the same as it had been in 1989 (12.8 percent). Moreover, the extreme inequality in poverty by race and ethnicity remained: 24.9 percent of African Americans, 25.7 percent of Native Americans, and 22 percent of Hispanics were below the poverty line in 1999. Three million poor people live in persistently poor rural areas with poverty rates of 20 percent or more. Also, the rate of poverty in rural areas was 13.4 percent, in contrast to 10.8 percent in urban areas (Miller and Rowley 2002, 1; Walsh and Duncan 2001, 118). Although there was a reduction in poverty among single-mother families, from 35.4 percent in 1992 to 24.7 percent in 2000, African American and Hispanic mothers remained extraordinarily likely to be in poverty (41 percent for African Americans and 44 percent for Hispanics in 1998) (Blank 2002, 1117; Gault and Um'rani 2001, 103–4). As Blank states: "Given the strong economy, this is perhaps a disappointingly small decline in poverty" (2002, 1117). Moreover, the decline in poverty was far less than the reduction in TANF caseloads, indicating that people leaving welfare simply moved from being "welfare poor" to "working poor" (Blank 2002, 1118).

Over the last three decades, the counties in this study have had consistently higher poverty rates than their respective states and the national averages (Table 16). This is true even in Mississippi, which has had the highest state-level poverty rates among the states in this study. These poverty rates have also persisted even in the presence of a strong national economy.

Table 16   Poverty rates and ranks for the persons in counties studied

	1980		1990		2000	
	Poverty rate	Poverty rank	Poverty rate	Poverty rank	Poverty rate	Poverty rank
Kentucky						
McCreary	39.5	34	45.5	23	32.2	61
Owsley	48.3	3	52.1	6	45.4	6
South Dakota						
Shannon	44.7	8	63.1	1	52.3	2
Todd	43.5	13	50.2	10	48.3	5
Texas						
Maverick	39.5	34	50.4	8	34.8	39
Starr	50.6	2	60.0	2	50.9	3
Mississippi						
Holmes	46.9	4	53.2	5	41.1	8
Sunflower	39.4	38	41.8	42	30.0	85

SOURCES: U.S. Bureau of the Census, 1980 Census of population, Characteristics of the population, Chapter C, Tabes 72 and 181. Poverty status in 1979 of families and persons; U.S. Bureau of the Census, Table CPH-L-184. The 100 poorest counties in the United States, 1979 and 1989; U.S. Bureau of the Census, 1990 Census, Summary Tape File 3, Table DP-4. Income and poverty status in 1989: 1990; U.S. Bureau of the Census, 2000 Census, Summary Tape File 3, Table DP-3. Profile of selected economic characteristics: 2000, http://www.census.gov/hhes/poverty/2000census/poppvstatoo.html/; U.S. Bureau of the Census, 2000 Census, Population by poverty status in 1999 for counties: 2000, http//www.census.gov/hhes/poverty/2000census/poppvstatoo.html/.

NOTE: The "poverty rank" is the county's rank among the hundred poorest counties in the country.

Despite the strength of the U.S. economy in 1999, poverty rates in all counties were two to five times greater than the national average. William O'Hare and Mark Mather (2003) define neighborhoods with poverty rates of 30 percent or more as having "high poverty" and neighborhoods with poverty rates of 40 percent or more as having "extremely high" poverty. Applying their definitions to the eight counties in this study, we see that all counties had high poverty and five of the counties had extremely high poverty.

The depth of poverty in these counties may be seen in the counties' ranks among the poorest counties in the country. The 2000 census indicates that five of the eight counties were among the "top 10" impoverished counties. The persistence of poverty in those counties is apparent when we look at these rankings across decennial censuses. Excepting McCreary and Sunflower counties, all counties have been in the top ten impoverished counties in at least one decennial census. Starr and Shannon counties stand out in their consistency among the counties with the highest poverty rates.

Table 17   Poverty rates for persons by cluster

	1980	1990	2000
Kentucky—state	17.6	19.0	15.8
Kentucky cluster	27.7	32.2	27.9
South Dakota—state	16.9	15.9	13.2
South Dakota cluster	48.6	50.6	45.8
Texas—state	14.7	18.1	15.4
Texas cluster	37.7	47.2	38.1
Mississippi—state	23.9	25.2	19.9
Mississippi cluster	38.8	41.1	32.6
United States	12.4	13.1	12.4

SOURCES: U.S. Bureau of the Census, 1980 Census of population, General social and economic characteristics, Tables 72, 181, 193, and 304; U.S. Bureau of the Census, 1990 Census, Summary Tape File 1, Table DP-4. Income and poverty status in 1989: 1990; U.S. Bureau of the Census, 2000 Census, Summary Tape File 3, Table DP-3. Profile of selected economic characteristics: 2000.
NOTE: See Appendix B for a list of all counties included in each cluster.

Poverty is persistent not only in the counties but also in the regions surrounding them. The persistence of regional poverty is exemplified by the statistics in Table 17, particularly in comparison to the national and state poverty rates. Poverty rates in these clusters have consistently been above the rates in their respective states and the national rates. The Kentucky and Mississippi clusters tended to have poverty rates between 150 percent and 200 percent of their respective state poverty rates, while poverty rates in the Texas and South Dakota clusters tended to be between 200 percent and 300 percent of their respective state poverty rates.

The general drop in poverty rates between 1990 and 2000 likely reflects the stronger economy in 1999, as compared with 1989. The relatively smaller drops in poverty rates in the South Dakota and Kentucky clusters between 1989 and 1999 suggests that these regions did not benefit from the strong economic growth during the 1990s.

The nature of poverty in these areas is revealed by considering poverty among specific populations (Table 18). Single-mother families with related children under eighteen face especially hard economic circumstances in all counties studied across both censuses. When compared with the high poverty rates for single-mother households at the national level, this group has been especially impoverished in the eight counties studied. Indeed, the poverty rates can be staggering. The 2000 census indicates that even during the

Table 18 Poverty rates for single-mother families with related children under eighteen

	1990	2000
Kentucky	51.8	42.7
McCreary	76.8	60.1
Owsley	84.3	79.4
South Dakota	48.8	37.9
Shannon	72.4	65.2
Todd	70.9	59.3
Texas	43.0	36.2
Maverick	69.7	61.0
Starr	77.1	73.2
Mississippi	61.4	48.1
Holmes	85.4	63.3
Sunflower	74.1	55.2
United States	42.3	34.3

SOURCES: U.S. Bureau of the Census, 1990 Census, Summary Tape File 3, Table DP-4. Income and poverty status in 1989: 1990; Kids Count Census Data Online, Table 17. Poverty status of families with related children by family type in the 2000 Census.

strong economy of 1999 the poverty rates for these families in the counties studied were all above 55 percent, reaching a high of 79 percent in Owsley County. In 1989, poverty rates were near or above 70 percent in all counties. When looking across the two censuses, one sees that poverty rates fell notably only in McCreary, Holmes, and Sunflower counties between 1989 and 1999.

When we change our focus to children under eighteen, we continue to observe high rates of poverty. Child poverty rates were generally at least three times the national average in 1990 and at least two times the national average in 2000 (Table 19). The county poverty rates also tend to be greater than twice their respective state rates. Child poverty rates exceeded 50 percent for all counties in the 1990 census and for six of the eight counties in the 2000 census. If we consider deep poverty (defined as having an income below 50 percent of the poverty level), we see that these rates, according to the 2000 census, are between two and more than four times the national average. Almost one-third of the children in both South Dakota counties are in deep poverty.

Family and community well-being may be reflected in other statistical measures. Subfamilies may indicate pressure placed on extended families to share housing to reduce the cost of living when someone loses benefits or a

Table 19   Poverty rates for persons under eighteen

| | In poverty | | In deep poverty |
	1990	2000	2000
Kentucky	24.8	20.8	9.4
McCreary	56.7	41.4	16.3
Owsley	64.3	56.4	25.3
South Dakota	20.4	17.2	8.1
Shannon	69.9	61.0	32.9
Todd	56.5	57.7	32.0
Texas	24.3	20.5	8.9
Maverick	58.3	40.7	16.9
Starr	68.0	59.5	28.0
Mississippi	33.6	27.0	13.1
Holmes	68.1	52.4	29.7
Sunflower	54.3	39.8	21.4
United States	18.3	16.6	7.4

SOURCE: Kids Count, Census data online, 2000 Census data—key facts.
NOTE: "Deep poverty" rates identify the percentage of the population under eighteen which is below 50 percent of the poverty rate.

job. According to the U.S. Census Bureau, "A subfamily is a married couple with or without own children under 18 years old who are never-married, or a single parent with one or more own never-married children under 18 years old. A subfamily does not maintain their own household, but lives in a household where the householder or householder's spouse is a relative" (U.S. Bureau of the Census, American Fact Finder). With the exception of the Kentucky counties, the percentages of households with subfamilies in these counties are at least twice as high as the national percentages (Table 20).

The South Dakota counties lie at an extreme in that they have double-digit percentages of households with subfamilies. A comparison of the percentages across the two censuses shows the changes to be generally nominal, with the exception of a decline in Shannon and an increase in Starr counties. The decline in subfamilies in Shannon County is likely due to increased housing construction during the 1990s after a decade of no federal funds for housing. Changes in the economies of the eight counties in our study between 1996 and 2001 can also shed light on community well-being since TANF. One element of economic change is population growth. The Kentucky and Mississippi counties stand in contrast to the South Dakota and Texas counties. While the Kentucky and Mississippi counties had nominal or negative growth

Table 20   Percent of all households that include subfamilies

	1990	2000
Kentucky	2.4	1.9
McCreary	3.1	3.3
Owsley	1.8	2.6
South Dakota	1.2	1.2
Shannon	22.0	15.3
Todd	10.5	11.3
Texas	3.5	3.5
Maverick	9.4	9.0
Starr	6.8	9.4
Mississippi	4.6	3.6
Holmes	7.5	7.2
Sunflower	8.5	8.5
United States	2.8	2.6

SOURCES: U.S. Bureau of the Census, 1990 Census, Summary Tape File 3, Table P005. Households, and Table P025. Subfamily type and presence and age of children; U.S. Bureau of the Census, 2000 Census, Summary Tape File 3, Table PCT6. Households by number of subfamilies.

between 1996 and 2001, the South Dakota and Texas counties were near or above the national population growth rates (Table 21). Some of these differences in population growth rates might reflect, in part, differences in the age profiles of these counties. The percent changes in population in McCreary, Holmes, and Sunflower counties also appears to be due to changes in manufacturing employment in these counties. Overall, loss in population will result in lost jobs in industries that produce for local consumption; a lower local population translates into less local demand. The population changes in the Kentucky and Mississippi counties would, therefore, have an adverse impact on welfare reform.

In relation to per capita income between 1996 and 2001, a majority of the counties experienced double-digit percentage changes over the five-year period. Owsley and Shannon counties experienced the greatest increases in per capita income, almost twice the national average. The Mississippi counties stand out in that they experienced virtually no growth or negative growth in per capita income. Holmes is the only county in which per capita income fell. Our discussion of changes in employment in these counties provides insights into the remarkable drop in Holmes County.

Table 21 Changes in population and per capita income (1996–2001)

	Population			Real per capita income		
	1996	2001	Change (%)	1996	2001	Change (%)
Kentucky	3,919,535	4,068,816	3.8	12,993	14,540	11.9
McCreary	16,788	26,996	1.2	7,433	8,518	14.6
Owsley	5,105	4,811	-5.8	7,893	9,723	23.2
South Dakota	742,213	758,324	2.2	13,986	15,374	9.9
Shannon	11,626	12,852	10.6	6,279	7,704	22.7
Todd	8,857	9,331	5.4	6,218	7,145	14.9
Texas	19,340,342	21,370,983	10.5	14,432	16,641	15.3
Maverick	44,581	47,993	7.5	6,161	7,164	16.3
Starr	51,008	54,983	7.8	5,214	5,710	9.5
Mississippi	2,748,085	2,859,733	4.1	11,584	12,655	9.3
Holmes	21,475	21,666	0.9	8,502	7,888	-7.2
Sunflower	36,271	34,247	-5.6	8,063	8,094	0.4
United States	269,394,284	285,317,559	5.9	15,469	17,173	11.0

SOURCE: Bureau of Economic Analysis (BEA), Regional Accounts Data, Table CA05. Personal income by major source and earnings by industry.

NOTE: Real per capita income was obtained by dividing the BEA data by the appropriate Midwest or Southern regional consumer price indexes (All Urban Consumers) and the U.S. consumer price index for the U.S. rates obtained from the Bureau of Labor statistics of the U.S. Department of Labor.

In summary, these counties not only suffer from persistently high poverty rates but the poverty rates of the populations who are the target of welfare legislation are especially high. The statistics suggest that these are indeed populations in need of help. From a policy perspective, one would hope that public policies directed at these populations err on the side of pulling them out of poverty rather them driving them further into it.

Summary and Conclusion

The poverty statistics for the counties in this study paint a grim picture, one that is, thankfully, beyond the experiences of most people in the United States. Unemployment rates are high, jobs are scarce, and the jobs which are available tend not to be the year-round, full-time jobs necessary for an effective transition of participants from welfare to work. Being generally rural with low population densities, these areas tend not to attract the types of businesses that would provide consistent employment for TANF participants. The sparsely populated, rural nature of the counties magnifies problems, like day care and transportation, that exist in populated urban areas. Despite this grim picture, the statistics also suggest that people generally want to work and would embrace the promise of incorporation into the labor force held out by PRWORA. High unemployment rates indicate that despite the obvious absence of jobs in the counties people still actively search for work. High percentages of people who hold full-time jobs, compared with the national average, indicate that people in the labor force do work. Some counties, like those in South Dakota, have relatively better educated populations. Indeed, it is not apparent that devolution of authority to states alone would be sufficient. The experiences of these counties are beyond what is typically true in their home states. We have no reason to expect that state-level officials understand these counties and their local economies.

Shannon County is among the counties in the study that is the worst off economically. It has the highest overall poverty rates (52.3 percent) and the highest poverty and deep poverty rates for children (61 percent and 32.9 percent), with 65.2 percent of single-mother families with children in poverty. Shannon County also has the lowest per capita income of $6,286, suggesting the absence of significant formal market economic activity. In the 2000 census, there were no households with incomes above $200,000. With respect to employment in industries, it has very little employment outside government-related industries. It has virtually no employment in export industries, with only 0.8 percent of employment in manufacturing. Further, it is missing the employment in local types of industries, with only 5.8 percent of employment in retail trade. The majority of its jobs are in industries that provide government-related services, such as education, health and social services, and public administration.

While Shannon County's labor market is weak, it is vibrant in the sense that people want to work and do work. While it has the highest percentage of people not employed (63.4 percent) among the counties in this study, it also has the highest unemployment rate (33.9 percent), the latter statistic suggesting that people want to work. While it has one of the lowest percentages of people with year-round, full-time jobs (40.9 percent of employed persons), it has the largest percentage of people with full-time jobs in a year (84.7 percent of employed persons). Thus, while a high percentage of people have jobs, those jobs are not for a full year.

Shannon County also has a very young population. Its median age is only twenty, a full fifteen years below the national median. Further, 45.3 percent of the population is under eighteen, and only 4.8 percent is sixty-five or older. These statistics indicate that it has a lot of young people who are dependent on parents. The statistic regarding the elderly is especially problematic from an economic perspective because it means that there are not many people receiving Social Security and retirement income. The absence of elderly people and employment in export jobs means that the county has few sources of export income.

While Shannon is the largest county in this study, it has the lowest population density, making long-distance travel a fact of life. Shannon County does have one of the better distributions of education, with 43.5 percent of the population twenty-five and older having more education than a high school diploma. Further, the large number of young people on the reservation could prove beneficial if they receive adequate education and training. The Bureau of Economic Analysis (BEA) statistics for Shannon are strong. It had the largest percentage changes in population and in total wage and salary employment and the second-highest percentage change in real per capita income.

Todd County is very similar to Shannon. While Shannon is extreme in many statistics, Todd is not far behind. Todd has among the highest poverty rates (48.3 percent) and poverty and deep poverty rates for children (57.7 percent and 56.5 percent), and it has low income levels ($7,714 per capita). It also has a young population, with 44 percent under eighteen and only 5.8 percent elderly. Its distribution of employment across industries is similar, with only 1.8 percent of those employed in manufacturing, and 6.7 percent in retail trade. Todd differs from Shannon County with respect to its labor market. Todd County appears to have a relatively more vibrant labor market, taking as given its low level of employment in export industries and in retail trade. Among the counties in this study, it has the lowest percent of its labor force not employed (49.7 percent), the highest percentage of its population in the labor force (61.9 percent), and the third-highest unemployment rate (18.7 percent). It also has the second-highest percentage of both year-round, full-time jobs (49.8 percent) and full-time jobs (84.5 percent). People in the county want to work and do work in jobs, but fewer are in year-round jobs than nationally. Todd County does differ from other counties in that it has the highest median income for single-mother families with own children under eighteen ($14,022).

For McCreary County, the 2000 census indicates two prominent sources of export income: (1) employment in export industries, and (2) ssi. Among the eight counties in this study, it had the highest percentage of people employed in export industries generally (35.9 percent) and manufacturing industries specifically (29.6 percent). It also has the third-highest percentage of employees with year-round, full-time jobs (49.4 percent). Its labor market is somewhat strong. It has one of the lower not employed rates for this study (52.5 percent). That number is tempered by its relatively lower unemployment rate of 11.5 percent. Thus, it appears relatively strong for the people who are working. McCreary also has the second-highest percentage of households receiving ssi (19 percent).

These sources of export income are likely the reason why McCreary County's median family income ($20,651) and per capita income ($9,896) are among the top half of the study counties, and its poverty rate (32.2 percent) is the second-lowest of the study counties. The county had a relatively high percentage increase in real per capita income between 1996 and 2001 (14.6 percent). It also had the lowest percentage of children in deep poverty (16.3 percent) and third-lowest percentage of children in poverty (41.4 percent) of the counties in this study, although its child poverty rate was more than twice the national average (16.6 percent). On the other hand, according to the 2000 census it was last among the counties in terms of median income for single-mother families with her own children under eighteen ($9,294). The presence of individuals receiving ssi, as well as the county having an above average percentage of households receiving Social Security Retirement Income (30 percent), are the likely reasons the county has one of the lowest percentages of households with income from earnings (65 percent).

The 2000 census statistics indicate that Owsley County is a study in contrasts. When compared to other counties in our study, it is second-highest in terms of per capita income ($10,742) and had the strongest growth in per capita income between 1996 and 2001 (23.3 percent). It is worst in terms of median income for families with children ($16,464), and among the worst in terms of median income of single-mother families with children under eighteen ($9,514), and children in poverty (56.4 percent).

The 2000 census indicates that Owsley has a relatively old population. It is the only county in our study with a median age above the national average (38.2 compared with 35.3 nationally). It has the highest percentage among the counties in this study of persons sixty-five or older (15 percent) and the lowest percentage of persons under eighteen (24.6 percent). As a result, the percentages of income received from SSI (27 percent) and Social Security Retirement Income (17 percent) are the highest among all counties in this study. Owsley also has the highest percentage of households that receive SSI (27 percent); it is 8 percent higher than the next highest county. Thus, the presence of an older population and associated passive incomes probably account for it having the lowest percentage of households with earnings (59 percent). These factors are also likely the reason the county has one of the highest not employed percentages (58.3 percent), the lowest labor force participation rate (46 percent), and the lowest unemployment rate (9.4 percent).

While these statistics suggest that the county's labor force is not as vibrant as those in other counties, Owsley did experience a 16.7 percent growth in wage and salary employment between 1996 and 2001. Of course, that growth was on a small initial employment base. The county's employment in export industries (21.5 percent) is below the national (25.3 percent) and Kentucky (27.1 percent) levels, although it does receive some income from export employment. Finally, it has one of the worst distributions of education among the counties studied, with a high percentage of its population having less than nine years of education (33.8 percent), and with less than high school (50.7 percent).

Regarding the Texas counties, Maverick has one of the lower poverty rates among the eight counties and is second-lowest in terms of child poverty and deep child poverty. Their poverty rate of 61 percent is extraordinarily high.

These poverty rates and the role of gender and family structure at the border are reflected in income-related statistics. While Maverick ranks second-best in terms of overall family median income among families with children, it ranks second-lowest in terms of median income among single-mother families. Unlike some of the other counties in this study, Maverick is marked by a high degree of income inequality. It is among the worst in terms of households with less than $10,000 in income, and it is second-highest with respect to households with more than $100,000 in income. Largely because of its enormous immigrant population, Maverick has the second-lowest percentage of households receiving public assistance. The BEA data indicate that it had one of the higher growth rates in per capita income between 1996 and 2001.

Maverick is also notable among the counties studied here for its low percentage of persons living in "rural areas" (places with fewer than 2,500 residents), which approximates the national average. Because the overwhelming majority of its population is concentrated in and around Eagle Pass, it is able to support many of the non-government-related industries that produce for local consumption. Table 11 indicates that industries that typically produce for local consumption serve as sources of export employment in Maverick. Maverick's percentage of employment in retail trade is 25 percent higher than the Texas and national averages. Part of the high percentage is also due to the shift in employment from manufacturing to retail trade discussed in the analysis of BEA data.

Maverick also has a relatively young population, with a median age 7.5 years below the national median. It has a smaller percentage of people sixty-five or older and a larger percentage of people under eighteen. It is not as extreme as the South Dakota counties in this regard. Again, this suggests that it will have more dependents than typical counties and, specifically, the Kentucky and Mississippi counties. Table 6 indicates that while Maverick has the lowest percentage of households with retirement income it is above the Texas and national averages with respect to Social Security income. This likely reflects an aging and disabled migrant farmworker population, which qualifies for social security yet never received pension benefits through employment.

Maverick, along with Starr, has one of the worst distributions of education among the counties in the study. Almost one-half of its population twenty-five and older has less than a high school diploma, with fully 40 percent having fewer than nine years of education. It is like, but worse than, the Kentucky counties in this regard and stands in contrast with the South Dakota counties. Educational deficits in South Texas are directly related to large percentages of immigrants from Mexico, where public education is affordable to the masses only through *primaria* or sixth grade.

On the other hand, Maverick's labor-force statistics suggest a labor force that is better off than many of the counties in the study. It had the second-lowest percentage of people sixteen to sixty-four who were not employed and the second-highest labor-force participation rate. Its unemployment rate is in the middle of the pack, suggesting that there are people who want to work. A glance at the work status of individuals changes the picture somewhat. Maverick County has the second-lowest percentage of people with year-round, full-time jobs and one of the higher percentages of people with full-time jobs. Thus, while people do work, they do not have the year-round, full-time jobs that would support the objectives of welfare reform. While Maverick does have some employment in export industries, it is below the national and Texas averages with respect to the groups of export industries identified in Table 12. Maverick's lower percentage of export employment likely reflects significant losses in manufacturing employment between 1996 and 2000. Again, we note that retail trade is a source of export employment in Maverick.

Starr County is like the South Dakota counties in terms of its poverty and related income figures. It has the second-worst overall poverty rate, child-poverty rate, and poverty rate for single-mother families with children. It is, however, in the middle of the pack with respect to deep poverty for children. The related median income figures reflect the same story. It has the second-lowest median income for families with children but is in the middle of the pack in terms of median income of single-mother families with related children. Starr has the second-lowest per capita income, suggesting that it does not have as much economic activity as other counties. Its percentage growth in per capita income between 1996 and 2001 was below that of either Texas or United States.

Starr County's demographic statistics are very similar to those of Maverick. It is large geographically, with the percentage of its population in rural areas approximating the national average but low relative to the other counties. Thus, it has the second-highest population density. It has a younger population, though not as young as the South Dakota counties, and the worst distribution of education among all of the counties. It also experienced one of the higher population growth rates between 1996 and 2001.

Starr County's labor-force statistics differ from those of Maverick County and are very similar to Shannon County's. It has the second-highest percentage of its labor force between sixteen and sixty-four which is not employed. Its labor-force participation rate is in the bottom half of the counties, though not the worst, and its unemployment rate is second highest. It did not experience a notable growth in wage and salary employment between 1996 and 2001. It is by far the worst in terms of year-round, full-time jobs. A mere 25 percent of working people have such jobs. That is only 43 percent of the national average. It also has the second-lowest percentage of people with full-time jobs. It and Owsley County are the only counties below the national average in this regard. It is like Todd County, though a little better, in terms of employment in export industries. Like Maverick County, its employment in the export-type industries is below the national average, however, also like Maverick, its retail sector functions as a source of export employment. The bulk of employment in official export industries is in agriculture, forestry, fishing, hunting, and mining. Starr County is far more agriculture-based than Maverick. As one would expect, the result is that a larger percentage of employment is in government-related industries that produce for local consumption. Starr has one of the higher percentages of employment in the education, health, and social services industries.

Welfare reform was implemented in Mississippi under strong economic conditions. Even so, in the early 1990s Mississippi remained among the poorest states in the country, even though economic growth was being fueled in the Gulf Coast region and along the Mississippi River by riverboat gambling. In fiscal year 1993 revenues from casinos were three times greater than predicted by the state, and job growth between 1992 and 1997 was 11.9 percent (Kirby et al. 1998, 11). Over the same period average wage and salary income grew by 19 percent and the unemployment rate fell from 8.1 percent to 5.7 percent (Brister, Beeler, and Chambry 1997, 8). The additional revenues from gaming that flowed into the state treasury were being spent on prison construction and maintenance, mental health programs, and education (Kirby et al. 1998, 16).

Nevertheless, poverty was still widespread and persistent. The state's 1995 median household income was $26,501, and the overall poverty rate was 21.4 percent. One of every three children in Mississippi was living in poverty (U.S. Bureau of the Census 1995). The percentage of children born out of wedlock and living in single-parent families was greater than the national average, and Mississippi had the highest rate of births to teen mothers in the nation (76 per 1000 female teens in 1996). In 1995, the state exhibited the highest rates of low-weight births, infant and child mortality, and teen deaths by accident, homicide, and suicide in the nation (Kirby et al. 1998, 11). Mississippi also continued to be predominantly a rural state, approximately 75 percent of its 2.6 million population residing in non-metro areas. Forty percent of the residents of the state were African American.

According to the 2000 census, there were 34,369 residents of Sunflower County, while as recently as 1950 there were over 60,000 residents. This dramatic decline in population has occurred throughout the Mississippi Delta, and mostly involves the out-migration of African American residents. The change over that fifty-year period is largely driven by the mechanization of agriculture. Tractors with large plows, cultivators, and mechanical cotton pickers, as well as the use of herbicides, drastically reduced the need for field workers. Where ten agricultural workers were needed previously, only one is needed now—to work as a tractor driver, mechanic, truck driver, or cotton gin operator. Furthermore, the few jobs that still exist are largely seasonal.

Small cities in neighboring counties are important to Sunflower residents as sources of employment and services that are unavailable within the county. The manufacturing plants that provide employment for Sunflower County are located mostly in cities like Cleveland, Mississippi (13,841), ten miles west of Ruleville in northern Sunflower County; Greenwood (18,425), which is thirty miles east of Indianola; and Greenville (41,633), which is twenty-five miles west of Indianola.

The 2000 census data also indicate that Sunflower County is "the best among the worst." Of the eight study counties, Sunflower County had the lowest overall rate of poverty (30 percent) and the lowest poverty rate for single-mother households with children under eighteen (55.2 percent). Also, it was the highest of the eight study counties in median income for families with children ($25,212), and per capita income ($11,365). Consequently, it has the lowest percentage of households receiving public assistance (6 percent). But when compared with nationwide statistics, Sunflower County looks bleak. Its poverty rate in 2000 was nearly three times that of the nation as a whole. Its income resources are barely half those of the nation.

In some respects, Sunflower's labor force is not as strong as those in other study counties. According to the 2000 census, it was the second-lowest among the study counties in labor force participation (50.5 percent) and unemployment rates (12.8 percent). On the other hand, it had the highest percentage of year-round, full-time jobs (51.1 percent). Further, it had a larger percentage of employment in export industries: manufacturing, agriculture, forestry, fishing, hunting, and mining (32.1 percent). The percentage of employment in these export industries was above the national average of 25.3 percent, as well as that of most rural counties.

However, this rather positive and hopeful picture of Sunflower County changed dramatically in the months following the collection of data for the 2000 census. The BEA data suggest that Sunflower was adversely affected by a 16.3 percent loss in manufacturing employment between 1996 and 2001. In most cases the manufacturing plants were located in neighboring counties. Interviews in the county confirmed this loss of jobs and revealed that the downturn began in 2000 and was continuing at the time of our interviews in 2002. Over that period Sunflower County also lost 5.6 percent of its population and had virtually no growth in real per capita income (0.4 percent), largely because of the plant closures and layoffs.

Holmes County has very high rates of poverty despite having some advantages not held by counties like those in South Dakota. In the 2000 census, it had the third-highest per capita income among all of the counties, the second-highest percentage of employment in export industries, with the second-highest percentage of people in manufacturing industries, and the highest percentage of households with incomes of $200,000 or more. On the other hand, it was eighth in terms of impoverished counties in the 2000 census, had the highest percentage of households with incomes below $10,000, and had one of the highest percentages of children in deep poverty. Holmes is similar to Owsley County in terms of retired and disabled persons. It has the second-highest percentage of households with Social Security income and the third-highest percentage of households with ssI. It also has the second-lowest percentage of households with earnings. While it has a younger population than the nation, with a higher percentage of people under eighteen, it has the same percentage of people sixty-five or older as the nation as a whole. Thus, it must have a lower percentage of working-age people. From 1996 to 2001, Holmes experienced the largest decline in overall employment among all counties with the change concentrated between 1998 and 2000. Holmes experienced a marked decline in manufacturing employment, which resulted in the only drop in per capita income among all counties over the period and likely contributed to the decline in population.

This statistical picture shows the incredible diversity among these rural counties, despite a shared experience of poverty. At the same time, other aspects of why caseloads declined, whether former TANF recipients are employed, and how family and community well-being have fared are difficult to determine from the numbers alone.

PART TWO

What the People Told Us

FIVE

Welform Reform on the Reservation, South Dakota

> On the reservation, there is no such [job] market. I mean, we're still dealing—
> this is Third World, let's just put it that way.
>
> —Rosebud TECRO director

Because of the culturally and historically distinct nature of American Indian reservation communities, the homogenizing pressures of welfare reform have been tempered by realistic social and economic alternatives to the nine-to-five capitalism envisioned by PRWORA's policymakers. While working is good, sitting around in an artificial community-service setting is not. While many households are ready and eager to make a greater transition toward the mainstream view of economic activity, the labor markets, physical infrastructure, and educational and training opportunities are completely inadequate to support this transition. Furthermore, differences among local administrative offices and tribal governments indicate that the opportunities for TANF participants are influenced by the degree of rigidity and monitoring or flexibility and cooperation built into program implementation, and that individual personality, administrative philosophy, local history, and physical logistics all have an impact on the relative success of welfare reform. At the same time, the development resources required to build up these local economies to the point of genuine and complete market integration are not only seriously inadequate but also declining rather than increasing. As a result, women in these communities, already in need of greater support, are facing increasing burdens on their time and resources. Administrative pressure to spend less time with their children and their extended family networks ends up isolating these women from the cultural core of how the uncertainty of the collective futures might be reduced.

This chapter represents the results of a series of interviews conducted on the Pine Ridge and Rosebud reservations between February and May 1999, and between April 2002 and October 2003. Directors and personnel within tribal, county, state, and federal government agencies, private businesses, and nonprofit organizations were interviewed about their involvement with, observations of, and responses to TANF. In addition, a total of 65 current and former recipients of TANF were interviewed about their experiences with and reactions to the requirements of TANF, 13 in 1999 and 22 in 2002 on Pine Ridge, 10 in 1999 and 20 in 2002 on Rosebud (for general characteristics of participants, see Appendix A, Tables 1–4).

Working for TANF

For many TANF participants, finding a real job through some form of training or community service for TANF is consistent with their own expressed goals for the future. When asked about their aspirations, participants mentioned wanting "to be self-sufficient with a paid job," "to get more education and get a good paying job," and "to hopefully find a job and better myself." Despite the dominant stereotype of lazy welfare recipients shirking gainful employment, most TANF participants agreed with the concept of working to receive money, and seriously wanted jobs. As one Pine Ridge woman put it, "I think it's okay, because at first, when I wasn't working, I get up early no matter what, but there's nothing to do. Sit around all day, clean your house, whatever. But you're required to work twenty hours a week, and you get to go do something for four hours. So I don't know. John [my employment specialist] makes it sound like I don't want to do it, but it's okay." The same sentiments were expressed by Rosebud participants. "I think it's good. I really do. I think it's good because it gives them experience, you know, and it also makes you feel better about yourself instead of just staying at home and get one check and then you run out of money, and then for the rest of the month you sit around and wait for the next check to come around. You know, it's just better that they work. I guess with me, it's got a lot to do with self-esteem. It just makes me feel better to be able to work."

Others were encouraged by the promise of a TANF placement giving them skills and experience to move toward real employment in the future. As one Pine Ridge participant explained, "I think it's a good idea, because it helps them to learn about jobs and have a job and maybe one of these days if some of them gets a steady job, they'll continue." A Rosebud participant agreed. "I think it's good. They're teaching us how to work, and I like it, but the money is not enough."

Views on TANF work requirements differed somewhat based on the age of the recipient. The younger women do not express the same resentments at the work requirements because they have never experienced any other program. For example, one young woman was required to begin work at her TANF placement site when her baby was only twelve weeks old, but as far as she was concerned, welfare had always been that way, so she accepted it. Therefore, after a period of adjustment, it seems that a work requirement for welfare will be considered natural. It was the women who were forty or older and who had received AFDC for many years who seemed to find the new work requirements the most abrasive. Once in middle age, it is much harder to develop the workplace skills that are needed to comply with the TANF work requirements. Working represents a complete change of lifestyle for the older recipients. As one younger TANF participant asked, "What are the old people supposed to do? Ever since TANF came in, the old ladies are confused. They have no job training, you know. That's not fair to them." Even though the participants were generally positive about the work experience that TANF provided, there were consistent criticisms about the way TANF was designed and implemented in South Dakota that focused on four key issues. First of all, participants found the rules to be too inflexible. TANF employment specialists were described as more stringent and rigid than a real employer would be about work hours. One Pine Ridge woman described the DSS rules: "They told me about holidays, that if it was national holidays that was the only time we'd be able to miss work." Another Pine Ridge woman addressed the problem of no sick leave for TANF workers. "I would have to say, also, [with a regular job] if you're sick and you miss a day, that you're paid. Whereas if I'm sick on TANF, I have to make up those hours. You know, if I'm sick one day, and I miss my four hours that day, well then the next day I get to go make up eight hours." Even the DSS admitted that the rules had become more stringent.

> That [sanctioning] has probably increased over the last two years. People become tired of all the requirements, and it is a fairly narrow area they have to tread in to keep on the system, they have to do the hours. And there too, now, it's no longer the case that they just take money away from people who miss hours. Now, the second time someone misses hours, they are sanctioned off 100 percent. Also, in the past they could apply at the first of the month, miss some hours, reapply in the middle of the month, have to go to a funeral and miss again, and even apply a third time in that same month. Now if you apply September 1 and are denied for any reason, there is no new application again until October 1. So if there is a death in the family, you have to wait a whole month to reapply. It's definitely meant fewer applications.

Employers also complained about the rigidity of the DSS requirements, such as the quantity of paper work involved in having a TANF worker placed with them. The DSS used weekly time sheets to determine whether sanctions should be imposed; so employers had to keep weekly time sheets for their TANF workers and submit them to DSS every week—on time, even if the rest of their staff was on a biweekly pay schedule. Some employers felt pressure not to report absences by TANF workers, even though it represented a disruption in their workplace, because it might result in sanctions that would hurt the TANF worker's children. The rigid imposition of sanctions also caused a constant flux in the TANF workers at a site, since once sanctions are imposed, there is no incentive to continue a relationship with your placement employer. This in turn reinforced some negative employer attitudes about TANF workers. As one Rosebud supervising employer said, "We went through a lot of them [TANF workers]. When they're off TANF, they're gone. When I started working here, I was just a TANF worker, and I had a lot of coworkers, and they're all gone. They're not around, you know. It's just like every other six months to a year, we have different workers. I don't know why."

Second, participants constantly mentioned that the benefits paid by TANF were too low, particularly for the number of hours that are required. TANF paid a benefit of $349 a month for a woman with two children in "shared housing." Shared housing includes publicly subsidized housing and housing with more than a nuclear family and constitutes about 90 percent of the available housing.[1] The only increase in benefits for meeting the work hours was a $50 bonus to help with transportation, clothing, and other costs associated with working. After one warning, the penalty for not putting in the required work hours a second time was loss of half the benefit check, and missing a third time was termination from TANF. As one Pine Ridge woman said, who had been on AFDC for seventeen years before the implementation of TANF, "I have to go to work every day in order to get this $50 check. If I don't, I'll be cut off." One Rosebud TANF worker said, "I notice that a lot of the women do get pretty upset when they're just on TANF and they're working all those hours and somebody else is working the same amount of hours and they get paid a whole lot more than they do." They also observed poor work habits on the part of people with permanent jobs, and found it unfair that they should be paid less for actually working harder than the full-time employees (Pickering 2004). The inverse of the concern about the low amount of benefits was the high number of hours.

1. A woman with two children in "independent" housing would receive $483 a month, a housing situation typical of most of South Dakota outside of Indian Country.

Many participants felt that thirty hours a week was already too many for women with children. As a Rosebud participant observed,

> Well, I just say about the hours I work, I think they have us do too many. I mean, it's like having a regular job, working for your welfare checks. I think we do too many hours. . . . I think they spend too much money on the day care, where people that are on TANF have to go and work, and I figure if they give them less hours, maybe it would help them to go out and look for a job, and have time to do things like that, instead of being at your site all day, and then not having a chance to go anywhere to seek work.

The prospect of increasing the requirement to forty hours was universally viewed as a nightmare for administrators and participants alike.

Third, the participants were disappointed that TANF did not support their educational aspirations. Because Shannon County has a high school dropout rate of over 70 percent, and the dropout rate for Todd County is higher than 30 percent, GEDs are often the key to becoming employable. This is particularly true of TANF participants, many of whom left school because they started their families early.

South Dakota's waiver program, "Strengthening South Dakota Families," which was in place from 1994 through 1999, was far more progressive than PRWORA in its strong support for education and treatment of participation in secondary education—regardless of the age of the recipient or family type— as fulfilling work requirements. Moreover, the waiver also counted vocational and college education as allowable work activities and even disregarded the earned income and other assets of all full-time students.

Following the expiration of the waiver in 1999, working toward a GED no longer constituted an accountable work activity unless the TANF participant was under nineteen. For those still in high school, if they did not continue with their high school education, they had to accept immediate placement at a work site to receive TANF benefits. Additionally, their parents could lose between $50 and $150 from their benefit amount for their teenager's failure to continue in school.

Regarding college education, South Dakota now allows participation in a program called Combined Work and Education Activity (CWEA) to count toward required work hours. This activity allows full-time undergraduate students (registered for a minimum of twelve credits) attending an accredited institution to fulfill work requirements by attending school provided they do not count more than fifteen credit hours toward the work requirement, and work the remaining required hours in another approved work activity. The students' courses of study must lead to learned skills that will help them find employment leading toward self-sufficiency; students must maintain GPAs of at least 2.5 and are allowed a maximum of two years in this program (South Dakota DSS 2003). At the same time, the benefits of the progressive elements of the South Dakota policy appeared to accrue largely to those with the private capacity to take advantage of them, a process known in the field and the literature as "creaming." One Social Services worker explained, "There again, the ones that were going to make it through anyway get through, but mostly they aren't trying for college. And also, if a TANF participant is doing community service, they get paid $50 like a bonus if they put in their hours, and it is paid after the fact. If they are in CWEA, though, they don't get the $50. So very few ever finished college or their GED while participating in TANF." Staff at Sinte Gleska University directly challenged the state for making the CWEA forms unnecessarily difficult to actively discourage TANF participants from considering higher education. One woman quoted former governor William J. Janklow's statement, "No one on welfare is going to get a master's degree in this state."

The expiration of the state waiver and its subsequent failure to strongly support college education and training resulted in missed opportunities to fill vacant positions requiring higher-level or specialized skills, such as nursing or special education. One Pine Ridge participant observed, "This is Martin, South Dakota, and there are no jobs. . . . Like I can go work at the nursing home and hospitals, but I'm not a nurse. So that would be an option, but I haven't gone to school for that." A Rosebud woman expressed her dissatisfaction with TANF's education policy. "You need to go to school to get ahead and make your life better. See welfare doesn't, they don't see, when you're on TANF, they want you to work for your TANF hours, and they don't count going to school, which they should. I mean, they want you to better your life and get off TANF, but they don't count the school hours as doing that, and they should, because they're bettering themselves to get off TANF and get a job. I thought that kind of sucked when I was on TANF."

Finally, they observed that TANF often conflicted with their children's needs, and therefore contradicted why they turned to welfare in the first place. The overwhelming sense from the TANF interview participants was that their primary goal is to provide for their children, whatever that requires. As one Pine Ridge participant explained it: "To me, it's like getting my kids through things, do you know what I mean? It's just being there whenever. It isn't about getting a job that's permanent because there is no such thing on this reservation." The costs of going to work come out of an extremely limited monthly budget, as one Rosebud woman described. "When I get my check, I pay them the rent, then I buy my kids the clothes they need, and then whatever, shampoo and all that, then I have about $50 left and I have to spend it on food, because it has to last us until the tenth." Therefore, any obstacles to fulfilling work hours are obstacles to paying for your child's basic necessities. "I need to get there," a Pine Ridge woman said of her placement, "because the money will stop if I don't [*laughs*]." When asked about her children, one Rosebud participant said, "They like it that I'm working, but I just don't make enough money. I don't make enough money like other mothers do. They have cars and all kinds of good stuff." As one Rosebud woman suggested, "I don't think they should be required to work until their kids get into school, because it's so hard with transportation, especially with TANF mothers, because they don't make very much, so you can't buy a vehicle, you can't be hiring people [to babysit] because it's just a once a month thing."

Reservation Labor Markets, Blood Quantum, and Tribal-Federal Relations

There were also some concerns among people generally that TANF participants could be competing with those already employed and those looking for work but not receiving TANF. These concerns stemmed from the extremely low demand for labor in both Pine Ridge and Rosebud. For example, while there was an increase of approximately a thousand jobs in Shannon County between 1996 and 2000, the sense was that the bulk of these were part-time and temporary positions, in large part created by a small but growing small business sector. With state and tribal budget crises, there is a growing concern that TANF will actually hurt the chances of poor people not on TANF to get real jobs. In turn, this low demand for labor has resulted in what mainstream society would describe as an "old boys' network" that controls the way many jobs are obtained (Mushinsky and Pickering 2005).

TANF recipients placed in work sites noted some tensions because they are doing the same or similar types of jobs as others in the community who have permanent wage jobs, but the TANF workers' benefit checks do not amount to minimum wage. As a result, one TANF worker in Pine Ridge noted of the permanent employees at her work site, "They worry about their jobs. They won't talk to you or anything like that. You ask them for help, or advice, and then they just ignore you."

Everyone throughout the community, including those working with TANF placements, stated that there were no jobs on these reservations. As a state JOBS worker explained, "We still work with unemployment for BIA General Assistance, we handle the unemployment forms. And we help with job placements. But there is still nothing for people to do, there is no work. There have been some changes in programs, so there have been some job loss. Like Head Start is hardly in operation anymore, and that used to be a source of quite a few jobs. When there is not much money around, there are not many job opportunities." As a result, the typical TANF placements were either make-work jobs in community service, with no real prospect of becoming a real position, or menial tasks that participants already knew how to do, with no real on-the-job training. Most of the reservation employers were doing as much as they could to create TANF work sites. The schools, tribal and district offices, hospitals, and even private sector businesses were taking on TANF workers. However, in most cases the positions were being created specifically to meet the needs of TANF recipients, rather than TANF recipients meeting the labor needs of the local economy. At best, they were providing public services without causing an increase in the costs of local government. As a result, many of the TANF participants complained that although they were placed in work sites, they had received no on-the-job training at all. "It's like, I didn't really feel useful. I mean, just like standing around and I could be doing something else, you know? Corine has her office in there, so I used to go in there and get on her computer, just to pass the time away. . . . I thought maybe right here I could help out the kids or something. But I just didn't feel useful. So I didn't even go in. I didn't care if they sanctioned me or not." A Rosebud program director who supervised TANF workers agreed. "They need to provide more training where they can train for different job skills. Or entice them some way when they come to work, you know, something to look forward to, but there's really nothing there for them. They're just stuck here, you know? The job skills we provide for them to learn, they learn that within a month, and then there's nothing for them after that. No jobs or nothing out there for them. So they just stay on TANF until their allotted time. They're in that system, and that's it." The same sentiment was expressed regarding Pine Ridge's Welfare-to-Work program. "There are hardly any jobs available on this reservation, and when there are you have twenty, forty, fifty people applying for one position. So the Welfare-to-Work clients, not all of those people are going to have a job when they're done with the program," a Welfare-to-Work program officer explained.

As a result, the types of on-the-job experience they were receiving were not for well-paid jobs or jobs likely to result in permanent positions. They were being placed in menial positions (janitors, receptionists, file clerks, and so on) for which it is assumed they will need little or no training. Migrating to jobs off the reservation presented a challenge, though it was another component of the Pine Ridge and Rosebud economies (Pickering 2000b). Daily commuting to work in larger towns and cities is difficult from Pine Ridge, since the closest major city is Rapid City, South Dakota, 40 miles from the northeastern corner of Shannon County and 120 miles from Pine Ridge Village.

There is an uncertain demographic impact from TANF that is difficult to assess because it is causing movement in two directions simultaneously, but Shannon County reported a 10.6 percent increase in population between 1996 and 2001. On the one hand, people cited many examples of Lakota people from urban areas moving back to the reservation. As one Pine Ridge social services worker noted, "We've heard from clients that say they have moved back here because they had either heard or feel that the penalties for not working aren't as stiff as they are off-reservation in the cities, because the cities are so on top of them, you know, getting into a work site and doing those hours every month or else. Whereas they see the social services on the reservations aren't as strict." A local leader from Pine Ridge agreed: "We have noticed a lot of people moving back to the reservation. They can't find work in the cities, or a lot of it would be young mothers with kids and they need family support and they can't make enough in the big city to do it, and so they come back. And it puts an increased burden on housing. It puts an increased burden on people, in that it seems like we're seeing more abuse and neglect, and child protection type of referrals." A woman from Rosebud provided her example: "The reason I moved back here when I was four months pregnant with him is because I knew I could get low rent housing basically, and I could pretty much get a job and live here on my own without any kind of help. I could do that here. Anywhere else, it would be kind of hard. Rent is higher, cost of living is higher. A lot of people ask me, 'Why did you come back?' Well, because I could afford it."

At the same time, people currently living on the reservation were talking about moving to urban areas where they could find actual wage work, rather than putting in the hours of community service that were required to receive the small amount of TANF benefits they were eligible for. As one TANF participant in Pine Ridge reported, "I decided to get off [TANF] and go back to school and maybe that way I could get a better, how do you put it, a better environment. Another thing I know is I want to get off the rez, where I know there's going to be jobs, and there's going to be people to help support you, so you can get a life is how I see it." Another consequence of the tight labor market on these reservations is that people generally conceded that factors other than qualifications influenced who was actually hired for any given position. Many people observed that one needed to have a relative or friend who was already working or had political influence to get a real job. "I guess a lot depends upon which family is in control of where," confided one Pine Ridge community worker. The consistent complaint of TANF participants was that permanent wage labor jobs are available only to those who are related to or close friends with the people who are in control of the tribal government or already in wage work positions, leaving them with little hope of ever obtaining real jobs.

A similar suspicion of favoritism was discussed in Rosebud. As one Rosebud TANF participant said, "If you don't have the training then, well, it's sort of true in a lot of places, but in here you also have to be related to somebody who's already in there, which really sucks, because you don't always get the job you're qualified for, you get the job that, you know, who your family is with. Unless your family is in there, which none of mine are, you don't get a job." Another Rosebud participant added, "You know around here, it's real political to get a job. You have to know the right people to get into a job so a lot of the families here they really struggle. Some of them will go without lights during the summer. Some of them will even move in to homes that don't even have water, but a lot of them have so much pride that they won't get on TANF."

In Pine Ridge in particular, there was also a strong perception that full-blood Lakota people were at a disadvantage in the local job market, and that people with white relatives or some white ancestry had more opportunities to be hired. More than 94 percent of the residents of Shannon County are Native American, predominantly members of the Oglala Lakota (Sioux) Tribe. However, only 31 percent are identified as having all Lakota ancestry by the tribal enrollment office, and 20 percent are less than half Lakota by ancestry (Pickering 2003). As one Pine Ridge TANF participant explained,

> Full bloods and people who probably have more Indian characteristics about them probably find it harder to get a job at the tribe than people who are half-breeds. I've noticed that for a long time. I think it goes back to the seventies with that AIM stuff going on here, the half-breeds are running everything and the full bloods and the Indians that are more Indian get the short end of the stick, and I think that it is that way today too. . . . There is internal racism, have racism in your own race. They don't like those guys because their skin is red and they have long hair, and they don't act like them or talk like them.

The history of how jobs are created and given out set the stage for a form of internal class conflict on the reservation. In the early years of the reservation, those who accepted jobs with the Bureau of Indian Affairs (BIA) were sometimes suspected of selling out to federal interests, of being co-opted by special benefits to favor outsiders over tribal members in decision making, and of succumbing to the pressures of cultural assimilation. The government exacerbated some of these tensions by showing explicit favoritism for "mixed-blood" workers, who the government agents felt were doing the best job of renouncing the "backwardness" of the tribal traditions of "full-bloods," and embracing the benefits of "civilization." At the same time, federal agents denounced full-blood leaders who attempted to resist the imposition of federal regulation by withholding rations and other government benefits from their communities. These categories of mixed and full blood had less to do with biological ancestry than with political and economic choices being made within the difficult context of reservation confinement and federal control (Biolsi 1995; Pickering 2000a).

These divisions between government "collaborators" and "resisters" developed into a form of class distinction on the reservation. Those who agreed with the BIA were more likely to obtain wage work and benefit from financial programs offered by the federal government. Those who opposed the BIA were unlikely to find wage work of any kind and would be found ineligible for or would not be informed about federal programs. Currently, full-time government employees are likely to have higher incomes than the rest of the population and are likely to have benefits. The remainder of the population, if they obtain work at all, are in general labor and service industry jobs that do not pay well, offer few or no benefits, and are usually part time or seasonal. While the economic distinctions between these two classes appear small in relation to national income levels, the distinctions within the reservation context are great nonetheless. Someone making $30,000 on the reservation is considered to be extremely well off, where the income per capita is only $6,286 per year. These class divisions are further reinforced by the perception, often substantiated in practice, that only the relatives and friends of people already working ever get jobs when a position opens up.

In contrast, Todd County is 85.6 percent Native American and 12.6 percent white. As a result, while the conflicts between full bloods and mixed bloods are still expressed, they are often less articulated than some of the conflicts between Native Americans and whites.

Racial issues between whites and Native Americans also play a role in how the option of migration is viewed. For example, these racial tensions led one Pine Ridge woman to stay on the reservation. "I know like one of the worst things is no matter where you go, like to any other part of the state, basically people are just like 'You're from there,' and they look down on you. That's pretty much the worst part, saying that, you know, Native Americans aren't able to get out and do things."

The Best and Worst of Devolution

Despite these common perceptions of limited job opportunities, Rosebud was generally more successful in getting TANF participants into real, permanent jobs than Pine Ridge. This leads to the question of the role of local administration, all governed by the same state TANF policies and one South Dakota Workforce Board, in implementing welfare reform. It also raises the question of how tribal governments in particular interacted with the South Dakota Department of Social Services on the one hand, and the federal programs available to tribes to assist with welfare reform on the other.

The combined complexities of multiple political entities and tremendous needs for a variety of social services has produced a complex system of offices and programs designed to help the reservation poor. There are federal programs administered by federal agencies, like Old Age, Survivors, and Disability Insurance (OASDI) and SSI; federal programs administered by the Bureau of Indian Affairs, like General Assistance (GA); federal programs administered by the state of South Dakota, including TANF and Food Stamps; and federal and tribal programs administered by the tribe, like Commodities, District grants, and the Low Income Housing and Energy Assistance Program (LIHEAP).

In such a complex environment, one would expect that a premium would be placed on interagency coordination and cooperation; and when TANF was first enacted, several community leaders felt that through it, they could see the beginnings of real interagency cooperation in the broadest sense of the term. Tribal government, state and local government, the churches, and volunteer nonprofit organizations all needed to be coordinating. TANF recipients need financial support, placements to satisfy their TANF work hours, support making the transition to wage work, support for basic survival in case they are sanctioned from TANF, and ways of solving short-term problems like transportation and child care. No one agency or organization can meet all these needs.

Loggerheads in Pine Ridge

Unfortunately, the experience in Pine Ridge over the last five years has been just the opposite. Given the special relationship between the federal government and the Oglala, and the sovereignty of the tribe over the lands within the reservation boundaries, the state has consistently tried to limit its economic obligations toward the residents of the reservation. For the most part, commitments on the part of the state to help with reservation projects are tied to waivers either of sovereign immunity or of tribal jurisdiction in favor of the state. These historic tensions between the tribe and the state continue to fester, to the detriment of poor people trying to manage the strictures of TANF. Implementation of TANF in Shannon County resulted in strained relationships between tribal and state agencies that ultimately made it impossible for TANF participants to transition from welfare to work.

For example, initially the federally funded Tribal Native Employment Work (NEW) program was closely aligned with TANF. Tribal NEW allows tribal governments that choose not to run their own tribal TANF programs to provide supportive services to reservation residents who are meeting work requirements. NEW funds are intended to address unique community needs while the state provides general TANF services. NEW funds may be put toward providing clothing, tools, or equipment needed for work and funding transportation—if there is a public transit system. Participants also receive a one-time $100 "allowance check."

The original intention was that participants in this program would meet their TANF work activity requirements and could receive meal reimbursement and other work-related expenses like clothing or licensing, as well as childcare referrals. The Tribal NEW program kept a list of businesses that were hiring and agencies that needed volunteers, such as Head Start. In 1999, there were ninety participants in the NEW program, twenty of whom were college students and seventy of whom were at work sites. TANF participants could also transition off TANF by obtaining a six-month position through the old Job Training Partnership Act (JTPA), now called the Work Investment Act (WIA).

All of this had changed drastically by 2003. The Tribal NEW director reported bluntly,

> We don't have anything to do with TANF anymore. The state stopped referring cases to us in December of 2001, so we have no more Tribal NEW referrals from TANF. The state said we were not following

the work requirements to a "T." And we said, "Well, we are a tribal agency, we aren't a state agency, so we do things differently." But before we could talk about it or work things out, they said they weren't going to work with us any more. We had our funding agency and we got on a conference call with the state . . . but it didn't do any good. So the placements are all back to DSS now. . . . Some of the things the state said, that the forms we used had to be the same as the state forms. And yet, it is a tribal program, so we shouldn't have to act like a state agency. So we said that, and they cut us off. . . . So now our priority is for unemployed people without a GED or high school diploma and no work experience. If they happen to be a TANF participant, it's just a coincidence.

A state Social Services worker confirmed, "There is no involvement with the tribe at this point." A similar end of cooperation was also mentioned at the state JOBS office: "We don't do TANF any more. Why? Ask . . . Social Services. They told us we are not to touch TANF. They took it from the tribe too. Now from my perspective, that's a hindrance, but in his infinite wisdom, it is now all with DSS. . . . Yes, the DSS told us to stay out of TANF. Now there is not much money around, so why duplicate efforts? It seems like a strange time to have so much territoriality going on. Makes sense to me to be cooperating and coordinating, but they don't want to know my opinion." To concentrate their remaining resources, Tribal NEW only had eighteen participants in 2003, two from each district selected from a waiting list.

Furthermore, those fortunate few who were Tribal NEW participants found new roadblocks from the state in continuing with the TANF program, despite the fact that both programs were designed to help with a transition to work.

The work allowance [for Tribal NEW] is $300 every two weeks, if they put in the hours. And that's another thing. The state Social Services is now using that work against them, if they get a work allowance, then they are counting it as income. Before, NEW was excluded when the state calculated their income. So we've had people in our program who have had their food stamps cut, and are ineligible for TANF, so they can't make it on just the work allowance. So this one woman, she went back on TANF and EBT [electronic benefit transfer], and even then she was ineligible for a couple of months because of the work allowance, so she really had a hard time.

Again, Social Services admitted, "Some things like Tribal NEW count as wages if they were to try for TANF, and some don't. There is some specific language about if it is on-the-job training and it ends up as a job, then it counts or, I don't even know, but it was some language in the statute that made the difference."

A similar fate befell a Welfare-to-Work program implemented by the tribe through Oglala Lakota College under a two-year grant. Tribes were able to apply for special U.S. Department of Labor Welfare-to-Work grants made available under the Balanced Budget Act of 1997. These grants were available to tribal governments, colleges, and private for-profit and not-for-profit Native American organizations on a competitive basis and were to be used to fund subsidized employment, on-the-job training, work experience, and postemployment retention services (U.S. Department of Labor 2003). Welfare-to-Work was intended to provide training, skills-building workshops, and other forms of assistance to individuals making the transition to permanent work sites. It was viewed as another area of great potential, like the Empowerment Zone, in part because it represented the first time that the College, the Tribe, the state, and private employers have collaborated on a project. Called Wanna Wowasi On Wakanyeja or Work Now for the Children, this grant was designed to help 150 TANF recipients transition to unsubsidized jobs by the spring of 2001. They also planned to make loans available to stimulate the creation of private childcare and transportation services, with the help of the Lakota Fund. There were 124 participants placed in work sites under this program. The outcomes of the program were disappointing in several respects, particularly to the program directors who applied for the grant with the promise of innovation and creativity, only to encounter rigid bureaucracy and an unwillingness to try new things (Albers 2001).

Because of the friction and lack of cooperation among the programs that might support TANF participants, none of the programs were providing what they felt were adequate services, and all complained of resource limitations. A state worker in Pine Ridge admitted, "We don't offer any training workshops like job readiness or anything. We haven't had funding for that for a long time. But I'm still hanging in there." The Tribal NEW director explained, "Of course we need more funding and more support staff. Now people are just trained in their work placements, mostly in tribal agencies. We can't do any life skills training or other workshops ourselves. We have just one staff member who carries all eighteen people as her caseload. There is no time limit on how long an individual can participate. They just have to meet the work requirements."

Another area in which state and tribal political relations blocked women's opportunity to pursue work and education was in the area of child support collections. Women could not even get their child support enforced because of conflicts between the tribal government and the state, but they were required to get a child support order to be eligible for TANF benefits. "Probably they need to start putting their feet down and find the fathers that make the kids, and make them pay the child support. Be responsible. They put them in this world." As one community advocate explained, "I agree people want to be off TANF. Believe me, they don't want to be on TANF. They don't even want to talk to those people up there at the state office, trust me. But they don't know how to go in and get a child support order. If they get a child support order, they don't even know what to do with it. But [the State] won't help these people here because they won't enforce it on the reservation." As one legal advocate explained, "If you've got a dad who is working at the Bureau of Indian Affairs and he's making $35,000 a year, the state of South Dakota will not enforce a child support obligation against him because they refuse to come to the reservation here and enforce child support." As a result, it is believed that some fathers move back to the reservation because they believe no one will come after them for child support there. Consequently, men can have a wage labor job and not share the proceeds with the kids they fathered, because state Social Services does not currently enforce child support orders in tribal court in Pine Ridge. As one TANF participant reported, "When I applied, I had to fill out child support papers and I even sent pictures and an address where he was, and I never heard anything from anyone. They just keep putting me off and putting me off. I gave them where the father was, where he was living, and everything they asked for and there was nothing being done about it. For me, that was really hard. It's the father's right to help with the child, but some of them don't do that. They come to the rez and stop paying, because on the rez they won't get bothered." A Social Services worker admitted, "In relation to child support, if the father is off the reservation, it can be enforced. If he is on the reservation, the tribe is not cooperating with the system, so the state can't enforce child support here. There are so many problems."

A total lack of infrastructure for childcare services accompanied the implementation of reform on the reservation in 1997, and TANF workers continued to struggle with child care through 2003. There were no formal daycare centers on Pine Ridge until 1997. As one community leader observed, "Shannon County has the largest by far number of TANF recipients in the whole state. And yet . . . we opened the first licensed day care in all of Shannon County. We're starting to get more day cares right now. The

Tribal Headstart is combining with the community colleges to open up four more daycare facilities that will be attached to the college centers." A TANF participant explained, "They [the children] get less things than they did before. Like whenever I was working, I would spend that much less time with my kids, just worrying about my hours for TANF, and I worried about my kids because of babysitters." Another woman agreed, "Sometimes I have to leave them to go to work, and one time I felt really bad because I wasn't there when something happened. But usually babysitting is always the problem."

Transportation was an unsolved problem for Pine Ridge TANF workers, despite its large size and widely dispersed population. The distances between most of the populated villages is between fifteen and ninety miles. While the casino does operate a van for its employees, there is no public transportation system in Shannon County. At the same time 64 percent of the 2002 interview participants from Pine Ridge did not have cars, making their transportation costly and uncertain. While some recipients called in favors from relatives or friends for rides, others reported paying as much as $40 for a ride to and from a meeting with their social worker or a day at their community work site, given the long distances, the poor quality of cars generally, and the lack of other options. Yet TANF benefits are only increased by $50 per month when a recipient puts in their hours at a work site. Transportation costs are not provided. "We don't provide any type of assistance with transportation because there are no public transportation systems on the reservation," a Shannon County social services worker explained. "We try to place them in an area that's close to their home, so it is within walking distance." This strategy meant that for remote communities, all the TANF participants had to find community work at only one or two potential sites.

Finally, virtually no one on TANF was receiving effective training, either off or on the job. Several TANF employers in Pine Ridge noted that they simply did not have the manpower to provide on-the-job training and felt that the state Social Services should be providing more training on the fundamentals of working at any site. Many Pine Ridge supervising employers cited problems with chronic lateness and absenteeism. Private businesses that did have TANF workers reported that some of the workers were good and others were not. As one Pine Ridge employer noted, "The shock of just going to work needs to be overcome before any greater strides can be made." Another TANF employer remarked, "I know at the store it's a struggle for [the TANF workers] sometimes, because they aren't used to coming to work and not used to dealing with that, and you know there are some we've hired a couple or three times and they finally kind of do it right. They get better in stages." The failure to provide TANF participants with some basic job training skills was having a negative impact on the number of placements available. One TANF recipient noted that her daughter, also receiving TANF, was having trouble finding a placement because many of the employers who initially offered to provide TANF work sites have now withdrawn from the program because of the difficulties they experienced with the TANF workers they were assigned.

As a result, there were few success stories that anyone in Pine Ridge could share about TANF participants becoming truly employed. According to a DSS employee, "I would say since July [2003] there have been only two or three who got off the system due to finding a real job. . . . The major explanation for caseload reductions is sanctioning." With so few participants actually finding permanent work, the transitional and follow-up supports have been less apparent in Pine Ridge. The TANF recipients observed that they had more support for transitioning to work under the former AFDC program than they do under TANF. They felt that AFDC covered more of their transportation and childcare costs than TANF did.

Collaboration in Rosebud

In stark contrast to the Pine Ridge experience, Rosebud was able to work collaboratively with state and federal programs in such a way that TANF participants in Todd County had a realistic hope of moving from welfare to real, permanent work. However, despite the tireless efforts of the tribal and state administrators to make TANF work, the inadequate level of funding they could access and the broader problem of economic development on the reservation still limited their success.

There has been a long history of conflict between the state of South Dakota and the Rosebud Sioux Tribe. These conflicts have centered around the jurisdiction and control that the state is able to assert over areas within the tribe's reservation boundaries. For every assertion of exclusive tribal jurisdiction, the state responds with a reduction in state-sponsored funding and services for reservation residents.

Nevertheless, on Rosebud TANF is being viewed as a helping program by the state, tribal, and nonprofit entities involved. Rather than setting people up to fail, these entities are working together to establish child care, transportation, and basic work readiness skills so that TANF participants can make a smooth transition to work. In 2000, the tribe consolidated their Tribal NEW, Welfare-to-Work, and WIA programs into the Tribal Employment Services. Through program consolidation, the Tribal Employment Services have been able to assist over five hundred people with job readiness, job placement, and transitional supports.

The Tribal Employment Services worked hand in hand with DSS to find work sites for those TANF workers ready and able to fulfill the work hours required by TANF. To the extent possible, TANF participants are being presented with choices about their work sites, so that their interests and abilities can be best suited to their TANF placement. Tribal NEW divides the TANF workers into three categories: (1) those ready to work ; (2) those close to completion of GED with some limited need of job skills training, but close to ready to work; and (3) those with drug and alcohol problems, learning disabilities, or physical restrictions that make it difficult or potentially impossible for them to find work sites. The first and second categories are now being placed in work sites. The third category continues to receive benefits without work requirements, although some forms of treatment or rehabilitation are being arranged for them.

The Tribal Employment Services programs are also offering some job training opportunities. Workshops on completing applications, resume writing, professionalism, team work, the office environment, and an introduction to the world of work have been offered to TANF participants. More funding is needed to expand the number of such workshops that can be offered. However, because the tribe's Welfare-to-Work program was created on a two-year grant, there is no certainty that the essential services they are now providing and need to expand will continue to be offered.

There seemed to be active coordination between the tribe, the state, and the local nonprofits in defining work activities and stimulating and expanding work sites for TANF placements. Interestingly, there is more cooperation between the tribe and the state around TANF than in any other setting. The Tribal Employment Services and state DSS adopted each others' forms, and the DSS worked with the tribe to count hours in each other's programs to meet TANF work requirements. Because the participation rates are state rates, the state has, for the first time, an economic incentive to have the tribe succeed. The tribes are the areas with the high caseloads, so the state needed reservations to find a way to reduce participation rates so the state could meet federal compliance targets. If the state failed to meet these targets on time, they could have lost $2 million in 2004 alone. Thus, the state is extremely motivated to help the tribe. Indeed, TANF may be helping to create some new models of tribal-state cooperation here in South Dakota.

The Rosebud program directors believe that their counterparts in the other tribes seem to be more interested in having their own program than working with the state. In contrast, the personnel on both sides of the table in Rosebud saw the benefits of cooperating extensively. The personnel even reported meeting outside work as friends, which further reduced the possibility of interagency hostilities. Not only did they know of each other's operations, but clients were not able to play one office off the other with misinformation, since copies of both tribal and state agency records were kept in both offices. While Rosebud began welfare reform with similar deficiencies in the areas of child care, transportation, and job services, it was able to construct two different sets of childcare centers beginning in August 1996, and then provide enough subsidization and funding to make them available for TANF workers and those newly employed from TANF (Biolsi et al. 2002, 139). For example, the Sicangu Policy Institute of the Sinte Gleska University helped establish one of the first childcare centers as a way of supporting TANF participants who wanted to continue their college educations.

While child care is being provided, it is not necessarily good child care (Biolsi et al. 2002, 138–39). The centers were responding to the need for child care created by TANF; one worker there noted that "most of them that do bring their kids [to the child care] are on TANF." The daycare services were not always reliable, as one former TANF participant reported. "I had Antelope Daycare be my childcare provider when I had those kids, and it was always a hit and miss with them being there. A couple of times if someone didn't want to show up and they had the key, there was no daycare, and they didn't inform you before hand there was no daycare." Several women talked about concerns they had with the quality of the child care also. One mother said plainly,

> My kids are not taken care of. I know they're not. I went there several, several times, and things were just so chaotic. The little girl was standing way on top of, you know how they build for kids to put their hats and coats and everything, they were standing up on there and the supervisor was standing there saying "I told you I was going to wait until you Mom came and seen you." I was like, "Well, what would have happened if they were to slip off there and hurt their arm or, you know, did something to them?" I said, "Geez, all to prove a point," you know, and I was just so upset. I think they're getting ready to close it down. That's going to be another problem for me. I'm not going to have any day care again.

Rosebud was also able to implement two different local transportation systems in addition to the van service available for casino employees (Biolsi et al. 2002, 135–36). The distances between the most populated villages on

Rosebud are between ten and twenty miles. DSS was making a concerted effort to arrange for work placement sites in the home village of each TANF participant so that transportation issues could be minimized. Nevertheless, there are TANF participants living in the remote parts of the reservation for whom locating work sites and arranging for transportation was a problem. By 2002, the Tribal Employment Services program, in coordination with DSS, was able to provide its own transportation services for TANF participants and transitional workers in Rosebud, both to work sites and to GED tutoring. Sinte Gleska University also operated a transportation system for students and workers that assisted many TANF participants.

They also had a coordinated plan for providing both workshops and general on-the-job training through community service sites to a significant portion of the TANF participants. Those who reported the best experiences in Rosebud were involved with the on-the-job training program or the JTPA program, now called WIA under current legislation. As one of the Rosebud participants explained, "One of the requirements at TANF is that you have to go apply like at JTPA. You have to go to TANF and fill out all kinds of job applications before you can even get TANF, so I had to go down to Rosebud and put in numerous applications and I did that for years." South Dakota's "On the Job Training" program provides a subsidy to offset the costs of private sector employers who provide training for participants to learn the skills required for their positions. Employers are expected to provide a real position to each subsidized TANF worker after six months, but are under no obligation to do so (South Dakota DSS 2003). Participants may also perform subsidized work in the public sector under On the Job Training. There was also a "Try-out employment" program to assist participants with work-related expenses for a period of not more than four weeks. Tribal Employment Services had success in placing TANF workers under all these programs, and in many instances in positions that became permanent. The Rosebud Hospital, for example, was on the Try-out employment program, and ultimately gave a housekeeping job to a woman who had been viewed as hard to serve.

The most remarkable aspect of the Rosebud TANF program was that participants were actually able to get real jobs, despite the recognized politics and personal influence that governed most hiring on the reservation. Rosebud displayed a better set of transitional and follow-up supports (coordinated between state and tribal programs) for those participants lucky enough to find real employment out of their TANF placements. As one woman who was on TANF when interviewed in 1999 who had made the transition to a full-time, year-round stable job by 2002 stated, "I built myself up gradually and TANF really helped me out. To be on TANF, to get me off and budgeting. I budget myself. Oh, I got a car, you know. I just saved and saved and saved. Finally, you know, it's good. TANF, I think it is, if you stick to it. Of course, there's guidelines and stuff, but I think it helped me a lot. Giving me the opportunity to get off."

In fact, in Rosebud, people looking for work felt that the TANF participants were being given an unfair advantage in accessing the limited number of job openings. One woman even stated, "I got on [TANF] so I can try to get a job." Another woman complained,

> I notice more TANF workers in places. But see, when they stick TANF workers in places, they always get hired on permanent positions. They're only there for what is it, gee, three–six months, and they have to get hired on or something like that, they said. And see, I don't think that's fair because other people that put in for those positions don't get it because the TANF workers get it. Whether they're qualified or not. Because they've been there so long, they already know the job and everything so they're the ones that get hired on, and the ones that put in for it, they don't get hired on. . . . I don't think that's fair to other people who put in for that position.

Unfortunately, the TANF program on the Rosebud reservation has had its staff reduced and its budget cut. What the TANF administrators needed most was economic development for the reservation, something completely outside their domain. As Thomas Biolsi calculated in 1997, the ratio of the population to jobs was 3.04 in Todd County, in contrast to 1.56 in neighboring Tripp County, putting substantially more burdens on those with jobs, and highlighting the critical need for job creation on the reservation (Biolsi et al. 2002, 148, 151).

Therefore, the successful placements were still limited, as one woman in the six-month On-the-Job training program explained: "I just took what I could get for now, whatever was open. [INTERVIEWER: Are you learning anything that will help you get a job locally?] No, because I know all of this already, so. And at home [*laughs*]. . . . I mean, in the next six months it's going to help me some, but after that it's going to go back to the way it was before, because that's all I'm going to have." Tribal agency personnel were frustrated at their inability to provide On-the-Job training or WIA slots because their budgets could not be stretched to include the salary for a new worker after the six-month training was completed. For example, the director of the Rosebud Tribal Employment Contract Rights Office (TECRO) explained,

"We have a training program with the tribe, JTPA, we had to quit using them, because we didn't have nothing for them when they completed their training. . . . The problem I see is that JTPA and the TANF program would probably do better in the private sector than working with government programs. I think it'd be better geared toward the private sector." The tribal social services office had the same problem: "I can't [take WIA or On-the-Job training placements] because my funding is only for two people, so I do put in my budget for funding to hire additional help, but I always get turned down."

The Everyday Economy and TANF

Another contrast between Pine Ridge and Rosebud was the level of recognition given to home-based enterprise on these reservations. The state and tribal agencies in Rosebud worked together to create community quilting centers, and to allow home-based artisans to use their talents to meet the work requirements of TANF. In contrast, for the most part, the only home-based enterprise allowed as a qualified work activity in Pine Ridge was child care. Ironically, home-based enterprise in Pine Ridge was even more extensive than it was in Rosebud. Nevertheless, members from both reservation communities saw home-based enterprise, subsistence production, and social networks of exchange as important components of both the survival of welfare participants and the future of economic development for these reservations.

Lakota households actively engage in a dynamic mix of home-based production, subsistence, and barter and trade, combined with temporary or seasonal wage work, that challenges traditional measures of economic activity. Comprehensive economic development needs to address support for economic activities occurring outside formal market relationships by recognizing the full contours of the everyday economy on these reservations. As a TANF participant from Pine Ridge said, "I'd say there's a lot of people that [do home-based] work. The thing is about people around here, you can get them to do just about anything as long as they know there's money involved, because money is hard to get, especially in the middle of the month it's the hardest." A Rosebud participant added, "We pretty much all work together. Like I said, we just all help each other. I can't really say because we just do it because they helped you and you do it because you want help back maybe later on down the line, you know?"

Because of the limited amount of cash in these communities, the everyday economy allows people to access a broader array of goods and services through trade and barter. In Pine Ridge, for example, 76 percent of households regularly trade, barter, and exchange goods, labor, or other household support (Pickering 2002). A TANF participant from Rosebud explained, "You know, with me, I don't have proper attire for the work I do, so just trying to do outdoor things or trying to make money outside of the home, whatever I can do, I do it. I babysit sometimes but a lot of the times when I babysit we're trading off because I trade off time for them, and then they bring their kids over. And those are friends that we do that. . . . The ones that I babysit for don't have the income to be paying it, so that's why we trade." As one Pine Ridge woman observed, "Around here, everybody trades for everything."

The self-sufficiency standard for Shannon County in 2000 dollars indicated that a single mother with two children under five would need $24,108 per year to make ends meet (Pearce 2000b, 67), and yet according to the U.S. census the median family income for a single woman with children is only $13,390. The hourly wage needed for this family to be self-sufficient is $11.41, whereas the vast majority of entry-level jobs for TANF participants pay minimum wage (Pearce 2000b, 67). Part of this income deficiency is met through the everyday economy. The scarcity of regular wage jobs and the limited amount of public benefits available means that many households are constantly piecing together different strategies to meet their needs. A Pine Ridge woman described an example: "At one point, [the electric company] they just turned me off. I mean you just don't plan those things. Things come up, and there's different reasons for something happening, like all of a sudden you have to get to Rapid City. You just don't plan on paying your light bill. It's like a necessity thing. And if you can wait 'til the next month, you do." Similarly, a small resource windfall can completely turn a family's financial situation around. A woman in Rosebud reported, "I won a drawing is what it was. I won $1,000, so I went out and got me a car." By having a car, she was able to apply for and keep a regular job, moving completely off TANF.

Other aspects of the economy turn on traditional Lakota cultural practices. Virtually all household participate in some ceremonies, powwows, funerals, or other traditional events each year that involve distributions of food and household goods, the average being twenty-six events per year but the range extending from a couple to more than two hundred per year (Pickering 2004). These events may run continuously for two to four days, twenty-four hours a day, and depend on a complex integration of social networks and market resources in what Tressa Berman has termed "ceremonial relations of production" (2003). In addition, subsistence hunting and gathering supplement household diets. In Pine Ridge, 80 percent of all the households, and 81.5 percent of households participating in TANF rely on some wild resources during the year to supplement their diets, suggesting that wildlife conservation and land use planning around native flora and fauna are also important components of the contemporary reservation economy (Pickering 2002).

TANF participants found the time constraints imposed by TANF work requirements directly interfered with important forms of household support accessed through the everyday economy. One woman explained, "A lot of people don't like to do [the TANF work hours]. Maybe it's just too time consuming, you know. A lot of times I'll have to work two or three extra hours in order to have a day off to go do my business, and to them it's just too time consuming. because my sister has three daughters who are under age, one just turned eighteen, the other two are seventeen and sixteen, and she doesn't want to do the hours, so she lives on food stamps." Welfare is simply part of a diverse mix of household resources, not necessarily significant enough to warrant the loss of other forms of support. There were initially just under 900 active cases in Shannon County in 1994, when the South Dakota waiver was approved, down to 750 in 1997. By 2002, that number had decreased to around 450 active cases. Similarly the caseload in Todd County started at about 650 when the state waiver was implemented in 1994, and declined to around 355 active cases by 2002. Both Pine Ridge and Rosebud DSS agreed that these remaining cases were hard to serve, and that new applicants were now almost exclusively repeat customers. Other programs, like LIHEAP and SSI, provide limited resources to meet the cash needs of the household. For example, while TANF caseloads were declining between 1992 and 2002, the SSI caseload in Shannon County increased by 36 percent over that same period, although it rose only slightly and then declined in Todd County.

Several TANF interview participants discussed the temporary nature of their use of TANF. A Pine Ridge participant reported, "Usually I work part time in the fall at the school, so a lot of times I don't get TANF for very long, and it depends on what I make, so it's just temporary." Similarly, a Rosebud participant noted, "I was off [TANF] for a couple of months, then I got back on. I didn't pay [the rent] for a couple of months, so it was either start paying or get evicted. So I just had to get back on TANF again."

Others spoke about the disincentives created by TANF. "Basically what they do is you have to fill out a form every month, and if you have any kind of income you made that month, they take it away from your check that you've made. And I know there's a lot of people that go out and do things like that, and they don't even report it, but why would you? I mean, I've cleaned people's houses just so I can get by, because he needs diapers and then there's also times that, my food is fine since I've been on food stamps, so I don't have to worry about that, but if he runs out of formula, because I'm on WIC [the Women, Infants and Children program] also, I give up my food stamps."

Some tribal members cite the long history of welfare programs on the reservation as a major contributing factor to the difficulties in implementing welfare reform now. As one community leader noted, "Welfare has created a state of dependency and apathy on the reservation, which has given the people no motivation to change their work situation." When one woman was asked if she was currently working, she replied, "No, because I'd have to report it if I was doing something else." Because other resources ebb and flow, the rigid view of "monthly income" by the Social Services office presented a severe hardship to families. One woman's experience dramatized the effect of this approach.

> Just a couple of days before the Christmas break, . . . I basically got my paycheck early, and that screwed up my monthly report, so the next month, I got fifteen dollars, lump sum. So they needed to have a little bit more understanding of what was going on, and not just cut me off. That was something I had no control over. Those two paychecks were supposed to last for two months. . . . How do you pay $380 when you only have $15? . . . It's like, you know, they want you to work and support yourself, they want to help you do that, but yet if you make a dime more in your work, they're going to take the dime away from you. And that's not helping anybody to get on their feet. . . . You really can't make money ahead on this system, because anything you make is taken away from you in a different way, you know?

When another TANF participant was asked if she had a second job, she replied, "No. If I did, it would come out of my TANF check. So, no point." In relation to home-based enterprise, another woman admitted, "If I do [bead work], I don't tell them because then they take it out of my check. Like I got sanctioned for TANF for not going to work one day, so in July I got a housekeeping job and I couldn't work, but I needed some money." When another participant was asked about income supplementing, she said, "Oh, yeah. You mean like going out and getting side jobs, things like that? You didn't want to make too much, because if you did then they'd take it out of your check." Yet another participant noted, "If I was to get an outside job or something, if they found out about it, they would deduct it off my check if I would tell and I only get $298 a month."

As a result, virtually all the participants interviewed asserted their preference for having a real job rather than staying on TANF. As one former TANF participant explained, "You don't have somebody looking over your shoulder all of the time. To me that was always a pain. You have to, how do I say it, report everything when you're on TANF. Now if I feel like going out and making more money, I can do it and nobody's going to say anything about it."

These disincentives extend to other public support programs as well. As one tribal agency director explained,

> The problem is that once they start collecting a check, most of them rent from the tribal authorities, right? The minute they go to work, their rent goes up. There's no buffer period for them to work their way into work. You get 30 percent of your income right there. It's gone. You're off food stamps. Boom. The minute you get money, you're done! I mean, how can you compete with that? Most welfare programs in the state of South Dakota give them a one-month buffer period. Well what's that going to get them? If they could just escalate a six-month period. Transition period. The Housing Authority especially. Because these people have to have clothing to work. And they have to buy food. Boom, right off. What's a hundred bucks for groceries? . . . It's hard to compete with welfare in the job market here. I think you see that on the reservations a lot. I tell that to everyone I talk to, I'm in competition with welfare, and I'm losing. . . . That's all they can acquire is low-level jobs. If I were in their situation, I would probably stay in the system as long as I could. I pay my low entry employees here higher than the other ones do, to try and get them to stay. But my pay is still, in my opinion, too low. . . . I start them out at $7.00 an hour, and a lot of them are starting them out at $5.00, geez, whatever the minimum is. $6.00? But the cost of gaining employment, what it costs you, is not worth the $7.00 an hour. You have to find a babysitter, you have to have transportation, clothing. And I can't solve that puzzle. I can't pay them $10.00 an hour. I can't afford to get them to work.

As a result, most reservation residents are moving in and out of formal work on a regular basis, but the kinds of support intended to help the working poor were not being fully accessed. For example, some but not all of the TANF participants were aware of the incentives behind the Earned Income Tax Credit structure. Of the 2002 interview participants, 45 percent had applied for EITC sometime in the past. One tribal agency director had people request that their required work hours be taxed. She explained, "People want to pay taxes, so they can qualify for the EITC." Most people were not aware that their income from self-employment could also count toward their EITC earnings. The TANF recipients observed that they had more support for making a transition to work under the former AFDC program than they do under TANF. They felt that AFDC covered more of their transportation and childcare costs than TANF does. They also felt that they needed to receive checks every two weeks, rather than once a month, to go to a work site. As one woman explained, "It's like they should at least try to split it and give it to them, so they'll spend a little bit in the beginning and a little bit in the middle, so it all doesn't get spent in the first week. And that's the problem I don't like about TANF is you have to wait every month."

The importance of the everyday economy to reservation residents has led to some alternative approaches to economic development. The Lakota Fund is the major lending institution on the reservation, in an environment where most people do not have access to credit or savings institutions (Pickering and Mushinski 2001, 2004). The Lakota Fund helps stimulate small business and home-based enterprise development through a number of small loan and training programs. Similarly, as of 2003 Sinte Gleska University had revitalized its program to support and stimulate small business and microenterprise development.

Supporting the home-based enterprise has been argued to be more effective than job training in providing a route by which reservation residents might escape the poverty trap. As one woman in Pine Ridge pointed out, this kind of home-based activity was the only realistic way for TANF recipients to leave welfare.

> I think if they want to do something like that, I think they should like maybe have classes, like vocational training classes, like teaching them how to sew, or teaching them how to bead, you know, something where they can maybe provide an income. Like take for instance maybe make beadwork, and they could turn around and sell it to someone. You know, teach them something where they can be useful, instead of them demanding you go to a work site and sit there like a wart on a log. They don't do anything. They don't provide training. . . . They should train them to get out there in the work force themselves, they want them off the welfare system so badly, you know.

Traditional Values and Contemporary Conflicts:
Family and Community Well-Being

The everyday economy is embedded in a set of traditional family and tribal relationships that offer key supports for TANF participants. This alternative system also has limitations, some of which are due to inadequate resources within this system, and some of which are the often unexpected results of a century of imposing modern Western concepts and practices on a traditional tribal society.

The extended family or *tiyospaye* was the central organizing feature of traditional Lakota society, and the values of the *tiyospaye* system continue to influence the way Lakota people think about society, politics, and economics on these reservations today. The extended family was often mentioned in relation to the care and nurturing of children when their parents had to work for TANF. Immediate family members still represent the bulk of the safety net available to the poor on the reservation. Of the TANF partici-pants interviewed, 77 percent mentioned receiving help from their mothers or other female relatives when they were sanctioned or needed child care, transportation, or housing. Most TANF participants rely on family members to watch their children. As one Pine Ridge participant explained, "They'll provide child care, but some people don't want child care, because they make you go get a physical, skin test. Some people don't like the child care. Then plus you have to get your kids a physical and immunizations. There's a lot that you have to go through for child care. I make their grandma babysit." A Rosebud project director observed the same thing: "I know they [TANF] provide babysitting costs, child care, but on the reservations there isn't very much childcare facilities available for them to use. So they depend on relatives. And with the drinking, you've got to understand, if they don't have a babysitter, what can they do? If it's me, I'm not going to leave my kids with just anybody."

At the same time, TANF was increasing the burdens on grandparents to provide full-time child care for their grandchildren. As an elder Pine Ridge woman noted, "And who is the one that are caretakers? Grandparents. And it's just making it harder and harder on the grandparents." Some parents even consented to changes in the custody of their children to help reduce the burdens imposed by TANF. Those who are least able to work within the extended family are viewed as the best members to receive custody of the children because they will be the last to have work site requirements imposed on them. A Social Services worker stated, "I think the caseloads are about the same as they were last year, maybe a little lower. Part of that is there are more grandparents and noncustodial parents. That's called Zero Plus, but now the custodian doesn't receive any benefits, it's just benefits for the kids." These changes in formal legal custody may have only a minor impact on the children involved, since there is a common pattern on the reservation of extended families living in close proximity and interacting actively on a day-to-day basis. As one community leader noted, "The parent will just give custody to another relative and the child will be able to continue to get benefits, and the parent will live with that person so you will have the housing overcrowding as usual. Children will legally, through the court documents, be passed around, but maybe remain in the same house." The State Social Services office estimated there had been a 15 percent increase in Pine Ridge TANF cases that were child only, amounting to two-fifths of the total caseload in 2003. However, Zero Plus did not necessarily compensate grandparents adequately for the costs of raising their grandchildren. As a Rosebud elder explained, "There's no money. I can't pay bills. . . . You know, everything is so expensive. You can't live on that TANF."

Even extended family support can be lost, however, when a participant's problems with alcohol, drug use, domestic violence, or lack of coping skills ends up burning their bridges to their family members. As one woman stated, "It's usually like for illness or like having a hard time, I would say like our family has a small group of family and extended family who help each other. As for the financial part of it, it's like nobody really has extra resources within a family unit to help each other, so like for us, we would probably go through either the district CAP office or use another program that provides assistance." The pressure on extended family to bail out someone with chronic problems can become too great. One woman went as far as to state, "Sometimes I think family members resent other people trying to better themselves. Just probably the family dynamics." One tribal employee noted the lack of family support for TANF participants trying to succeed in their work site. Relatives become jealous of a family member who gets a work placement, and so they go out of their way to report them to DSS for any infractions on the TANF rules. Rather than build up their self-esteem, their family members try to drag them back down. These issues are going to make it hard for these women to get themselves to work, feel good at work, and be able to be productive at work. The Lakota community has traditionally been based on the concepts of generosity, giving, and extending the concept of family to all living things. As one woman explained, "Anything they need help with, you just let the family members know and you try to help." When another woman was asked if she and her children had ever gone hungry, she said, "No. I have too many relatives for that." However, TANF participants themselves expressed skepticism about the willingness or ability of the community to help them out if push came to shove. One woman characterized her community as "everyone out for themselves." Another asserted that in her HUD cluster housing community, no one would share with each other. As resources are contracting rather than expanding, it becomes more difficult to find help in the community apart from immediate family members. As one woman recalled, "A lot of times I think what's lacking is the parents not being there, you know, the parent isn't home. Maybe it's a single parent family. . . . Because back in the old, old days, a child was raised not only by the parents, but by family members, all the *tiyospaye,* all the families, you know. And it isn't like that now. And having just one person watch them, that's a lot of work. That's a lot of responsibility, and that doesn't happen nowadays where everybody is involved in raising the children, so it's a lot different." Another woman noted her disappointment in the family supports for her son. "His father, he's from around here. He's got all kinds of relatives that live here, but basically I can't depend on them. In the beginning they say, 'Oh, I'll be there for him, and I'll be there for you,' but they're not. They have their own kids and their own lives to deal with, and I don't really try to depend on them." People are going to find ways of helping themselves, but things like generosity and reaching out to family members may not be realistic for those who are the poorest of the poor.

However, the traditional value placed on women and the obligations of men toward women have been severely eroded by the incorporation of these Lakota communities into the peripheral end of a global market economy. In some ways, TANF seems to be bringing underlying tensions around gender relations and their impact on families under the spotlight. Several of the TANF recipients joked that if the men are not willing to support them by going out and getting jobs, at least they should be willing to take care of the kids while the women are forced to go to a work placement. The entire burden of taking care of the household, cooking, cleaning, child rearing, and now wage work are all being heaped on the women, but the men are not required to do anything. From the perspective of the women receiving TANF, all the men have to do is meet their individual needs in any way they want. "It's kind of not fair, because the mom is stuck with the kids, yet they have to go to work. And the dads could be somewhere else and just sign up for GA and get it, and not have to do anything." The gender burdens feel extremely unfair to these women. As one woman explained it,

> After I went through my divorce, he left me with the [rent] bill, and so I'm paying back-rent plus my rent, and that comes right out of

my [TANF] check before I even get it. I got it signed over to them,
my rent's paid. . . . The only thing there was that he had an adjustment period because of the divorce, and he was just really confused
and hurt, and just didn't understand why, and now he pretty much
knows. And his dad is still dogging him. I got a protection order
and everything against him, but he still goes around. I mean, it's
just really really hard to settle him down after he gets him all riled
up, you know. It's just really really terrible.

There is also an implicit, if not explicit, group willingness to privilege
young males by not reprimanding them for failure to take responsibility for
children they father. Sons see their fathers abandon them, never provide for
them financially, and start other families with other women and learn from
that example. The counterexamples of long-term stable relationships between
men and women are rare. Only 45 percent of the Native American families
with children in Shannon County are headed by married couples. Another
41 percent of families with children are single-mother headed, a status that
is consistently associated with poverty. Assistance in getting child support
and other methods of forcing delinquent ex-spouses and boyfriends to pay
for their children are not forthcoming. There is a crying need for programs
for young men. They need to be reached and trained and told that they
have responsibilities and there are consequences to their actions, and there
has to be some follow-through with some forms of enforcement.

Concerns of domestic violence are throughout both reservation communities. As one woman admitted, "I almost got killed in a relationship that
included drinking and at the time that happened, I think I was at my very
lowest in my life. I felt like I had no self esteem. It was like beaten out of me.
And once that happened to me and I was away from that individual for maybe
a month or so, it was like I woke up, or my eyes opened, or my mind cleared
or something, and I felt like 'I don't want to live like this anymore. Why do I
continue living this way? So I kind of like regained my bearings so to speak,
and uh, decided to make that change right there." While other interviewees
were more guarded, incidents such as being unable to finish high school because
of a broken arm, and moving out of the family home when the children's father
was released from the penitentiary alluded to problems with domestic violence.

One woman captured the connections between domestic violence, poverty,
and barriers to employment.

I'm sure they'll hire me back at the casino, but it's just a matter of
getting over there and getting my teeth done, and it's just such a

big hassle. I'm just real self-conscious of it, and you can't make tips with no teeth [*laughs*]. It just don't work that way. I've been trying to get mine fixed for, geez, three years now. . . . I've learned to hide it really well, after two years of going like that, you know, you just learn to hide stuff. . . . I got a divorce. That's what happened to the teeth. I had two busted ribs and two knocked teeth. So that was it. I was done. I didn't want it to be passed on to my children, because sooner or later it would have been. My girls were still real tiny babies then, so I figured, "We'll get rid of you now, and that way maybe they won't remember you."

The same woman went on to explain,

I was abused very badly when I was growing up, I had to drop out of school. That's why I had my kids so young, because I was scared to go anywhere or do anything, and I had a boyfriend, and that's just where I started out when I was fifteen years old. . . . And I enrolled in school trying to make myself feel better about my whole background and what was happening to me, and I was just really strong when I had kids, because I said "I'll never let my kids be beat that way, ever." I mean, I start shaking when I see violence happening in front of me, like what I do, it's like it's me again. So violence is just not part of my life.

Some of the erosion of family relationships and obligations is directly attributable to problems of substance abuse. While the stereotype of drunken Indians has been greatly overplayed, the rates of alcoholism among the Northern Plains tribes are around 25 percent, higher than in the United States generally, and higher than for reservations in other regions (Spicer et al. 2003). This leads to special challenges for both TANF participants and their children. As one TANF participant from Rosebud recalled of her ex-husband: "He was into drugs, so he wasn't giving us nothing. He left me with all the bills. He never had to pay nothing. I'm still paying on the bills that we owe. They're all in his name, and the court order says he's supposed to pay half because we were married at the time the bills were created, but he hasn't spent a dime, not one dime." One woman said of the community since TANF, "To me it looks like it got worse. Because a lot of these people are unemployed and they don't have no income, and they take to drinking. It's like they have no home to sit in, no will to go on, like to better themselves or anything, because there's nothing to do it with. Because they can't get

TANF unless they put in hours, and there's not enough work sites around here." Another woman noted, "My daughter has one [Employment Specialist] that, she didn't show up at eight o'clock yesterday morning, so they closed her case. Ready to give up. Hopelessness, I think that's what makes people drink a lot, because they can't get help, they can't do what they want to do, it's a standstill." A Social Services worker stated quite adamantly,

> I believe, if the jobs are here, with some period for adjustment, that 75–80 percent of the jobs would be filled if there was a job for everyone on the reservation. People would rather work than not or get TANF. Sure, there are a few with severe alcohol problems, and we need drug and alcohol rehabs to be taken care of internally for employees. Now, if you miss work on the reservation and you have an alcohol problem, there is no place to go for help. Enough shut down now with the tribe. A good deal of these problems would go away if five hundred to a thousand jobs were created here, after an adjustment period for the employees and the enterprises.

One former participant in Rosebud sent her fifteen-year-old son to treatment for marijuana, explaining, "Well, I think they go through that stage, like I've had a lot of my male friends now come up to me and say, 'What are you doing, sending your son off to treatment? We all did that when we were that age.' And then some of them still do it, and some are running around drinking, so I always look at them and say that I want my son different than you. . . . I don't mean to hurt their feelings, but I said I want my boy to be different than a lot of the men I've chosen to be with and even around."

Some attributed substance abuse and violence to the economic context of forcing people to work where there are no jobs. One Rosebud women reported, "He left after a week [of my working]. Maybe it was two weeks. He got mad and said he doesn't want to see me anymore. And that made me feel worse. . . . But he is in and out all of the time, so we're used to that." Another Rosebud woman said,

> I ended up quitting college for a while because he had complaints that I stayed away too much with the working and the shop and the college at the same time. So then I quit college for a while, so then I had to go back on TANF. . . . I was making more money than him. Like I could make one week, and then make more money than he would make in a month [selling quilts]. So that kind of got a little threatening to him, and he didn't like it very much. And I

always wondered, "Oh, God, what if I got this job?" because I make like $3.90 more than him, so he was threatened by that right away. So it's hard for the women because it's like they have to make sure that they don't make more than the men. Otherwise that could be threatening to the men. And that's not fair, but that's how it is.

Others saw the work requirements of TANF as helping improve women's self-confidence and independence. A woman working in the Rosebud school system said,

> I think that it's hard on people who aren't used to working, but the people who really want to improve themselves or work, I think it's helped them. . . . It's making people really take a look at their lives and, well, it seems to be more helpful rather than, you know, just staying in your situation. It's saying "Here's something that's going to help you," and "here's some skills that's going to help you," so in that way it seems to be helping. And it seems like there's more accountability and self-determination and being more responsible for their own lives, instead of somebody always being there to lead them through things. . . . I think it's, the way I see it, it's giving the women more self-confidence so they feel like they can actually do these things, because I think my niece was really, she always felt like she couldn't learn and she couldn't work, and she was really depending on social services all the time. And now she's kind of, um, opinionated [*laughs*]. . . . But I can see the change in her. It's a good change.

A Rosebud participant agreed: "It's emotional for me. It's got a lot to do with your self-esteem, and being able to get up and help yourself, and not having to sit at home and wait for a check, or wait for a man to show up and help you, and you know, it just makes me feel a lot better to work." Another Rosebud participant added, "I just feel better working instead of being on TANF."

Conclusion

In the setting of the Pine Ridge and Rosebud reservations, imposing work requirements before you have stimulated a viable, "independent" economy is like putting the cart before the horse. The requirement that TANF recipients look for work is becoming the engine for creating that work. However, without concrete economic development, the work being created is defined by bureaucratic needs rather than the needs of the economy. As a result, the opportunity for a long-term productive impact is being squandered (Pickering 2001). Rather than simply exclude the lifetime limit for recipients in areas of high unemployment, it would seem more logical to suspend implementation of TANF in those areas altogether. The funds that are going to be spent in managing the bureaucratic monitoring of individuals in artificial work sites could be spent creating real economic development that would result in actual jobs for recipients down the road. The overwhelming conclusion is that some common sense and flexibility at the local level could solve many of the harshest aspects of TANF. As a woman from Pine Ridge expressed it, "It's up to the person, and their circumstances, and whatever reasons they have. Because we're not all the same."

SIX

Welform Reform in Appalachia, Kentucky

Coal has always cursed the land in which it lies.
—Harry M. Caudill

Households in the Cumberland Plateau confront ongoing hardships from the historically constructed poverty that surrounds them. Nonetheless, Kentucky implemented progressive education policies and stimulated cooperative approaches to job creation and economic development to help ease the more onerous aspects of making the transition from welfare to work. Extended families coordinating their efforts in the complex and integrated "everyday" economy also provided support to households struggling between welfare and work.

It would be tempting but incorrect to attribute the changes in the education systems of McCreary and Owsley counties to welfare reform. Many of the positive efforts we observed should be viewed as a consequence of a major education reform by the state of Kentucky. In 1989 the Kentucky Supreme Court found that the public education system of Kentucky was unconstitutional and mandated the state legislature to undertake broad and sweeping reforms. In June 1990 the legislature passed the Kentucky Education Reform Act (KERA). The legislation did, indeed, prescribe several major changes, among them financial reforms, school restructuring, curriculum changes, and student and family services. As a result, Kentucky was showing significant improvements in human capital investments prior to welfare reform. Thus, when K-TAP became a reality, local school administrators, teachers, community leaders, and at least some parents, were already addressing the need to keep children in school in order to avoid creating another generation of poorly educated young adults heavily reliant on welfare and other human services.[1]

Perhaps the experiences associated with education reform prepared McCreary and Owsley counties for welfare reform. Our interviews revealed an unusually

1. For a review related to KERA, see *Review of Research* 1996.

high degree of community involvement in efforts to support TANF participants' transition from welfare to work. We attribute this high level of support
to several factors. Prominent among them are community leadership and
organization, small county populations, and racial and ethnic homogeneity.
However, in spite of the more progressive approach in these counties, history
and geographic isolation continue to plague efforts to raise the quality of life.

This chapter represents the results of a series of interviews conducted in
Owsley and McCreary counties between April and October 1999 and between
September 2002 and March 2003. Directors and personnel within county,
state, and federal government agencies; private businesses; and nonprofit
organizations were interviewed about their involvement with, observations of,
and responses to TANF. In addition, a total of fifty-one current and former
recipients of TANF were interviewed about their experiences with and reactions
to the requirements of TANF, twenty-one in Owsley and thirty in McCreary
(for general characteristics of participants, see Appendix A, Tables 5–8).

TANF Administration

When welfare reform came to McCreary County, it caused a widespread
sense of concern. With unemployment running above 20 percent, there was
good reason for worry. Since the mines closed in the mid-1970s, all eighteen
of them, jobs have been scarce. Many workers went to large urban centers
"up North" in search of work, although some later returned to be near family.
Among those who remained, census data show that over a third commute
to jobs outside the county, mostly in the towns of Oneida and Somerset.

For three-quarters of the last century McCreary County was "company
owned." Stearns Coal and Timber Company owned the forest and the coal.
Even today many McCrearians blame the Stearns Company for their current
economic hardships. It maintained a monopoly of the coal and timber. By
doing so, it effectively squashed any and all entrepreneurial efforts by smaller
firms and individuals. It also followed the once common industrial management pattern of paternalistic dominance of its workers and their families.

By 1990 the structure of work had changed rather dramatically. Employment in the service sector, manufacturing, and retail trade had become the
base of the local economy. Most of the service sector jobs were in health
and education. The manufacturing was largely in textile and leather fabri-
cation, where pay is relatively low and employment somewhat unstable.
The retail sector in McCreary County is similar to retail jobs elsewhere—
seasonal, part time, low wage, and providing limited or no benefits. Thus,

with the transformation of the local economy, there came a noticeable shift from jobs in the mines, which paid relatively well, to jobs in retail shops, "cut and sew" factories, and a mixture of good and bad jobs in the service sector, which paid relatively poorly.

Compassion, concern, and caring were easily discerned sentiments as people talked about the hard-to-place families. Only a few of them were seen as headed by a "ne'er-do-well" father or mother. More often reference was to their inability to read or write, to their fear of leaving the community to work, to mild mental or physical disorders, or to substance abuse. The concern was succinctly expressed by one community leader: "What are they going to do when their welfare payments end? Not many of them will ever be able to hold a job."

At the time of our interviews in 2002, no K-TAP participants had been sanctioned in Owsley County, and only a few in McCreary County. Case managers appear to be patient and forgiving; interviewees reported no instances of families being sanctioned for missing appointments. Managed caseworkers in Owsley County had been diligent in keeping all participants eligible until they were able to make the transition from welfare to work by finding community service work for them or getting them into job training programs. In at least a few instances, participants had been persuaded to declare previously "hidden" work, which enabled them to meet the work requirements of the able-bodied K-TAP program and thus maintain their eligibility for food stamps and Medicaid. The energy, compassion, and creativity of Owsley County's two caseworkers appeared to be a major factor in the numerical success of welfare reform. As one of them said, "We have to be creative in figuring out what can be counted toward their work requirement. We try to get in-home employment for people who can't leave home. These would be people who don't drive, or have a learning disability. We have some people who are afraid of getting out in social situations. Or they may have a disabled child they have to care for."

In the January 1999 Owsley County activity records, of 123 K-TAP participants mandated to work, 83 (67 percent) were working in unsubsidized employment while continuing to receive some support from K-TAP. Another 37 (30 percent) were meeting their work requirements by doing "community service." Two individuals were engaged in the Other Work Employment Program (OWEP), and one person was enrolled in adult basic education. The state expected Owsley County to have an 83 percent participation rate. They had exceeded that with a rate of 87 percent. One of the caseworkers said with pride, "We [Owsley County] have the highest participation rate in the state, and we have the least resources."

When we interviewed current and former K-TAP participants, all of them agreed that welfare reform had been a good thing, at least so far. As one participant remarked, "When welfare reform was announced, we expected a disaster. But it hasn't happened." There was the sense that it had been good in several ways. It had gotten some people to go to work; people who could find jobs. It also had gotten others to begin improving their job readiness by attending literacy classes, working to get their GEDs, or doing community service work to improve their employability. In most cases, they viewed the new work requirements as fair, and even beneficial. As one mother said, "I was really shy until I started doing that community work. It got me to where I could open up more. Instead of working for free [doing volunteer community work], I could get out there and do it myself and get paid for it. You get more each month working than you get from K-TAP." Caseworkers also noticed a positive change of attitude among welfare participants. According to one nonprofit service provider, "They are beginning to accept the notion that welfare payments are not going to be there forever, that they have to work, and that is a good thing."

Hardship and Welfare Reform: The Struggle to Break Free

What these details do not reveal is the struggles of young parents trying to break free from their own childhoods of poverty. Most of the people we interviewed started out "in the hole." Many of their parents were divorced or never married, and most of their parents never finished high school. Substance abuse and family violence were all too common in their childhood homes. Their parents worked at low-paying jobs and had insecure employment. As a result, their families had very limited resources. Just getting by, with help from government programs, family, and local charities, was a common experience.

It is important to bear in mind that with the loss of employment in the Cumberland Plateau during the Great Depression of the 1930s and with the closing of the mines in the 1970s, many people moved away in search of employment elsewhere. The people we interviewed are the children and grandchildren of the families that were left behind to eke out an existence in a very depressed local economy. It is noteworthy that many of those who moved away in search of employment had returned upon their retirement, often with quite good pensions and Social Security eligibility. The resources of these family elders were an important part of the extended family support system, which is almost certain to decline as they die.

The official rate of unemployment hovers around 10 percent. However, local reckoning puts the true unemployment rate at 40–50 percent. Thus, discouraged workers, people who would like to work but have given up looking, make up an estimated 30–40 percent of the potential labor force, which causes problems for the Family Support Services case managers and K-TAP participants. The architects of K-TAP reasoned that in counties with low unemployment rates all able-bodied adults between the ages of eighteen and fifty should be able to find at least eighty hours of work per month, especially when community service and self-employment are accepted as meeting the work requirement. However, if the true unemployment rate is 40 to 50 percent, as locals reckon, K-TAP participants may be expected to face great difficulty in finding unsubsidized employment to meet their work requirements.

However, lifestyles resist change. At least half of those we interviewed appeared to be repeating their parents' mistakes: many were divorced or separated, most had dropped out of school before completing high school to work in marginal and unstable jobs with low pay and no benefits, many of the men were permanently disabled from job-related injuries, and many children and parents alike had serious health problems, which was evident in the high levels of SSI eligibility.

From a purely financial standpoint, the transition from welfare to work is not easy. Several interviewees indicated that they ran out of money before the end of the month (or the next payday). These financial shortfalls led to food insecurity. One mother told us, "Sometimes at the end of the month, before food stamps come in, I have go to the food pantry." She was not alone. We asked, "Have you or your children ever gone without eating because you didn't have money to buy food?" Some indicated they had, but not the children. As one responded, "Yes, lots of times, near the end of the month. Lots of times I don't eat so the girls can eat." Another said, "I've gone without eatin', but they [the children] don't know about that. I've gone without, but not my kids. End of the month is hardest." Another reported, "Yes, I have skipped meals so the kids would have food." Clearly, parental sacrifice is a near universal norm.

Health care is another area where existing supports appear to be inadequate. The healthcare needs of children of respondents were met to a large extent through Medicaid and Kentucky Child Health Insurance Program (K-CHIP), but not the healthcare needs of adults. Individuals eligible for K-TAP benefits were typically eligible for Medicaid under the Kentucky plan. Medicaid was administered by Family Support Services. Children of K-TAP participants also received a "medical card." Even when the parents were not eligible for a K-TAP cash grant, they and their children could receive a medical card if the family income was below a certain threshold.

For low-income families with an adult working, K-CHIP provides health insurance for children living in families with incomes below 200 percent of the federal poverty line, even when the employer does not. Initiated in July 1999, the program requires participants to pay a premium of $2 to $20 a month depending on income and to make minimal co-payments at the time of service (Kentucky Cabinet for Families and Children 2003). However, that left many low-income adults without health insurance, even though they were working, since employers rarely provide health insurance benefits to employees, particularly part-time and seasonal workers.

Even with medical assistance, respondents reported that they frequently did not go to the doctor, or get prescriptions filled, because they did not have money to pay for them. For most prescriptions a co-payment was required, and although it was nominal, sometimes there was little or no cash available and a choice had to be made between medicine, food, diapers, fuel, and other essentials. This was also the case when the physician or health professional recommended nonprescription items such as aspirin, cough medicine, or medical supplies. Items that cost only a few dollars were sometimes well beyond the means of many respondents at certain times. As a consequence, they failed to receive health care, which, in some cases, resulted in lost days at work and ultimately loss of employment. When a parent is ill, "We just tough it out," as one woman said. In the Cumberlands, "yarb doctors" are still quite common ("yarb" is used locally for "herb"). These are people who have specialized knowledge of the medicinal values of plants that grow naturally in the forests. The concoctions made from these plants, "home remedies," were widely used and preferred by some, especially the older residents.

Lack of affordable, quality child care also keeps some welfare participants from seeking employment or returning to school. The administration of child-care payments was structured to incorporate a co-payment starting with families whose income was $900 a month, up from $400 a month in 1997. The co-payment began at approximately 5 percent and gradually increased to 11 percent depending on the number of children in care. Transitional child care was available, "if funding permit[ed]," for up to twelve months for eligible participants, and childcare assistance was terminated when income crossed 150 percent of the poverty line (Kentucky Cabinet for Families and Children 1997, 2003).

Transportation is a huge problem for families trying to transition off welfare. Many families have no vehicle at all, and those who do often have older ones. Several of the interviewees with vehicles admitted to having no car insurance, even though it was required by the state. For example, one interviewee said, "I dropped the [car] insurance. I couldn't afford it. It was insurance or food, so I dropped the insurance." Repairs were a constant drain on resources, and the unreliable nature of the vehicles led to missed appointments with social workers, doctors, and job interviews. Although cash supports of up to $500 per year for car repair and a maximum of $400 per year for expenses related to participation in Kentucky Works was available to K-TAP participants (Kentucky Department for Social Insurance 1997), missing work because of "car trouble" sometimes resulted in their being fired. The isolation of Owsley County also hampered the efforts of the Family Support Services Office to get K-TAP participants involved in welfare to work programs. According to one of the case managers,

> A lot of things that are offered, such as Work Investment Act programs, but our regional offices are located so far away [41 miles] that our clients don't actually get help. Places closer get it all. We're sort of pitched in the back. Seriously, that's how a lot of the programs are. It's hard for a lot of our people to get out to Hazard [location of many regional programs]. But people who live in Perry County [where Hazard is located], it's very available to them and, of course, they're going to get the lion's share. I think the location of the regional office in Hazard is central for our region, but it's just difficult for our clients to be able to get there. A lot of our clients don't have vehicles and there are no taxis. So a lot of our clients are very limited so far as transportation.

Drug and alcohol abuse is another serious and pervasive barrier to work for some welfare participants. As one professional put it, "I can't say whether there is a correlation or not to the socioeconomic status of the K-TAP participants. It seems to stretch across economic boundaries. I know that half, probably more, have been substance abusers themselves or have immediate family involved in the drug scene. This sometimes has resulted in them having had children removed from the home due to drug abuse." In his view, drug and alcohol abuse was a leading cause of families being on welfare. One of the interviewees echoed this assessment of the drug abuse problem. "It's really bad. People get caught up in it in their everyday life because there is not anything for them really. Got a lot of time on your hands, no jobs, and I think that's why a lot of people do it. Makes lot of people [have] marital problems. It's in just about every other household around [here].

It's very common. Very easy access. 'Meth' is being made actually in the neighborhood."

Despite these significant barriers to employment, caseloads had been declining. When K-TAP was initiated in McCreary County, there were 742 cases being handled by the Social Insurance Department. By December 2002 that number had declined to 345, including 188 adults with average monthly grants of $237. Females accounted for 77.66 percent of the adults, and 58 of the 188 adults were employed.

The passage of welfare reform legislation created a great deal of anxiety in Owsley County during the fall of 1996. As one official bluntly stated, "We feared for the worst." The official message was "Get a job!" But the people of Owsley County had been struggling for years to find adequate employment, and welfare reform did not include job creation as one of its goals. Thus, it was not surprising that people were anxious about what would happen in the months ahead. The emphasis was on moving welfare participants off the rolls and into the workforce with a small amount of assistance for job training, job search, transportation, and child care. Nevertheless, by April 1999 there had been a 32.5 percent reduction in the number of families receiving assistance through K-TAP since it began in October 1996. When K-TAP went into effect, Owsley County had 240 families on their roster of managed cases. By April 1999, 162 cases remained, and by October of 2002 144 families, including two married couples, comprised the TANF caseload. There was near consensus among community leaders that about half those who left welfare had found employment as paid workers. For some that had required relocating outside the county. According to a Family Support Services caseworker, among those who found work in the area, "many have obtained jobs with the school system, with local nursing homes as certified nursing assistants, some are working in factories. I have some who are cashiers at our local [retail] businesses—convenience store, grocery store, Dollar Store." Unfortunately, most jobs were part time, paid minimum wage, and offered few, if any, employee benefits. There were other welfare families that had left the county (and K-TAP), but local informants did not know whether they had found work or not.

The remaining half of those who left K-TAP did so for one of three reasons, according to caseworkers. First, some became ineligible because their family situations had improved to the point where their income levels were above the threshold of eligibility (reconciliation with a spouse, marriage, child support payments increased, etc.). Second, in a few instances the children had reached the age of maturity and thus the family became ineligible. Finally, some families were simply "making do" without the K-TAP payments, which raised the question of how they were providing for their basic needs. A similar assessment was given by case managers in McCreary County.

Education

Prior to welfare reform, Kentucky had implemented several progressive policies—among them education initiatives and a coordinated and collaborative administrative effort to improve economic conditions—that effectively supported people leaving K-TAP and reduced caseloads. Another explanation for caseload declines may be found in the extended family support and "everyday" economy of poor households in the Cumberland Plateau.

There is no question that lack of education is a major barrier to getting off welfare. Welfare and workforce development administrators in Kentucky were acutely aware of the education deficits that prevailed among the state's adult population. While about two-thirds of adult K-TAP participants in Kentucky had a work history in 1997, only half had high school diplomas (Kentucky Department for Social Insurance 1997).

Kentucky has an exceptionally progressive attitude toward education as a legitimate work activity. An education bonus of $250 per individual is now available to both adults and children who receive high school diplomas, GEDs, or postsecondary degrees. Supportive services offered to students include some of the following: child care, transportation, car repairs, registration, and activity fees (Kentucky Cabinet for Families and Children 2003).

Virtually every interviewee who had not completed high school said they needed more education to make better lives for themselves and their families. We found they were very appreciative of the support provided by Family Support Services caseworkers for the advancement of their educations. The following comment was typical: "They helped me to get in this training [course] and they're going to help me go to college too."

We also asked participants about their occupational aspirations. At least half of them wanted professional jobs such as dietician, teacher, nurse, social worker, architect, and child development specialist. These aspirations were long standing, but achieving them had been delayed by past circumstances, including teen pregnancy, early marriage and child bearing, divorce and nonpayment of child support, lack of funds, and lack of family and community support.

We observed that some K-TAP participants, and former participants, were or had previously been engaged in educational activities that counted toward their work requirements and prepared them for future employment. K-TAP policy allowed participants deemed "not work-ready" to engage in supportive activities to facilitate work readiness, including up to six months of "continuing education," "life skills training," and "job readiness and basic skills" that was usually provided by a Community Service Agency (Hudson Institute 1997). These educational activities covered a wide range of experiences, such as adult literacy classes, GED preparation, Certified Nursing Aide certification, computer use and keyboarding, attendance at area community and technical colleges, enrollment in University of Kentucky extension classes, and courses in small business entrepreneurship. Participants were given up to six months of cash assistance to pursue these educational opportunities before they were required to begin participation in work activities, rather than only two months as the federal option provided (Kentucky Cabinet for Families and Children 1997).

Allowing mandated K-TAP participants to meet their work obligations by attending school was a deliberate Kentucky policy that was enthusiastically supported by Owsley County Family Support Services caseworkers. "We prefer that [attending school]. I'm an education advocate. I think a GED or high school diploma enhances their chances for a better job. And we give a $250 educational bonus to those that get their GED or finish high school. We push that constantly." The school board also was providing space for several adult education programs. The Parent and Child Education (PACE) program required parents and children to participate together in a program that took the parent through literacy training and on to the GED. At the time of our visit in 2002, there were fifteen enrollees, and eleven of them were K-TAP participants. The Kentucky Vocational and Adult Education Program (KVAE) was also supported by the school board. KVAE was an adult literacy and GED preparation program, but did not require parent and child both to participate. In the spring of 1999 there were ten GED students, mostly K-TAP participants. However, during the course of the 1998–99 school year there were seventy-six adults enrolled in KVAE.

For those who completed high school or earned their GEDs, or who had already completed some college, K-TAP allowed them to pursue their career goals by allowing them to fulfill their work requirements by taking college courses. As one participant stated, "K-TAP gave me the opportunity to get my GED and better myself by getting higher education." Participants were allowed to complete up to twenty-four months of postsecondary education without having to participate in any other work activity (Kentucky Cabinet for Families and Children 2003). Women were making great efforts to go to school and get jobs. Their motivation was to do it for their children, as much as for themselves. The director of the McCreary Community College

Center believed there was a "spin off" as well. Some K-TAP participants at the college were reportedly getting their friends to go to school too. These "welfare moms" were becoming role models for other low-income mothers and young women.

"The challenge is to bring the men along, not beat up on them," the college center director continued. She believed the programs were encouraging women to have higher expectations and to recognize that there were jobs for them. But she worried about the men left behind, stating: "We need to educate them for jobs that are not traditionally men's work [in McCreary County]. Agriculture is gone. Mining is gone. Timber is about gone. There is very little construction work. Where are the jobs for men? We need to train them for jobs in the service industry—computers, electronics, business, and teaching. And help them to feel good about doing these kinds of jobs." One K-TAP father confirmed the director's commitment to encouraging the men. He was taking classes at the college center and had his heart set on becoming a high school math teacher.

School attendance is not compulsory after age sixteen in Kentucky. There were numerous reasons for dropping out of school, none of them pleasant. Pregnancy was a common explanation: one K-TAP recipient said, "I went to twelfth grade, but didn't graduate. I got pregnant and my mom threw me out. I lived with cousins and lived with the child's father for a year and a half." Another said, "I quit to stay home to take care of my little girl." She was fifteen years old at the time.

Poor performance was the reason some dropped out of school. One woman told us, "I was kept in sixth grade for three years. Then I quit." One cannot avoid wondering why she was required to repeat the sixth grade for three years. Did she have a learning disability? Perhaps she needed glasses? Was there a family situation that distracted her attention from school matters? Child abuse by parents was also cited as a cause for leaving school; as one woman reported: "The only reason I dropped out [of the eleventh grade] was my mom and dad. When you go to school with a busted mouth, two black eyes and bruises all up and down your body, it's time to leave [home and school]." Others said they left school because of a parent's illness and the need for them to help take care of the parent. In addition, some dropped out because they "were bored" or "just didn't like the teachers."

The removal of lack of education and job skills as barriers to employment requires community efforts, as well as individual commitment. Changes in the educational systems of McCreary and Owsley counties reduced dropout rates. Modifications of the curriculum were producing a higher quality education. In addition, the community colleges were creating opportunities for education consistent with the needs of expanding employment in the county and region. The future for students appeared more promising. Reducing the historically high dropout rate was one of the priority goals of the educators and community leaders of both the McCreary and Owsley County school districts. While that effort did not address the educational deficiencies of most K-TAP participants, there was a conscious effort to help the next generation obtain quality educations to enable them to avoid the need for welfare assistance. Making school exciting and meaningful to the students was the goal. "You go, you sleep, you graduate" was no longer an acceptable attitude in the schools, according to the assistant superintendent, a native of McCreary County, who taught in central Kentucky schools and served as a guidance counselor, curriculum supervisor, and assistant superintendent before returning to his home school district in 1997. Under his guidance the high school curriculum was revised to create greater flexibility for student choice in courses, and the district had recently created an alternative high school as one way to keep students in school to graduation. There were forty-two slots in the alternative school, where the emphasis was on work skills. The student-to-teacher ratio was about half that of the regular class-room. Efforts were being made to initiate a collaborative program with the Job Corps to get local high school students (potential dropouts) into the program during which time they would live at the Job Corps campus during the week and be at home on weekends. The curriculum of the Job Corps campus, located in McCreary County, emphasized technical skills training.

The effort to open doors to more opportunities for high school students was not limited to technical training. The campus of the McCreary Community College Center is located adjacent to the high school, and high school seniors were taking courses at the college center. The path from high school to the community college center was literally a brief walk through the woods— "A pathway to the future," said the director of the college center. She believed that more people were going to school as a result of welfare reform. Since two years of college education were allowed under K-TAP, the college was committed to opening the doors of the college center to K-TAP participants as well as other young people of McCreary County. There were at least a dozen K-TAP participants studying at the college.

The Owsley County School Board also had several programs serving low-income families—adults and children. Most of the programs were in place prior to welfare reform, but conversations with school administrators made it clear that serving K-TAP families was an important goal. The Universal Food Program provided hot breakfasts and lunches to all students attending school. This meant that during the school year every child in Owsley County who attended school received at least two nutritious meals five days each week. According to one school official, "Monday morning breakfast is the favorite meal of the week, with some children occasionally behaving as though they have had little, if anything, to eat since Friday lunch." According to the school superintendent, "This program also is an effective incentive for school attendance, which averages about 94–95 percent in the elementary school and around 90 percent in the high school." The school board also provided free transportation to the Appalachian Technology College in neighboring Lee County for high school students who wanted to take courses there. These were primarily vocational-technical courses, which appeal to students not planning to attend college.

In 1998 the school board initiated the School-to-Work Program. Juniors and seniors could register for the program, which allowed them to spend two hours of their school day working in a local business, government office, or nonprofit organization to gain work experience. In the first year, twenty students were enrolled in this program. However, interviews in the community revealed there were some who questioned the value of the program. One concern was whether the "work experiences" were genuine and have the intended effect. Another doubt was raised about whether the students most needing work experiences were the ones enrolled in the program. The claim was made that most of the enrollees were among the best students in the high school and were planning to attend college rather than go to work when they graduated.

In Owsley County, the "Action Team" (a local nonprofit organization) had initiated several projects designed to help low-income people increase their education and gain skills that would make them more competitive in the labor market, either as employees or as entrepreneurs. The Action Team was created several years before welfare reform as an antipoverty and economic development pilot project based in Berea, Kentucky. While they were cognizant of K-TAP participants' needs, their programs were designed to serve a broader clientele of low-income families as well as county-wide economic development. The vehicle for some of their educational projects was distance learning, and equipment was provided through the Center for Rural Development in Somerset with funds from the U.S. Small Business Administration. Maintenance of the program was through a variety of local groups and individuals in the city of Booneville, including the Farmers' State Bank. With distance-learning technology, the Action Team was able to initiate several projects.

They held workshops on entrepreneurship using the curriculum and staff of the University of Louisville. According to the Action Team Director, "There

were nine people took that class called 'Kentucky Entrepreneur.' Six of them
were K-TAP participants. That was followed by a class on business planning
called 'You, the Entrepreneur.' Five students enrolled and three were K-TAP
participants." The entrepreneurship training by the Action Team was not
limited to adults. "We have a $20,000 grant that will be spent on a student-run
store that will be in this building. That will be started in the fall [2002]."

The Action Team also was a prime mover in the creation of the Fund for
Excellence (FFE), a largely locally funded program designed to encourage
children to remain in school and to pursue post–high school education.
"The kids start in seventh grade. This graduating class, this year [2002],
was the first FFE class and their class had the highest percent graduating in
the history of the county." The FFE continued to be supportive of students
even after they graduated from high school by providing small scholarships
with funds earned by the students and their parents. These funds were
invested, and the earnings provided small scholarships for graduates continuing their education.

Therefore, welfare reform may have been a modest force in generating
the apparent increased community commitment to keeping children and
youth in school, at least through high school graduation. No doubt there are
other forces at work here too. Nevertheless, more effort may be required by
the educational leaders, and by K-TAP officials, to encourage more welfare
participants to take part in educational and job training opportunities. For
example, education and training that is targeted at available jobs would be
helpful, according to welfare participants.

Working Together for a Change:
Administration and Economic Development

The K-TAP plan emphasized the need for a "multi-agency approach," and
former governor Paul Patton established a cabinet level "task force" that
included the secretaries of the Cabinet for Families and Children (CFC); the
Cabinet for Economic Development; the Cabinet for Workforce Development;
the Cabinet for Arts, Education, and Humanities; the Cabinet for Health
Services; and the Cabinet for Transportation to address moving K-TAP participants into employment (Kentucky Cabinet for Families and Children 1997).
One might argue reasonably that welfare reform had stimulated increased
community efforts toward better welfare administration and better economic
development in McCreary and Owsley counties by getting people to work
together for a change.

Administration and Coordination

K-TAP also emphasized a "community-based approach" to reform that sought to incorporate the strengths of the private nonprofit and for-profit sectors. As such, K-TAP sought to address both the characteristics of individual participants and the "regional distinctions of their communities." Thus, during the development phase of K-TAP the CFC held regional meetings across the state to provide local governments, private organizations, and citizens the opportunity for "public comment" on its K-TAP plans. Welfare participants were also advised of reforms, and their input was solicited. Meetings were held with leaders of business and industry to discuss labor demand and their potential contributions (Kentucky Cabinet for Families and Children 1997).

As a result, the decline in caseloads was a bit of a surprise even to the people in Family Support Services. The Family Support Services supervisor in Owsley County explained, "My theory on that [the amount of reduction] is that we did it very gradually. We did it in a manner that we did everything we could to help these people [make the transition from welfare to work]." He also gave credit to others in the community. "It was not just us. It was not this agency solely that did it. It was every community partner. It was all of them pulling together saying, 'Listen, this is what we got to do and this is how we're going to do it. Each member has to do his part.' And it worked."

Regional policy was developed by the CFC in partnership with the Cabinet for Workforce Development, which oversaw twenty-six local "Job Service Employer Committees" responsible for providing information on local labor market conditions and recommending appropriate workforce development activities. The departments of Social Insurance, Social Services, and the Office of Family Resource and Youth Services (all divisions of the CFC) were responsible for service delivery and worked with the Workforce Development Cabinet and private and nonprofit organizations at the local level. The Department of Social Insurance was responsible for the determination of eligibility for K-TAP, food stamps, and Medicaid. The department referred "work-ready" K-TAP participants to the Department of Employment Services, a division of the Workforce Development Cabinet, which was responsible for contacting employers and connecting participants with jobs. The Department of Social Insurance also contracted screening, testing, and placement duties to local community service organizations and contracted childcare and transportation service to public and private providers (Kentucky Department for Social Insurance 1997).

The "multi-agency" and "community-based" approaches were integral to the K-TAP program. The CFC continued to contract with the Workforce

Development Cabinet to provide employment services to work program participants. Moreover, increasingly progressive programs continued to emerge over time, including the creation of a partnership between the CFC and the Kentucky Association of Health Care Facilities, where selected Kentucky Works program participants were trained and hired as nurses' aides. The association had also agreed to consider OWEP placements in nonprofit nursing homes. Positive incentives for employers to hire K-TAP participants were also put in place. Tax-based incentives were made available to those who hired K-TAP participants and offered child care, education, and training (Hudson Institute 1997). In addition to the federal "Work Opportunities Tax Credit" passed by Congress in 1996, which provides a federal tax credit for companies that hire cash assistance participants or members of a family who have been on assistance for at least nine months, the state created the "Unemployment Tax Credit," offering a $100 credit against the Kentucky income tax liability of employers for each eligible individual hired (Kentucky Cabinet for Families and Children 1997).

One K-TAP respondent described the changed situation in an appreciative manner. "The seventies and eighties, it wasn't like now. At the time there wasn't anybody that would have enough faith in you to help you. Most people would say, 'Well, you ain't got no education. You can't do nothing.' Now there's somebody on every corner, just about, willing to help you if you're willing to try." As we talked with people in the community, we found confirmation of what she was saying. We recalled the Owsley County Family Support Services supervisor's comment that "it was all the community part-ners working together" that explained the dramatic drop in the number of people on welfare. What had they been doing to create the sense that there was support "on every corner?"

In Owsley County an interorganizational alliance of representatives of government agencies, the private sector, and nonprofit organizations was formed in Booneville. They were meeting monthly to share information about their individual efforts, to discuss ideas for future actions, and to coordinate the work they were doing. A similar organization had existed previously, but the new organization emerged in response to welfare reform, at least in part.

"Food Place" was created to respond to emergency food needs of families in Owsley County. Previously there were no food pantries in the county. Instead, several agencies responded as best they could to emergency situations. These included churches, nonprofits, and government agencies, but there was no coordination. Food Place replaced the piecemeal approach by opening a food pantry where all previous providers could refer families in need. It was managed by a ministerial alliance and funded by donations and gifts from individuals and the organizations that previously offered food assistance. Being formally organized as a food pantry enabled Food Place to access a food distribution center in Lexington and to distribute federal commodities.

As we talked with community leaders, it became clear that virtually every organization—public, private, and nongovernmental—had played a role in efforts to raise the educational attainment, meet basic needs, and create jobs in Owsley County. There appeared to be two keys to this remarkable level of community involvement: leadership and community organization.

Virtually all the leaders of local organizations were born and raised in Owsley County, although most of them had school and work experiences outside the county. Perhaps most significantly, they had returned "home" to make their livings, raise their families, and improve the situation in Owsley County. Many of them were from the same age cohort as the K-TAP participants, which meant they had known each other since childhood, or at least had known each other's families. A good many had married into local families. Thus, there existed a social network of kin and friends among local leaders.

This social network, which appeared to embody a considerable amount of trust, took on a quasi-formal structure as an "interagency meeting." Initially they met sporadically, perhaps every couple of months over lunch. When K-TAP was initiated they began to meet monthly and to take on a more formal character with a regular meeting place, a host, a recorder of meeting activities, and a distribution of minutes. According to one long-standing member,

> We try to get someone from every agency to attend. And if you do that and you get in there and just go around the table, real informal, and go around the table and say, 'Joe, you got anything new? What's new down at your office?' And if there is (anything), I share that information. It's a good thing for us to get together and share ideas. And we usually have it down at the Action place [Action Team offices]. That's a good place to have it. It's in town. And then we get minutes and notes of the meeting. Sometimes we meet together with the Industrial Board.

Given that Owsley County has a very small population, it was not surprising that there was considerable overlapping membership among the boards of community organizations and government bodies. Thus, to some extent, sharing of knowledge among organizations was endemic and informal, but it appeared that the quasi-formal interagency meetings served a coordinating function, particularly with regard to family and social service efforts.

In McCreary County a similar interorganizational "coordinating" group emerged shortly after the implementation of K-TAP. However, it did not develop the formal structure of the group in Owsley County. Nor was it as inclusive. The McCreary group consisted primarily of representatives of organizations directly involved in the delivery of social and family services. Nevertheless, its monthly meetings held at the Whitley City Motel and Restaurant were well attended and, according to the Family Support Services director, "very helpful."

Economic Development Efforts

Perhaps the most critical barrier to getting off welfare is lack of employment opportunities in or near the community where one lives. Thus, community economic development that increases the jobs available and raises incomes is of utmost importance. The leaders of McCreary and Owsley counties were making strong efforts in this area. Although most of the development activities in the counties existed prior to welfare reform, there were some new initiatives directly related to the changes in the welfare system. And the sixty-month time limits of K-TAP had introduced a sense of urgency among leaders.

Local leaders were well aware of the need for economic development. In government, business, and education, nearly everyone interviewed expressed a sense of urgent need to expand economic opportunities and improve the skills of local workers. The plight of welfare participants was a point of concern, but their vision of the future encompassed the well-being of all workers. There was keen awareness and acceptance of the view that if welfare reform was to work in the long run, they would need more employment opportunities. This view was expressed repeatedly and emphatically by community leaders as well as K-TAP participants.

To a very large extent the economic development efforts in McCreary County were led by the County Judge Executive's office. Economic development efforts resulted in the establishment of Outdoor Ventures Corporation (OVC), a tent-making factory with U.S. government contracts, which employed 120 workers and had surprisingly progressive management. The company ran an on-site educational program for its workers. State funds paid the teacher, and OVC employees attended classes four hours per week at the factory while being paid for class time. Seventy-five percent of the workers had completed a basic math course, and OVC was planning a reading comprehension course. Also, a free health clinic was held every fall for all workers and their families. This included free blood pressure and diabetes screening, as well as flu shots, all at the company's expense. As the plant manager saw it, it was a way to raise the productivity of his workers. "Better skills, better health, better attitudes toward their work and themselves. It's good for them and it's good for the company."

McCreary County was selected as the site for a new federal penitentiary complex near Pine Knot. The $100 million complex will eventually house 1,200 inmates, including 150 to 200 male inmates in a minimum-security facility, and employ more than 400 persons with an annual payroll of $17 million. In anticipation of the coming penitentiary complex, personnel from the community college center and the high school had been meeting with prison officials and local economic leaders to initiate curriculum changes and special instructional programs designed to prepare McCrearians for employment at the facility.

Local leaders were also successful in attracting a major retail facility to Whitley City, a Pamida discount store. Pamida is a subsidiary of ShopKo Stores, with 165 locations in rural communities, primarily in the Midwest, Western Mountains, and Pacific Northwest regions. The store in McCreary County provided employment for approximately forty workers. Pamida also served as the anchor for a new shopping mall on U.S. 27, which included a dozen or so smaller retail shops.

While it would be incorrect to portray the economic development efforts in McCreary County as a response to welfare reform, it is clear that community leaders are keenly aware of the need for employment opportunities to meet the goal of welfare-to-work. But economic development is, of course, of benefit to all McCrearians. McCreary County appeared fortunate to have local leaders who were civic minded and dedicated to raising the quality of life for all in the county. The OVC plant manager's explanation for his policies articulates the sentiments of all the leaders we interviewed, "What I own today was owned by someone else sixty years ago. Sixty years from now, someone else will own it again. My life isn't going to be remembered, but I want to feel like I've done some good for the community and the people."

Families in the Everyday Economy:
A Multiple Resource Strategy

All of the interviewees combined multiple sources of formal market and unreported income, both cash and in-kind support, in a household survival strategy. This was true regardless of whether or not they received cash grants from K-TAP, and regardless of whether or not they were employed. Extended family members also emerged as important sources of both cash and in kind support. Formal wage work, government checks, and gifts of money were key means of obtaining cash necessary to participate in the formal market economy. For virtually all low-income families, these sources of cash were not sufficient, and additional cash was obtained by "doing odd jobs," the local term for unreported income or working "off the books."

Market Activity

Wage work, often part time and seasonal, provides a source of cash that is needed to access goods and services available only through formal market transactions. In our interviews with current and former K-TAP participants, virtually everyone knew of families who were working and no longer received cash grants from K-TAP. Many of the respondents were among those making the transition from welfare to work. As required by K-TAP, they were working or volunteering. Nonetheless, all of them continued to receive assistance from other government programs, family and local aid groups. The income they received from working was too little to make them "self-sufficient." As shown by Christina Smith-Fitzpatrick (1999), most poor Kentuckians are working poor who rely primarily on earnings from work, but often complement this income with welfare assistance. Fifty percent of families who received cash welfare benefits in Kentucky between 1995 and 1997 included a wage worker (Smith-Fitzpatrick 1999).

Public Supports

Public assistance programs are another common supplement in the everyday economy. Among the K-TAP participants and former participants, food stamps, heating assistance, Medicaid, K-CHIP, Women, Infants and Children (WIC), free school lunches for the children, use of the local free health clinic, free child care from family and some nonprofits, job training and education from nonprofits, food banks, clothing banks, the Family Resource Center at the school (for school supplies and some clothing), and government and nonprofit transportation programs were all mentioned as providing some support. Occasionally child support was obtained through public judgments; however, these could be difficult to enforce. One divorced mother told us her ex-husband was $15,000 in arrears with child support payments.

K-TAP itself was part of the mix of the everyday economy. We learned from a Family Support Services manager that "when the first sixty months of K-TAP were up [in October 2001], there were only fifteen cases [whose eligibility expired]. Almost all of them had some other income in the home. In some cases there were other individuals in the home (or multiple individuals) who received SSI or Social Security." One cannot help but wonder how many K-TAP eligible families also have other sources of income in the home which make it possible for them to "make ends meet." They must, because the K-TAP grant alone cannot provide for the basic needs of a family. The case manager continued, "Only one of the fifteen families was discontinued without any 'known' source of income other than K-TAP. But we did find her a job at the local nursing home and she continues to work there today." According to another case manager, "A lot of them have a disabled child or spouse and they're getting SSI. That [money] replaces the K-TAP payment that they lost. They didn't really lose a lot. And a lot of the people in this area have unreported income."

Some families that voluntarily left K-TAP were encouraged to do so by their caseworkers in order to save their eligibility for a future time when they might need the welfare payments even more. One of the case managers explained it this way. "Sometimes a mother [or father] may be working at a part-time job that pays $400-$500 per month. Once this income is considered in the case, it may cut their K-TAP grant from the full amount to, say, $50 per month. Because they have another means of support at that time, it may be more to their advantage to let the K-TAP check go, especially if their children are very young, and not use up their K-TAP months. That way, years from now, if they face a hardship, they can reapply for their remaining months of K-TAP."

Unreported Activity

The unreported economy is huge in the Cumberland Plateau. By the "unreported economy," we mean to include all exchanges of services and goods that are "off the books." According to a government official in McCreary County, "I would say it's two to three times larger than what you see on paper [statistics describing the formal economy]." Other community leaders estimated the unreported economy constituted half to two-thirds of the county's total economy, the value of all economic transactions. "They [low-income families] do what they have to do to survive."

Unreported work, for mostly legal but sometimes illegal activities, can be for cash or in-kind goods and services. Respondents described a variety of legitimate but unreported "odd jobs," such as cleaning, child and elder care, farm work, or logging. Given the nearness of the forest, especially in McCreary County, it is not surprising that many worked at activities related to timber.

Cutting logs, hauling logs, clearing brush, and cutting firewood were cited as sources of unreported income, especially for men. For women, the odd jobs were more traditional domestic tasks, such as cleaning homes, caring for children, cooking for an elderly person or family, and "doing hair." Other ways of earning unreported income included mowing lawns, picking up cans, picking wild berries and nuts, working in tobacco fields, house painting, doing light construction, repairing vehicles, and running a "taxi" service. One individual reported selling her household furniture and personal items in order to "raise money."

Some of these entrepreneurial activities became small businesses, such as the man who purchased nonperishable goods in Lexington on a weekly basis and resold them from his garage "store." Buying and selling used items, such as household appliances, hand tools, clothing, and antiques, was common. Many who engage in this routinely attended the "flea markets," which are institutions in the eastern Kentucky counties. In all these instances, the goods or services being sold were legal; however, the failure to purchase appropriate licenses or to pay taxes was not. Buying goods in the unreported economy involved some risk, however, as one respondent explained: "I don't like buying things from people, because you never know whether they were stolen or not."

Illegal activities, in the usual sense of the term, are another means of earning cash in the unreported economy. While virtually everyone interviewed knew about these activities, perhaps even knew the persons involved, only a few individuals were reportedly engaged in them. Drugs and alcohol seemed to be the primary trade goods, especially since some Cumberland Plateau counties are "dry." Running cock fights was also reported and confirmed by a deputy sheriff. For a few individuals these activities provided income, but for most people they were an opportunity to spend money rather than earn it.

A major component of the unreported economy does not involve the exchange of money. Rather, goods are exchanged for other goods, services are exchanged for goods, or services are exchanged for other services. The possibilities are enormous, and a great many are realized by residents. The monetary value of such exchanges is usually modest, although the use value may be quite large. "Bartering is still very big in McCreary County," according to one official. The same could be said of Owsley County. For example, in order to build a new house, a man cut saw logs from his woodlot and hauled them to the sawyer, who cut them into lumber. Since the home builder was short on cash, he cut and hauled more logs than were needed for his house. He gave the surplus logs to the sawyer as payment for his services. The principle can be extended to many other kinds of exchanges, and the practice apparently is quite common in the everyday economies of the Cumberland Plateau.

If K-TAP participants are willing to report these activities, case managers will credit them toward their work requirements. But persuading participants to report their unreported work was a challenge. Money earned and reported may cause a reduction in their cash grants, even though the time worked counts toward their work requirement. "It's a bit of a balancing act for them," according to a case manager.

The Extended Family Supports

Parents, grandparents, and other family members often are called upon to help welfare families absorb the shortfalls resulting from the loss or reduction of welfare benefits. It would be difficult to overemphasize the importance of the extended family for financial, social, and emotional support. We asked respondents, "What would you do if you did not have money for food, clothing, housing, utilities, transportation, or school expenses?" Far and away, the most prevalent response was, "I would ask my parents [or other family members] for help." In a few instances, women said they would ask their boyfriends for help. Most of the respondents had lived outside their "home county" for an extended period of time during their lives, but family drew them back. In most instances the returnee looked to the family for support. However, in some cases they returned to provide care for a parent, grandparent, or other family member. Gifts and loans from family and boyfriends were important supplements to meeting household needs. Trading goods and services with family and friends, either for immediate or longer-term returns, was also common among the families in the Cumberland Plateau.

A few of the families we interviewed owned land or their own homes. Often this was the result of their parents, or other kin, giving them the land. They then pulled a relatively inexpensive trailer there, forming an extended family compound. In other instances, a parent simply gave permission for his or her child to move a trailer onto the land. Thus, it was quite common to find the nuclear families of an extended family living within a short distance of each other, often within walking distance. This spatial proximity facilitated the social relations and support network of the extended family.[2]

For example, grandparents were seen as having a key role to play in encouraging education. Many grandparents are a key financial resource in

2. This practice was also highly prevalent in the *colonias* of the Texas counties.

their extended families, drawing upon their pensions and Social Security to assist their families. "Grandparents who have worked away and retired back in McCreary County are an important resource [for] money, experience and skills," according to the college center director.

We should hasten to add that not all families lived in such harmonious relationships. As noted, some K-TAP participants reported quitting school because of abusive home lives. Gender roles and the strains created by TANF were often elements in family tension. In the Cumberland Plateau, where traditional gender roles are often strongly affirmed and men folk still joke about "keeping the woman barefoot and pregnant," welfare reform and its mandate that women work outside the home created pressures to redefine gender relations in some families. This caused tensions in some families. "Most men want their wives to stay home with the kids," said one mother. Another, whose husband was unemployed, stated, "Sometimes it's hard because I control the money. Sometimes it bothers him if he wants something and doesn't have the money."

The director of the McCreary Community College Center expressed concern about a backlash in a culturally conservative community such as McCreary County, where some women feel guilty about leaving their children to work outside the home, male partners feel threatened by women working outside the home, and there are many in the community who believe strongly in the traditional gender roles of women as housewife and mother. This observation was confirmed by the professional staff of several nonprofit organizations working with K-TAP participants.

The phenomenon of threatened male partners is real. Respondents related stories of family violence erupting when the male partner suspected "his woman" of becoming too friendly with one of her male coworkers. In most instances, quarreling was reported to have been the extent of the hostility. However, there were a few cases of serious physical injuries being inflicted on women by their male partners.

Research indicates that most incidents of family violence go unreported. And while it would be inaccurate to characterize all of them as related to the strain created by welfare reform, local residents did express the belief that reform was causing trouble at home for some women. As one K-TAP participant stated, "You're going to have to have a really understanding husband because there's going to be a lot of changes going on when the further you better yourself, the less dependent you're going to be on him. He's going to feel a little left out because you're not going to be around him. That's the biggest thing I had to work through."

At the same time, K-TAP women were becoming role models for their women friends, who were saying, "If she can do it, so can I." The director of the community college center saw K-TAP students bringing their friends to take classes. Several of the K-TAP participants who were interviewed expressed the same sentiment. For example, "K-TAP gave me the opportunity to get my GED and better myself by getting higher education." And another woman said, "Having to work is for the best. I feel better about myself." This sentiment was echoed by another former K-TAP participant. "My self-esteem is higher. The kids were embarrassed to say their mom was on welfare."

In sum, the extended family functioned as a "shock absorber," one that largely worked. However, persons interviewed wondered how much families could absorb because many members of the extended family were themselves already stretched financially, especially parents and grandparents who may have been receiving financial assistance or living on Social Security benefits and pensions. Furthermore, the potential tensions between men and women may be even more difficult to manage as welfare reform forces changes in gender roles.

Conclusion

Based on interviews with welfare participants, former participants, and community leaders, there appeared to be several major barriers to transitioning from welfare to work on the Cumberland Plateau. Participants had the potential to remove some of them, but others required dedicated and sustained efforts by political and business leaders in the community and beyond. Despite the struggles and hardships that continued to face families in poverty, Kentucky made a commitment to education as a road out of poverty for all its citizens, including those on welfare. The emphasis in Kentucky on "community-based" responses and coordinating beyond the walls of the welfare office also created synergies of opportunities for families and economic development for the region. The resourcefulness of poor families in orchestrating resources garnered from formal work, public benefit programs, unreported activities, and the strong network of extended families ultimately explains the ability of these counties to make welfare reform work.

SEVEN

Welform Reform in the Rio Grande Valley, Texas

If we want to measure success by getting people off of the welfare rolls, well,
I'll tell you right now that the programs have been very successful.
But, I mean, is that what we want to measure it by?
Or whether we made a difference in those peoples' lives?
Whether we increased the capacity of the workforce?
—Maverick County TANF Administrator, Spring 2003

The state of Texas devolved significant authority for administering welfare reform to the regional level.[1] As a result, differences in regional administrative structures and capacities have had significant impacts on policy implementation and services in Maverick and Starr counties, which, in turn, have had direct effects on TANF participants' ability to achieve positive outcomes. The Texas welfare reform program is among the toughest in the nation in terms of its work requirements and adult time limits. At the same time, Texas has among the lowest levels of TANF cash assistance and offers among the fewest opportunities for education and training. Devolution to the county level exacerbated the effect of these deficiencies. Thus welfare reform in Maverick and Starr counties was marked, ultimately, by sharp caseload declines, resulting largely from scores of participants quitting the program.

The vast majority of the TANF participants interviewed in these counties were not able to take advantage of new programs theoretically available under welfare reform because they either did not exist in these counties or, if they did, they were never informed of them. The interviews, supported by the secondary literature on reform in Texas, indicate that welfare reform in the Valley, as it related to TANF participants, amounted to little more than a concerted effort to push them off the rolls as quickly as possible and keep them off. For most of the thirty-one families who had left welfare at the time of their interview, this strategy had produced neither significant positive nor

1. We use the term "Valley" here to refer to both the Lower Rio Grande Valley and the Middle Rio Grande Valley of Texas, which, combined, runs from Brownsville-Matamoros on the Gulf Coast to Val Verde County (north of Laredo). Most residents of South Texas, however, consider "the Valley" to be limited to Cameron, Willacy, and Hidalgo counties, which form the southernmost tip of the state.

negative impacts on their material well-being. For the majority of the thirty-one families who were in the program, its effects were similarly weak. This was largely explained by the low level of TANF benefits offered in Texas, the temporary nature of welfare use by most families, and the minor role played by TANF as a component of household survival in these counties.

However, although most of interviewees who had left TANF experienced few serious negative impacts on well-being, the implementation of reform in the context of weak labor markets and social service systems was not benign. Those families with the weakest personal networks, in other words, those who relied most heavily on public assistance, did experience the most extreme forms of material hardship, including homelessness and hunger, as direct results of reform. Moreover, many families who escaped extreme material hardship lost access to educational and training opportunities.

This chapter is organized around three broad themes. First, we consider why the number of TANF cases declined rapidly once work participation requirements were imposed. The evidence supports the argument that policy, specifically, the punitive aspects of welfare policy, fueled caseload declines. Second, we explore what happened to the families that left TANF as well as those "left behind" in the program to explain its impacts on household survival strategies and well-being. Finally, given the poor condition of both the local labor markets and the service delivery systems in each county, we turn to the "everyday economy" in the Valley to explain why the material hardships expected to accompany welfare reform were not more severe or widespread. The answer to this question is straightforward: AFDC in Texas never offered so much assistance that its retrenchment could "cause" severe hardship. Still, the ripples sent out by reform through other areas of the everyday economy, specifically, its impact on access to other public programs and family networks, threatened the well-being of most respondent families. Primary data were collected through in-depth interviews with 62 current and former TANF participants and approximately 110 community leaders from the public, private, and "third" sectors in Maverick and Starr counties (for general characteristics of participants, see Appendix A) between October 2002 and June 2003. A preliminary round of interviews with 10 TANF participants was conducted in March of 1999.[2] Primary data were also collected through participation in various community events ranging from food pantry distributions, to county commissioners meetings, to observation of interactions

---

2. Data from the 1999 participant interviews inform the analysis but are not quoted or included in numeric calculations here.

between TANF applicants and caseworkers in local Texas Department of Human Services waiting rooms.

Administrative data were collected from various state and federal agencies, including the Texas Department of Human Services (TDHS) and the Texas Workforce Commission (TWC). Demographic and economic data were collected from the U.S. Bureau of the Census, the U.S. Department of Labor, and the U.S. Department of Commerce.

The main lesson from the Valley case studies is that the institutional structures, both formal and informal, that obtain within a place as well as the ties that connect locales to broader political and economic forums (i.e., regions, states, and nations) strongly condition the impacts of welfare reform on families under devolution. When enacting PRWORA, legislators championed the idea of "local control" and greater responsibility for third-sector and private organizations (Coates and Himmelfarb 1996). In Texas, a "business-oriented" approach was pursued, following the belief that a rising tide would raise all boats (Texas Department of Human Services 1996; Pindus et al. 1998). In reality, devolution of control over welfare to state and local elites in Texas and the Valley resulted in a nightmare that could have been predicted by anyone familiar with state and local institutional structures.

Background: Valley Life, Poverty, and Politics

To understand the impacts of welfare reform in the Valley one must begin with the fact that they were conditioned, first and foremost, by the very limited role cash welfare assistance played in the lives of most families. When welfare reform was implemented in Texas in 1997, the state offered one of the lowest cash payments in the country. The maximum TANF benefit for a family of three was $188 a month, and the average grant was $160 per month. Because no family, even one receiving food stamps and housing assistance, could survive on such a pittance, families were necessarily engaged in other forms of income-garnering activity to survive in the "everyday economy."

The impacts of reform in the Valley were also conditioned by the unique character of Valley poverty, which distinguishes it in important ways from that found in the other regions included in this study. Perhaps the most distinct characteristic of Valley poverty is that it is fueled to a large extent by the constant influx of new immigrants from Mexico, most of whom lack the equivalent of a high school education, speak very little, if any, English, and have little to no economic resources beyond their own labor power. Immigrants enter and exit the Valley every day, legally and illegally, to work, to enroll their children in Texas schools where they will learn English, to stake a claim on the "American Dream" by building a home in the unincorporated and unregulated developments known as *colonias*, or merely to pass through to parts farther north (Richardson 1999). Understanding the matrix of immigration, education, and homeownership in the *colonias* is crucial to understanding poverty in the Valley because it provides the institutional foundation upon which families work toward a better future than that available to them in Mexico.

While problematic in many respects, the *colonias* are communities in which new immigrants find family, friends, shelter, and information leading to work and other resources. They provide a unique opportunity through which the poorest of immigrants, as well as long-time Valley residents, may become homeowners, a status they likely could not attain anywhere else in the country. Homeownership acts as a huge incentive for low-income families to stay in the Valley. Many families interviewed for this study, all of whom had annual incomes well below the poverty line, owned their own homes or were living with relatives in the *colonias*, paying very little or no rent.

The *colonias* began to develop during the 1950s when large landowners in the area began to divide large tracts in unincorporated areas, some of it in flood planes, into lots which they sold to families without providing paved roads, sewers, or potable water. Contracts were, and still are, made between sellers and buyers outside the banking system. Under these contracts, known as "contracts for deed," the buyer acquires no equity until the property is fully paid off. One missed payment may result in the loss of not only the land but also everything the buyer has built on it. Not all deed holders in the *colonias* enforced this option, however, and because lots can be purchased, as one Maverick County leader put it, "for $50 down and $50 a month for the rest of your life," the contract for deed was a useful instrument for many families.

Many of the families we interviewed explained how they built their homes themselves with the help of relatives and friends. They often lived with in-laws or in apartments during the early years of construction and moved into what was a hollow shell of a home as soon as the roof, doors, and windows were installed. They then spent the next three to ten years finishing the home, investing in it whatever money they earned beyond that needed to meet basic needs (see Richardson 1999; Federal Reserve Bank of Dallas 1996).

Because of the contracts for deed and lack of infrastructure, *colonias* are often portrayed as highly exploitative "rural slums," and in many cases, they are. However, there are more than fourteen hundred *colonias* in Texas alone, and there exists enormous variation among them. Moreover, not all deed holders are poised to foreclose on residents for one missed payment. Because older *colonias* were built just outside city limits, many have long been integrated into municipal service systems through incorporation or other arrangements. In many places, you cannot tell when you have left the city limits and entered a *colonia*.

Despite state efforts to stop the spread of *colonias,* enforcement at the local level is difficult, and they continue to grow (Federal Reserve Bank of Dallas 1996). In Starr and Maverick counties, newer *colonias* are located in isolated rural areas far from municipal services and do exhibit the Third World conditions stereotypically associated with the term, including deeply rutted dirt roads which become impassable during the rainy season.

The point is that the *colonias* are an alternative institution that affords many families what they themselves consider a "decent" standard of living in spite of their low and sporadic wages. Chad Richardson (1999) conducted a survey of hundreds of *colonias* households and argues that there are positive elements to *colonia* life and that they serve an important purpose. He notes that homeownership in the *colonias* exceeds the U.S. national average and that many residents choose to live there because they can build their own homes. Among other benefits, residents of the *colonias* express a sense of ownership and investment in their neighborhoods and homes (Richardson 1999, 45–47).

The *colonias* therefore create a strong incentive for low-income families to stay in the Valley, which, in turn, contributes to high poverty rates. They also affect the hardships associated with poverty. In short, a limited cash income goes much further when housing costs are low, and few of the families interviewed were living in abject poverty (see also Richardson and Pagán 2002 and Sharp 1998). On the other hand, the *colonias* also represent something of a trap. Although residents often become homeowners, they fail to acquire any equity until the deed is fully paid, and even then, they are unlikely to accrue much wealth through the property.

Another characteristic of the Valley which leads residents, both new and old, to stay is the existence of an ethnic community in which strong network ties provide access to key resources. Network ties bring new immigrants to the Valley and lead many to stay. The highly porous Texas-Mexico border (tightened only somewhat by new homeland security measures) allows *colonias* residents to work in the United States while sustaining important ties in Mexico (see Richardson and Pagán 2002 and Richardson 1999). Many of the families we interviewed had relatives who lived minutes away in the border towns of Piedras Negras, Carmargo, and Ciudad Miguel Aléman. Some went to Mexico once a week to attend church, and many, including professional workers, regularly went to Mexico for health care. The others had relatives one to two hours away in the large Mexican cities of Monterrey, Nuevo Laredo, and Reynosa. They interacted with these kin quite regularly, and mutual assistance flowed both ways. Of course, ties to San Antonio, McAllen, Laredo, Houston, and Dallas were also strong, as were ties to employers, relatives, churches, and other third-sector organizations in the states where they migrated for work. Thus, for many poor families, the *colonias* of the Valley function as the key node in an internationalized survival strategy through which resources obtained across an enormous span of economic, geographic, political, and legal space are combined.

Family and community networks are the main avenues through which the scarce resource of *trabajo* or "a job" is obtained. The overwhelming majority of respondents who were working found their jobs through personal contacts, and almost every respondent stated that in order to find work you needed to "know someone." The work available to the Valley's less educated residents has always been and remains highly "flexible" and informal, both in terms of labor demand among employers as well as in terms of the process through which jobs are found and distributed. Valley poverty is overwhelmingly the "working poverty" that accompanies less than full-time, year-round secure employment characteristic of traditional agriculture and the new low-end service and retail industries. The majority of respondents interviewed for this study had, at some point in their lives, been migrant farmworkers, and almost every one of them had parents who had worked in agriculture. Some had recently returned from migrant trips during which they worked up to fourteen hours a day, every day, in fields, canneries, and packing sheds from Illinois to Washington State. Migrant work is a family affair, and some began working in the fields when they were as young as eight. One man described bringing water to his father at the age of four! Others did not make their first foray into the fields until they were eighteen or nineteen, often after marrying into a migrant family. These latecomers described the work as brutal and could not understand how their spouses tolerated it. Most families who had recently migrated did so as a last resort to deal with financial crises. In a few cases, this was combined with a desire to avoid using their limited months of TANF eligibility.

Like the *colonias,* the institution of migrant farm work does not hold up well to mainstream U.S. standards. However, again, it does allow new immigrants and other residents who lack certain skills, particularly the ability to speak, read, or write English, to make a living on which many do not merely survive, but are able to build homes and, in some cases, send their children to college. While migrant farmworker families are arguably the most severely exploited group of workers in the nation, their rates of home-ownership are high, and many consider themselves well-off, especially as compared to family and friends in Mexico (see Richardson 1999).

It is also important to recognize that the institutions of the *colonias* and migrant farm work are grounded in a traditional family structure dominated by men, many of whom maintain tight control over their daughters and wives. This is achieved, in part, via control of women's access to public space, be it the corner store, the café, the disco, the school, or the workplace. The prevalence of traditional gender roles in the Valley adds an additional obstacle for women seeking, or forced, to exit welfare for work. One welfare worker in Starr County related that he had worked with many young women whose fathers prohibited them from leaving home to attend college. Others explained that it was not unusual for a man to prohibit his wife from leaving the home for any reason (i.e., "to buy a gallon of milk") without notifying him. One professional woman explained her seemingly natural deference to her husband:

> Well [*laughs*] . . . it is hard, it's hard, but it turns into a habit, sir, that after the years it's just natural. . . . Either you get used to it or leave. . . . And sometimes you're just afraid to face, you know, to face the world alone, especially if you were born in a family that you see your dad, you know, tie your mom. It's going to be that way. Ok. You grow up believing that the man is the man, he's always going to be the man. He's always going to be the boss. Alright . . . you grow up believing that that's the way it's going to be for you too.

Indicators of the starkly gendered social practices and gender inequality in the Valley appear in U.S. census data (1990 and 2000). Relative to the other areas included in this study, Valley women have lower levels of labor force participation, education, and rates of household headship. The effect of gender relations on education is compounded for women who grow up in Mexico and cannot afford to pay to attend school after completing *la primaria* (sixth grade). More generally, among our respondents, women who grew up on both sides of the border often left or were removed from school as young girls to either work in the home, the fields, or to get married. In their own words: "I had to work in the house, taking care of my younger brothers and sisters." Another stated: "The reason I got out of school was because I got married [when I was sixteen] and my husband, he didn't let me go to school no more." A respondent who graduated from high school and wanted to go to college explained, "[My parents] didn't let me. My parents were very old fashioned." Others had quit school to escape home lives of abuse. In the words of one welfare worker, many merely "exchanged the control of their fathers for the control of their new father, their husband." It is important to acknowledge that most women interviewed did not simply "quit" school or "drop out." Rather, they were pushed out by parents, teachers, husbands, and other circumstances beyond their control.

Low levels of education, little work experience outside domestic work and farm labor, and high rates of marriage and child birth at a young age contributed to extensive dependence on men and left some respondents vulnerable to domestic abuse. Although we did not ask respondents if they had ever been battered, one related how the boyfriend of another respondent had beaten that respondent in front of her when he had found the two having lunch together in the friend's apartment. The woman was not allowed to have guests in her own home without his permission. Such abuse was reported to be tolerated in particular by undocumented women whose batterers threatened to report them to the Immigration and Naturalization Service (INS) if they attempted to leave or file a report (see also Richardson 1999). According to a caseworker at a local women's shelter, these women did not report the abuse because they feared being separated from their citizen children.

Threats of violence against women were not limited to the domestic sphere. Two women social workers related incidents in which jealous and allegedly abusive husbands threatened them. One related the following: "One day I called this family . . . and this guy [answered], I thought he was coming to kill me because . . . I said, 'I want to speak to Ms. [last name].' And he said, 'That was her first husband and . . . and she's gonna know who I am when she gets home.'" She added, "[The woman] didn't show . . . for school for the next five days and we were kind of worried and when she came back they said he had beaten her up pretty bad. And then he threatened me for about three times. You know, 'I'm gonna [*indicates a threatening tone*].'" The public character of such acts, among others, indicates that physical violence toward women likely remains a socially acceptable instrument of male control in the Valley.

The impacts of welfare reform cannot be understood without understanding how the program interacted with these conditions. The *colonias* and migrant and seasonal farm work both represent what Richardson (1999) cites as Mexican culture's encouragement of "adaptability" and the tendency of people "to respond to needs and new situations by informal means" (1999, xv). Informal means are far from a panacea, however, and these institutions both buffered and exacerbated the potential negative impacts of welfare reform. Moreover, they provided neither an adequate nor safe alternative for women and children who were worst off and who became more dependent upon network members as a result of welfare reform.

With these conditions in mind, we now review the political and administrative institutional conditions to which welfare reform was delivered under devolution. While high rates of immigration, the *colonias*, strong network ties, migrant farm work, and *machismo* go a long way toward explaining the persistence of high poverty rates in the Valley, they do not, of course, tell the whole story. While census and BEA data clearly show that poverty in the Valley is systematically produced through official labor market conditions, less obvious are the key roles played by local and regional political institutions.

In *Poorest of Americans: The Mexican-Americans of the Lower Rio Grande Valley of South Texas* (1989), Robert Lee Maril provides a historical account of the development of contemporary Valley poverty.[3] He sees the historical geographic isolation of the area as underlying its weak labor markets and ineffective political institutions, writing: "To this day [1989], the Lower Rio Grande Valley of South Texas and the Mexican state of Tamaulipas remain isolated from both Mexican and American economic, political, and cultural centers" (Maril 1989, 23). In spite of the growth of the 1990s, Maril's observation remains largely salient.

The economic history of the Valley varies over time and across counties in terms of levels of farming, ranching, and manufacturing. However, the one aspect that has been of consistent importance has been that of trade with Mexico (Maril 1989), which under NAFTA has become an even more significant part of economic life. And while in relation to the border boom towns of Laredo and McAllen, Starr and Maverick counties have merely picked up scraps from the explosion in trade between the United States and Mexico, they are boom towns themselves relative to places like Shannon and Todd counties, South Dakota. The growth of the retail, services, and transportation sectors contributed to tangible gains in labor market demand as evidenced by solid declines in unemployment between 1990 and 2000 as well as declines in poverty (see Chapter 2 and Sharp 1998). In sum, the economic isolation of these counties is already becoming a thing of the past.

---

3. Maril uses "Valley" to refer only to those counties of the Lower Rio Grande Valley of Texas. This area includes Starr County but not Maverick, which is located in the Middle Rio Grande Valley and is as much West Texas as it is South Texas. Nonetheless, almost all of what Maril writes about the Valley applies to Maverick.

Local and regional political institutions, on the other hand, which also developed through isolation, may prove more resistant to change. Indeed, this chapter shows that the political history and political geography of a region are as crucial as labor market conditions to the outcomes of welfare reform. The experience of Maverick and Starr counties provides strong support for the argument that regional administrative regimes of varying political character are decisive factors in the outcomes of reform.

Maril documents the political history of the Valley as marked by "political bossism," which arose during the mid-nineteenth century and functioned to bring political stability to outlaw territory. Starr County is remarkable among Valley counties in that the political machine established in the 1890s reportedly "ran the county well into the twentieth century" (Maril 1989, 42). The legacy of that machine, combined with Starr County's reputation as a major center of smuggling, earned Starr the moniker of "the last frontier" among Valley residents.

The price of stability over the long term was local government that was neither accountable nor effective. Jobs in public education, law enforcement, and city and county government were distributed on the basis of connections and political allegiance. In Maril's words: "Unqualified and or incompetent workers are routinely hired; they then maintain and often run agencies and programs to the immediate loss of those served. Public monies are mismanaged, not necessarily with the intent to defraud, . . . but from incompetence or a lack of proper supervision" (Maril 1989, 94).

Locals who ventured to speak to us about politics echoed Maril's findings. They named contemporary political bosses who stood behind elected officials, described "*pachangas*" or election parties held just outside the polls and to which voters were literally hauled, paid, and offered food and beer for going. The vote haulers were women from large and well-connected families who were paid a lump sum per election. In short, politics in these counties are fierce battles between competing factions of elites for control over the distribution of what scarce resources exist, largely public contracts and jobs. The overwhelming majority of persons interviewed believed that good jobs in public agencies were allocated on the basis of personal connections. Some also believed that public benefits, such as transportation assistance, were allocated the same way. Accounts of graft and intimidation were fairly widely reported. For example, the director of one Valley agency engaged in economic development described a visit from "some goons of an unnamed county agency" immediately after receiving a large grant and being told: "You just sign the check and we'll do the rest. If you don't, well, people like you don't last very long." Other examples of corruption and bad judgment included the confession of the Starr County sheriff in 1998 to taking bribes from a local bail bondsman (Thorpe 1998), the confession of a Maverick County DEA agent to charges of aggravated assault by a public servant and deadly conduct for shooting an unarmed, undocumented immigrant in the back (Colloff 2001), a permanent injunction against the Starr County Judge for violating *colonias* development ordinances (*McAllen Monitor,* January 28, 2001), and a number of lawsuits and injunctions against several welfare-to-work organizations in the Starr County region (Smith 2001; Bisbee 2001).

Maril also notes that weak and undiversified private sectors created intense competition among localities for control over state and federal programs and the jobs they provide. This fractured the ability of leaders to work together within the counties as well as with the leaders of neighboring counties as a region (see *McAllen Monitor,* February 11, 2001). Finally, Maril notes a near complete absence of civic responsibility for the poor among Valley elites, whom he describes as "desensitized" to the poverty around them (Maril 1989, 157). All of these factors exerted profound effects on welfare reform.

Explaining Caseload Decline in the Valley: Institutional History and Punitive Welfare Policy

The Politics of Devolution in Texas

Annual caseload data from the TDHS show that TANF caseloads in a cluster of persistently poor rural Valley counties peaked in 1995 before beginning a gradual descent that grew steeper following the implementation of welfare reform in 1997. Within the cluster, the decline in Maverick was notably sharp, falling by 60 percent between October 1996 and October 1999 (Table 22).

The Starr County TANF caseload trend was also notable, however, for the opposite reason. In contrast to the national trend, its TANF caseload continued to climb between 1994 and 1997 before holding constant through 2000. The divergence in the paths taken by Maverick and Starr is even more striking when one considers that in 1994 Maverick had 1,446 TANF cases compared to 1,634 in Starr, but by 1999 the Maverick caseload had fallen to 475 cases while Starr's stood above its 1994 level at 1,763.

Additionally, while both counties experienced significant declines in Food Stamp cases, Maverick's 42 percent decline was almost double that in Starr. Similarly, Maverick experienced a much sharper decline in "family and child" Medicaid recipients, as its caseload fell by 18 percent versus only 4 percent

Table 22   Caseload declines in Maverick and Starr counties (October 1996 to October 2002)

	TANF cases		Food stamp cases		Medicaid recipients	
	Maverick	Starr	Maverick	Starr	Maverick	Starr
October 1996	1183	1798	5312	7952	8660	11982
October 1997	955	1980	4416	6997	8196	12340
October 1998	681	1779	3752	6485	7662	11986
October 1999	475	1763	3313	6266	7119	12272
October 2000	474	1724	3102	5838	7093	11528
October 2001	457	1498	3291	5799	7529	11533
October 2002	495	1338	4073	6179	8443	12433

SOURCE: Texas Department of Human Services.

in Starr between 1996 and 2000. These differences in caseload trends, particularly the radical divergence in TANF cases, are largely explained by one straightforward fact; the imposition of mandatory work requirements and time limits in Maverick County in 1997 and their suspension in Starr until 2000.

According to Maverick County administrators, following the passage of PRWORA aggressive efforts were made to discourage families from going on TANF, including increased surveillance, home visits, and electronic efforts to detect fraud. All nonexempt families were subject to state and federal time limits and required to begin immediate participation in work requirements. In the words of Maverick administrators, these policies precipitated the mass exodus from the program of all families with "any other means." In stark contrast, Starr County administrators stated that in the wake of federal welfare reform, "nothing changed," nor did anything begin to change until the year 2000 when the state of Texas essentially forced the regional board responsible for administering TANF in the county to enforce work requirements.

The question, then, is why were work requirements imposed immediately in Maverick but delayed in Starr? And given that work requirements were imposed in all the other persistently poor counties included in this study, what accounts for Starr's special exemption? The answer to this question is less straightforward and ultimately points to the importance of economic and political history and the county's relation to the other counties in its workforce board region. It is also related to the Texas approach to reform, which held as its top priority minimizing spending on the TANF program by avoiding the significant costs associated with providing welfare to work services, particularly child care (see Winston 2002; Sabo et al. 2003).

Maverick and Starr counties lack sufficient labor market demand and social service infrastructure to successfully move families from welfare to work. The difference in policy was not due to any real difference in the availability of services. Rather, it stemmed from key differences in the political and economic structures of the respective regional workforce boards to which they belonged, including the relevance of each county's TANF caseload to its board's meeting state "performance" criteria and the ability of key board member organizations to capture monies spent in each county. It was of crucial importance to the interests of the organizations sitting on the board that oversaw Maverick County that its TANF caseload decline sharply. In contrast, the organizations sitting on the board that originally oversaw Starr County had no such interest. Indeed, it was in their interest to exempt Starr.

When the state initiated the restructuring of its workforce development system in 1995 by organizing itself into twenty-eight regional "Local Workforce Development Board Areas," Starr was placed under the South Texas Workforce Board (STWB), headquartered 150 miles upriver in the metropolitan area of Laredo (Webb County). The placement was based on Starr's long-standing political ties to the other counties in that region, particularly those established through the "South Texas Development Council," a regional council of governments established in the early 1970s to coordinate local efforts and which administered the JTPA program in the region. Although Starr was much closer to, and more integrated economically and educationally with, the Lower Rio Grande Valley Workforce Board (LRGVWB), housed in the McAllen area (Hidalgo County), the decision was made by then governor George W. Bush and Starr County leaders to put the county in the STWB. The Starr County judge we interviewed and who was not in office at that time believed that the placement with the STWB made no sense and hypothesized that the decision was based on "the need for appropriate numbers."

Once Starr was placed with the STWB, the board voted to exempt the county from welfare to work requirements. According to a STWB board executive, the decision was based on a "recommendation by a board committee that evaluated the services available in the area. . . . [A]t that time they felt that there was not sufficient resources for the clients to actually go out and get some type of service."

Although services were lacking in Starr, they were also largely absent in Maverick, however, this did not prevent the implementation of work requirements there. Moreover, according to the executive, services remained lacking in Starr three years later when work requirements were imposed. Thus, the lack of services does not explain Starr's exemption. The real explanation is found in the politics and economics of social services in the

Valley and the role that each county played in its respective workforce board area.

In theory, workforce boards were supposed to be led by representatives from the private sector with the public sector (education and other third-sector organizations) and labor playing supporting roles. However, in the Valley, where the private sector is relatively weak and employers tend to be small and use personal networks to hire employees, business owners were largely uninterested in participating in workforce development programs or sitting on workforce boards. They were further deterred from participating to the extent they saw the councils of governments, which essentially became the workforce boards, as vehicles through which local "politicos" distributed public largess to friends and supporters.

Thus, the workforce boards that oversaw these counties were dominated not by the private sector, but by the community colleges, Community Action Agencies (CAAs), childcare providers, and other entities with historical experience delivering workforce-related programs and a strong interest in how funds were distributed. Each played a dual role as both a provider of services as well as a decision-making board member. Thus, the process of reform in the Valley was as much a matter of to whom the public funds, particularly the windfall of childcare, training, and construction monies, which accompanied reform, would be distributed as whether or not services were available in an area to help participants transition to work. Starr County TANF participants were exempted from work requirements not because services were nonexistent but rather because the major agencies that controlled the STWB while simultaneously competing for its funds did not provide services in Starr County or within its commuting range.

For example, a key member of the STWB and provider of services was the Laredo Community College (LCC). LCC did not have a campus in Starr and was located far outside commuting range. By exempting Starr, the STWB reduced its responsibility to spend TANF, Welfare to Work, WIA, and Child Care Block Grant funds on Starr TANF participants who would use those monies to pay providers located outside the Laredo area. Exempting Starr allowed the board to spend more of its funds through its own member institutions. Starr County leaders made exactly this point when explaining why they eventually chose to quit the STWB to join the LRGVWB in 2002.

Another reason Starr was exempted was the relatively small size of its TANF caseload as compared to that of Laredo (Webb County). In the eyes of the STWB, reducing the caseload in Starr was not central to its success at meeting federal performance criteria.

The situation in Maverick County and its Middle Rio Grande Valley Workforce Board (MRGVWB) was similar in that the board was controlled by service-providing entities incorporated outside the county but different in one crucial respect: as the largest county in the MRGVWB area—and as the county with the largest TANF caseload—reducing caseloads and enforcing participation in work activities in Maverick was central to meeting performance criteria.

As in Starr, Maverick County was placed under the MRGVWB on the basis of its long-standing political ties to the nine-county Middle Rio Grande Valley Development Council—also a council of governments. These same nine counties became the MRGVWB following the passage of welfare reform in Texas in 1995. In contrast to Starr, many of the institutions which held key seats on the MRGVWB also delivered services in Maverick. For example, the board's largest subcontractor for services, Southwest Texas Junior College (SWTJC), had an extension campus in Eagle Pass, which included a business and technology program. This presence in the county reduced the political obstacles to service delivery but did not eliminate them completely. Maverick County leaders alleged that the board tended to concentrate its spending in the smaller yet more politically powerful counties of Uvalde, Zavala, and Dimmit, which house the main organizations involved with the board. The interviews with Maverick County TANF participants indicate that few monies for assistance with child care, transportation, and education or training were available. Nonetheless, the main difference between Starr and Maverick was the fact that, in terms of meeting "the numbers," MRGVWB administrators had little choice but to aggressively attack the Maverick caseload.

These institutional differences at the regional level were the product of specific, historical-political relationships. They provide the underlying explanation why similarly distressed counties were treated differently and why caseloads took highly divergent paths under devolution. Ultimately, the politics of service delivery unleashed by devolution trumped a reasoned consideration of labor market conditions and the availability of welfare to work services. This explanation is bolstered by the fact that in 2000 the Texas Workforce Commission (TWC) forced the STWB to designate Starr a mandatory work county although the availability of services had not improved at all. An STWB executive explained why the state made Starr a mandatory county at that time: "The state wanted the entire border area to be full service [i.e., mandatory] . . . it was an election year." As in Maverick, the implementation of work requirements and time limits led to an immediate decline in caseloads (see Figure 3).

The next question is, once work requirements were imposed, why did caseloads in both counties drop so drastically? In this case, the most obvious answer is perhaps the most likely. Texas provided a parent with two children a maximum cash grant of $188 a month, and the average grant for a family of three in 1997 was $160 per month (Winston 2002). When policies of diversion and work requirements were implemented, especially in the absence of supportive services, the benefit was simply not worth the cost. One married TANF leaver with a large family expressed the general sentiment: "It's not worth it. . . . It was too much, too much. . . . And then they want you to work for eight hours every day for free? . . . And if you don't do it, they will give you a citation? . . . They will sanction you? . . . They gave me and my family $250 a month. It's not worth it." According to Maverick administrators, the caseload declines were fueled by decisions such as this; participants with any other options simply quit the program. Moreover, most of those we interviewed who had quit, like the man just quoted, were hardly any worse off for it. At $188 per month, TANF was at best a tertiary source of income, behind official and unofficial work, family support, and other forms of public assistance, particularly food stamps and housing.

It should be noted that participants who chose to quit or discontinue their application responded just as the architects of the program had intended. The program consisted of four main components that may be described as "hurdles" or obstacles to receiving assistance, none of which addressed participant needs for substantive education and training and all of which were designed to move them into the low-wage labor market as quickly as possible. Each component interacted with the broader household survival strategies of respondent families in a systematic manner that encouraged withdrawal. We examine each in detail.

First, before being certified to receive benefits, all applicants for TANF were required to attend a "Workforce Orientation for Applicants" (WOA) held at their local workforce development center. The purpose of the WOA was to inform applicants of work responsibilities and time limits under TANF and encourage them to seek other avenues of support. In Maverick County, the WOA turned out to be a highly effective deterrent to participation because applicants were misinformed at the WOA about the effect of lifetime limits on their children.

Almost half of the Maverick respondents stated they were told that their use of TANF would count against their *children's* lifetime limits such that when they were adults and had families of their own they would not be eligible for assistance if they had been on TANF for five years. As one explained: "From what we were explained, . . . if my daughter grew up and she had kids and she needed help with TANF . . . [if] they found out that I had already spent-out the five years then she couldn't receive it because I'm her mother and I already spent-out the five years. And it didn't matter if she was a different family already, but since she was with me at the time, her name was included, so then she wouldn't qualify." This functioned as an extremely strong incentive for most to exit the program. When asked how that had made her feel, the woman replied: "Well, it made me feel that I had to get out of it because I didn't want my daughter to have that problem when she was older if she needed help, you know, she could go out and get it and not be told, 'Sorry, sorry you can't get help.' Maybe at that time I couldn't help her out either, you know, if she really needed it."

Those who continued with the application process were then required to attend a two-week "orientation." This was combined, to some extent, with the third component in the sequence, the "job search." Some respondents found the orientation useful. As one put it: "They taught us as to what to expect on an interview. What to look for. What to answer. They got us to write, like resumes. . . . It was very helpful." Others, particularly those who had been isolated at home, stated they enjoyed the experience of meeting new people. More generally, however, the orientation was characterized as a "waste of time." One woman reflected the general view: "Well, . . . I know how to make an application. I mean, I didn't really learn anything new." The savviest respondents perceived the real purpose of the program. As one put it: "I don't know, they're trying to get us, I guess, fed-up so we could just like, turn away [from] that and just keep on with our lives in a different way."

The overwhelming majority of respondents worked or had worked, and some stated that the orientation was an obstacle to finding work, particularly those who worked in the fields. Those respondents explained how the scheduling of the orientation, which ran from eight in the morning to noon or late afternoon (depending on the day), conflicted with their ability to find day labor. As one man who was exempted from participation because of a disability put it in reference to his wife: "Look, she goes [to orientation] from 8 a.m. 'till 1 p.m. or 2 p.m. They want her to look for work [afterwards] but . . . you're not gonna find work at that time. To work starts in the morning. That's what I told them. [INTERVIEWER: What did they say?] Nothing, 'Those are the rules.'" His family was under sanction for not complying with work requirements.

The third component, the job search, ran concurrently with the orientation and up to four weeks after certification. A few respondents reported finding work during the job search. Most stated that they were required to garner twenty signatures per week from employers to prove they were looking for work. The actual number of signatures required, according to state policy, was likely closer to fifteen on average (it varied by individual based on their benefit levels). Looking for work in these counties without a personal contact was largely futile, and the job search quickly became a perfunctory exercise in collecting signatures, a process frustrating for TANF participants and local employers alike. The following statement about the job search was widely heard: "I can't be going place to place to get a signature. And then they cut your TANF if you don't take them? . . . I don't know, I mean. . . . It's too much hassle." Some respondents related that local store managers were annoyed with being hassled for signatures and were sometimes rude in declining to sign them: "The people, they get mad, they don't wanna [sign]. Like, because there's a lot of people already, so it was like, 'Come on' [*exasperated*]. It's like, it's nonsense because they're already fed-up and everything. . . . They would just turn away, they wouldn't even look at you, they would just turn away."

Some caseworkers also saw the requirement that one obtain a signature in person as unreasonable, particularly for those without vehicles, and told participants to "just use the phone" and sign the form themselves. Others came to the same conclusion independently: "I would just call by phone . . . because I didn't have daycare. How was I gonna be carrying my baby and going to [apply for jobs]? No!"

Although in theory Choices provided $15 per week to help cover the cost of transportation during the job search, many respondents never received this assistance, and those who did said it was not sufficient to meet the expense of looking for jobs forty to sixty miles away. As one Starr County participant stated: "There's not that many places here so, where else do we go? They would say, 'Go to McAllen' and all that." While the majority of participants reported having a car in their household, many did not have their own vehicle, and neither Starr nor Maverick offered any public transportation other than for medical appointments. Fulfilling the job search requirements therefore necessitated extreme reliance on family and friends for rides.

Exemptions from the job search and other work requirements were nearly impossible to obtain. Participants who lacked access to a vehicle were told to "look for a ride." According to one: "[Caseworkers] didn't care if you didn't have the means to go to their places. If you don't go, well, they take away the benefit. There were some girls that would go walking, or they would ride with another friend or something."

One woman who lived in a remote part of Starr County had neither a car nor a driver's license yet was not exempted from the participation requirements. To fulfill them, she had moved into her sister's apartment in McAllen. As she put it: "[I moved] just so that I could be closer to where I could get signatures." As in most other cases, her sister drove her around to look for jobs. When she eventually found work at a hot dog stand she had to quit after three months because "my sister, she was living with me in McAllen . . . and then she left so I had to leave the job. And then the store closed down anyway."

Another respondent who found work during her job search, indicated that asking for a signature may have sent employers a negative signal. In her explanation of how she found a job, she made special note of the fact she made no mention of needing a signature: "I didn't tell him to sign my paper, I just saw a manager and I came up to him and I asked if he was hiring. He said to go the next day and I went, but I didn't make him sign my paper or anything." According to some local welfare workers and employers, some saw a request for a signature as a sign that the person was on TANF and didn't really want to work. Most local employers contacted were unaware of welfare to work programs and the benefits associated with hiring TANF participants. Administrators in both counties admitted that efforts to inform employers about programs and refute stereotypes about TANF participants had not been top priorities.

Those who neither quit TANF nor found a job during the orientation or job search were reevaluated and (theoretically) eligible to receive more intensive services to address barriers. For example, GED and English as a Second Language classes could be attended if Workforce Investment Act (WIA) or Department of Labor Welfare to Work monies permitted. For a variety of reasons, however, most respondents eligible for such services were not receiving them. Instead, they were placed in community service positions, where they worked merely to maintain their eligibility for TANF. This was particularly problematic in Starr County, where program mismanagement and political strife reigned.

When we arrived in Starr in October 2002, local welfare workers stated they had no funds to provide any services beyond the Choices program. Not a single TANF participant in the county was receiving program-funded education or training. The lack of funds was the result of a combination of mismanagement of program funds by the regional workforce boards, poor performance by the private contractor for services, a political conflict between Starr and Hidalgo County officials, which had erupted during the transfer of Starr from the STWB to the LRGVWB, and the expiration of the Department of Labor's Welfare to Work program. Because of these developments, every TANF participant interviewed between October 2002 and March 2003, many of whom did not speak English and lacked a high school–level education, was performing all of his or her mandated hours in community service. Moreover, because Texas mandated TANF participants to perform work hours equivalent to the sum of their monthly food stamps and TANF benefits divided by the federal minimum wage, most were performing more work hours than mandated by the federal law.

While Maverick County did not experience the management problems or the degree of politicization of program funds that Starr did, the ability of TANF participants to access services was severely constrained by two other factors: extremely limited state funding for child care relative to demand and the imposition, in 2002, of restrictive federal policies regarding education, which capped the percentage of a region's caseload a board could count as completing work hours in education at 30 percent. As a result, TANF participants in Maverick were almost as unlikely as those in Starr to be in education or training programs.

In sum, the lack of jobs combined with a lack of opportunities to pursue education left most TANF participants warehoused in dead-end community service placements. A Starr County welfare worker summed up the effect of the overall situation on TANF participants: "While most people want to work, they feel they are handcuffed because there are no jobs here. . . . Of course, most are undereducated and are only qualified to work in the fields. Now that that [work has] decreased they don't have that outlet. So you have 'em shackled. They look for a job and they can't find one so you put 'em in community service and they feel that they are working for free."

Participants' accounts of community service placements were mixed. A few enjoyed the work, learned new skills, and made new friends, who, in some cases, became important network members. These aspects were often combined with less positive ones. An oft repeated complaint was that community service placements were more inflexible than a real job in terms of getting time off to deal with day-to-day exigencies, such as medical appointments. Indeed, every minute of a thirty-five-hour work requirement had to be accounted for with no time counted for lunch or breaks. The rigidity of the system reached its apotheosis on major national holidays such as Christmas. During these times, when most businesses and work placement centers were closed, participants were held responsible for completing work hours and subject to sanctions for failing to do so. The experiences of one married mother of five who worked seasonally in the fields, did not speak English, and did not have a high school–level education captured many of the difficulties associated with community service.

"Maria" stated that she was required to perform fifty-one hours of community service a week (the maximum number of work hours a married couple family could be required to complete under the federal law was fifty-five). Although she was working every hour that her placement site was open (nine hours a day Monday through Friday), she needed another six hours a week to avoid sanction. When asked how she was expected to make those hours, she indicated that she was told to engage in homework: "Well, they told me do something else, like sell tamales or something." She explained how this problem was exacerbated at the holidays: "Sometimes when it is a holiday like today [Christmas Eve], it does not count. I have to make it up. For example, work on Saturday or working after six p.m. . . . . What is going to happen is that . . . they're going to reduce the grant by $80 or $75. . . . It's impossible." Although Maria enjoyed the work and supported the policy of work requirements, she felt that fifty-one hours per week was excessive and that forty hours, "*el normal,*" would have been sufficient. Most respondents reported spending between thirty and forty hours per week in community service.

While the idea of performing some "community service" in exchange for benefits enjoyed near universal support among our sixty-two TANF respondents, the reality was marred. In addition to the excessive and inflexible hours, in some cases irresponsible supervisors at work placement sites combined with callous caseworkers to impart additional hardships on participants. There is very little known about the experiences of TANF participants at community service placement sites. Our data indicate that supervisors had significant power over participants to either help or harm them, and they did both. Some were described as kind and helpful, and a major benefit of community service for some was the creation of new network ties to influential individuals. For example, one woman volunteering at a community-based agency in Maverick was referred to training by her supervisor. In addition to the training, she received a $350 stipend and a $200 grant for clothing. Moreover, when her TANF caseworker refused to credit the training as fulfilling her work hours, the supervisor intervened on her behalf.

On the other hand, Maria, along with three other respondents placed at the same site, reported very serious difficulties with the secretary responsible for verifying their work hours. She described her efforts to get the secretary to credit her hours as follows: "Sometimes she's angry, . . . and I go and ask her to [verify] my hours and she says she is too busy." At other times, she simply was not there to do it. She related a recent example: "Friday she was not there. . . . Nobody could [fax] my hours so . . . on Monday I

[went] early . . . and . . . gave the sheet to [her boss] and I told her, 'I need that you [fax] my hours otherwise they are going to sanction me.'" The boss agreed, and then failed to fax her hours. When she tried to explain what happened to her caseworker, he reportedly replied: "It's not my problem, it's your problem . . . because you get the check. . . . You should have left the sheet [for the secretary to fax]." She then explained that she had previously tried that approach and the hours had not been sent, thus she never merely left them, noting: "[I tell her], 'Do them, send them,' that way I am sure she is sending them. . . . I have to be there, watching her."

It should be noted here that the women at this site, as well as others, were performing nontrivial jobs, such as cleaning, child care, and reading utility meters for municipalities, work that had to be done and saved the entities with which they were placed from having to pay regular employees. At the same time, the work was boring, taught them no new skills, and would not lead to permanent positions. As one woman put it: "Right now I'm doing janitorial work, maintenance . . . it's the same as if I would be at home. I would clean, just the same thing I'm doing over there."

By no means did all community placements involve boring menial work and irresponsible supervisors. A woman who was volunteering at a community-based organization described her experience as follows: "The volunteering, to me, is helping me. Like right now, I didn't know nothing about offices. So I've been learning a little bit of how to file, the way you're supposed to be answering the phone, how to treat people when they come in or when they need something, ask them. I didn't know nothing of that. That helps me." At the same time, however, she felt that the likelihood that the placement would lead to a real job with the agency was low. She was also angry that she was no longer allowed to fulfill any of her participation hours in school. She had been pulled out of her GED class to do community service despite her sixth grade education. She echoed many other respondents who stated that no employer, outside of growers, would hire her without a GED.

As noted above, respondents were nearly unanimous in their support of the notion that one should be required to "do something" in exchange for TANF assistance. They also believed that education and training were legitimate activities that should have been counted toward program participation. Many held high professional aspirations to which the policy presented a barrier. Thus, among their recommendations for policy change, allowing more time for education topped the list. Another oft repeated suggestion was to provide real opportunities for on-the-job training that would lead to hard skills and a real job. As one woman put it: "Instead of putting people in community work, tell 'em, 'Hey, that's the job you gonna have.' And we start working at that job, and if we like it, we stay there. . . . In that way we could get out of TANF. . . . But if . . . we're giving our time to go over there the forty hours and then just getting the TANF, not getting the benefits of a [real job], the benefits that the rest of the workers have. I say it's, it's better if they do it that way."

This recommendation articulates the basic idea underlying the training component provided through the WIA. Only a handful of respondents in both counties, however, had access to the program because of funding limitations, a shortage of public and third-sector agencies qualified to participate, and the politics pervading the system. The few respondents fortunate enough to be served by the WIA program, however, did obtain decent, full-time year round jobs at their placement sites and reported being much better off for it. For example, one married man had been given a placement at a community-based agency. During his six-month period of subsidized training he was paid $6.00 an hour to work forty hours a week while learning new skills. Following the training period he was hired as a regular employee and given a raise to $6.36 per hour. He was then encouraged by his boss to attend additional training, which resulted in another raise. He praised the program, describing his caseworker as "excellent, excellent" and said of his boss: "My director, he motivated me into going to Austin for training to get certified and he pushed me to it. He gave me the confidence, and I went up there and I passed so I got a different position and a better pay. Right now . . . I'm earning $7.52, which is, like within a year's time, you know. I think it's great." He also received high praise from his supervisors, who characterized him as an excellent employee whom they could hardly believe had been on welfare.

At the same time, although such respondents were among those faring the best, their low wages left them facing continued hardships and heavily reliant on family supports. With regard to transportation, the man stated: "I have no [automobile] insurance, no inspection sticker, no license plate and I [take a] risk every day coming to work and back." In another case, a young woman who had gone through On-the-Job-Training was making only $5.86 per hour, 14 *cents less* than the $6 she had received during her training, and saw little opportunity for advancement at her new job: "I don't wanna stay there like [my bosses] have, twenty years, thirty years . . . and they're in the same thing? I don't want that." These limited cases indicate that those offered substantive services took advantage of them and improved their lot. Unfortunately, few were given the opportunity. Although the board could not provide data on the number of TANF participants in Maverick receiving WIA funded training, one executive stated, "We're talking like three to four or five to seven."

In sum, the Choices program was very successful at accomplishing its goal of reducing caseloads through diversion and punitive policies. The effectiveness was further enhanced by administrative conditions which functioned to amplify the punitive aspects of the policy and mute its few supportive elements. In both counties welfare reform was implemented before adequate infrastructures of service delivery were in place. For example, access to child care during the early years of reform in Maverick County (1997–99) involved a bureaucratic process including an automated telephone system and the exchange of forms through the mail that took at least two weeks to complete. This was in lieu of an on-site childcare specialist to assist participants in person. When a specialist finally did arrive in 1999, that individual described the situation as follows: "When we first took over the program it was in really bad shape and ah, it was quite an experience. . . . It was new, it was, it was—awful." Board officials admitted that the delay likely resulted in the loss of some participants.

A similar process of imposing mandates without providing the means to meet them was repeated in Starr when it became a mandatory work county in 2000. Starr participants were mandated to fulfill work requirements at the same time that its board was fined $3.5 million for poor performance by the state (Cortez 2001).

The practices of some frontline caseworkers at local TDHS and TWC offices also contributed to caseload declines by deterring applicants from applying for TANF, failing to inform people of available services, distributing misinformation about how TANF time limits affected children, and in some cases, treating people so poorly that they would not return to the office under almost any circumstance. There was more evidence of problems with caseworkers in Maverick County where changes in the "culture" of welfare had been in place since 1997. The director of the agency responsible for the operation of the Choices program in Maverick credited their high performance on state evaluations to the "internalization of the work-first philosophy" among his staff stating: "We don't sit back [and wait] for [noncompliant participants] to show-up. They don't show-up, we go knock on their doors and we bring 'em in. If they still don't show-up, then the end result is, of course, no benefits."

A Starr County office director noted that his caseworkers had recently been given license to question TANF applicants more intensively about their expenses and sources of income and were under less pressure to avoid errors and "client complaints." He stated that the approach had deterred some applicants, particularly those with other sources of cash income.

Aggressive efforts at deterrence, which were stressed in TDHS training literature (see Fisher 1999), likely explain why participants in the Texas counties more often reported bad experiences with caseworkers than those in the other regions examined in this study. Accounts of treatment by caseworkers varied considerably, but the overwhelming majority of participants in both counties described interactions that were both good and bad. Also, a few Maverick participants reported treatment that can only be described as abusive. The following two characterizations were representative of descriptions of caseworkers: "Well, I guess it's really who the worker is. . . . There's some, . . . they're like they're in a bad mood or it's like, if they're giving you [their own] money like, . . . they make you feel bad. . . . But, it's not all of them." Another explained: "I guess, when they're 'in the mood,' . . . and they wanna go ahead and do their job, they'll do their job and they'll treat you like a human being. Versus if they're having a lousy day, or if they just woke up on the wrong side of the bed that morning, they'll treat you [*long pause*], like a dog, to be honest."

At the extreme, the treatment some reported receiving by caseworkers indicates that the welfare office can be a hostile place. One of the main advantages of being off welfare cited by most was not being subject to humiliating treatment. One leaver was working twenty-four hours per week as a home health provider yet mandated to complete six hours per week of community service to remain eligible for her family's food stamps. She reported that her caseworker once asked her: "Is your husband working now? He can't find a job? What is he doing? Is he always just scratching his balls? Watching TV?" Another stated: "They gave me such a hard time. . . . I was very happy to go and tell them I didn't wanna participate anymore because they was very ugly. They would come here [to my house] with lies that, say, 'Oh, I saw you with your husband Saturday. We [have] pictures at Wal-Mart.' I was like . . . 'Oh my God?' you know? . . . She told me that Wal-Mart worked for them." Although reports of such explicit abuse were not common, many expressed feeling "humiliated," "disciplined," and generally looked down upon by certain caseworkers.

In some cases, local administrations responded to allegations of abusive treatment and requests to be transferred to other workers. One Maverick County respondent stated that her caseworker was fired after the following incident:

> I think I was pregnant with her [*points to daughter*] and one of the caseworkers that I had, he was very rude, I mean he was, you know,

like screaming, "You better do that!" and "You better do!" And then, at that time, my blood pressure got up and they got me some sugar, . . . because of the mean thing that he was telling me. . . . So I went and talked to the . . . director, . . . and I got the letter from the doctor, what had happened to me when I came to renew the food stamps and Medicaid, . . . [how he] got [my] blood pressure up, and they got me the sugar, and it was popping me like that. So I mean, they punch him out [fired him].

It is crucial to note that this woman's husband had a contact in the TDHS office. In most cases, respondents reported tolerating poor treatment. There were three main reasons. First, many believed that complaining would either be futile or exacerbate the problem. They saw caseworkers and office managers as part of a team that stuck together. Second, most felt guilty for even asking for help and thus believed they had no right to complain. Finally, many were so confused about the program's benefits and their responsibilities that denigrating treatment may have been perceived as routine.

Yet another issue raised by many clients was caseworker withholding of information about benefits. Some became indignant when, during our interviews, we asked them about certain available benefits and programs of which they were totally unaware. A few expressed the belief that certain caseworkers withheld such information to keep benefits for their favored clients: "Some of them, they do help you and some, they are, 'No, you need to go to another place' or to do something else. They're really, like if they have special people, like their relatives, they can give them the help instead. I think so." Among the thirty-one TANF participants interviewed who had exited the program, only a few reported ever receiving postemployment transitional assistance with transportation or child care. Most never knew such benefits existed.

All of the above contributed to rapid exits from the program and an unwillingness to return to welfare offices to seek postemployment services once work was obtained. Only one of the thirty-one families off TANF reported receiving postemployment child care. A member of the executive board at the MRGVWB shed light on why this was so. She explained the consequences of not keeping one's postemployment appointment. In so doing, she emphasized the distinction between what was "supposed" to be happening at local office versus what may have been happening:

If you are receiving TANF . . . and you get a job . . . it's supposed to be, I always say "*supposed* to be" [*her emphasis*] because . . . I'm not sittin' there and I don't know what they tell 'em but, what they're supposed to be counseling with these clients about is the importance of—whether you get a job or not, it doesn't matter, still keep your appointment . . . [because] that opens up the doors to other programs. . . . [F]irst of all, they get guaranteed daycare. . . . And you can get up to maybe even twenty-four, but [at least] twelve months of additional Medicaid services. . . . If you don't, you're terminated with another code that disqualifies you and you are not eligible for any of those things. . . . Once again I go back to "supposed to," because these are things—procedures—that have been set up and you can only hope that they're always followed.

From this limited evidence, it is impossible to ascertain the extent to which the many misunderstandings of policy held by TANF participants were due to their own misinterpretations or forgetfulness or to caseworker error or abuse.

The Limited Impacts of Reform:
TANF and the Everyday Economy of the Valley

It would have been reasonable to expect that the significant caseload declines precipitated by TANF in the context of extreme unemployment and deep and persistent poverty would have caused widespread and significant material hardships for many families. Our interviews indicate this did not occur. The *colonias*, migrant and seasonal farm work, strong family networks, myriad forms of monetary and in-kind exchanges, and access to other, more substantial public assistance programs buffered the impacts of reform. This complex of institutions, and the relatively minor role played by TANF within it, allowed most respondents to forgo the program without suffering catastrophic effects.

The Official Labor Market

During the late 1990s and early 2000s, the official economy of the Valley in general was booming, and Maverick and Starr counties clearly benefited from it. Indeed, while the economies of most of the other counties included in this study have been largely stagnant or in decline, Starr and Maverick have grown markedly and appear on course toward continued expansion. Whether or not growth will be accompanied by reductions in poverty is an altogether different question (see Sharp 1998); nonetheless, approximately half of the Maverick and Starr respondents who left TANF (sixteen out of thirty-one) reported exiting for work.

As was characteristic of the economic growth in the Valley more broadly, in almost every case respondents who were working were earning near minimum wage, working less than full time, and receiving no benefits. Data on occupations and wages provided by the MRGVWB on 125 TANF participants who left the program for work during 1998 and 1999 show that almost all had merely moved from welfare to the ranks of the working poor. One-third (32 percent) were working as nurses' aids or home healthcare assistants, and one-fifth (19 percent) were in fast food. Ten percent were in seasonal work performing "canning" while 8 percent were in "pottery making," and 8 percent were in retail. Not including one individual who became a truck driver (making over $18 an hour), the average starting wage was $5.34 an hour.

Consistent with these data, the most frequently cited occupation among our TANF respondents who were working was "provider." A provider is a home health worker who performs domestic services for the elderly and disabled such as cooking, cleaning, laundry, and hygiene. On average, our respondents worked no more than fifteen to twenty hours per week and one as few as nine hours. Pay ranged from minimum wage to $6 per hour and there were no benefits.

Provider work was a double-edged sword. Low wages and benefits on the one hand were combined with the advantage of flexibility. Providers tended to work for relatives and often lived very close to them, a huge benefit to those with transportation problems. Some described the work as satisfying; including one woman who was taking care of her grandmother and enjoyed the opportunity to spend time with her. However, the work was also difficult and, in some cases, entailed lifting clients in and out of beds, chairs, and bathtubs. It was also emotionally draining. As one provider explained: "It's hard, because . . . they're rude sometimes and they don't know it, you know? . . . [A]nd they don't want for you to go right away, they want for us to stay even a longer time with them . . . to keep them company."

Because the hours were few and wages low, most providers were receiving food stamps. One had to perform volunteer work hours in addition to her provider work to remain eligible for food stamps. Many respondents expressed the desire to become certified as a nurse assistant (CNA), and nursing was listed as a "demand occupation" in both board areas. Nonetheless, only a few had received such training.

The other jobs held by women leavers were in other, largely "feminized" industries, specifically retail, fast food, field work, local medical offices, housekeeping, and third-sector agencies. On the other hand, male leavers reported working on oil rigs, in engine repair shops, construction, and the fields.

Local leaders reported that demand for labor was so slack that hundreds of applications were submitted for almost every job that opened up and college graduates were competing for entry-level jobs at places like Wal-Mart and Denny's Restaurant. The scarcity of jobs was reflected in almost every participant interview in the refrains "you have to know someone" and "if you have a job, you take care of it." In some cases, "taking care" of one's job went beyond being a reliable worker and entailed accepting highly exploitative working arrangements. One respondent explained how she was told by an employer that if she wanted a job, she would have to put in extra unpaid hours. Another explained how limited job opportunities led her to forgo pursuing wages owed to her by her employer. She had found a job as a cashier in a retail franchise earning $5.75 per hour. She was promoted to manager and given a raise to $9.00 per hour. After managing the store for a few months, she was still receiving only $5.75. She asked her supervisor numerous times to correct the problem, but he only replied that he had processed the raise and the problem was with the company's headquarters. When a new supervisor eventually took over, she complained to her: "I told her . . . and she's like, 'They still have you down for $5.75. He never changed it.' . . . And she's like, 'I'm so sorry to tell you this . . . but I know for a fact that you're probably not getting your retro pay.'" She added: "They owe me like maybe $1,000. . . . That's not right because I worked the hours. . . . But I'm like, I can't quit because of that. Because what are we gonna do? . . . I'm not gonna quit over something like that . . . you know, because here [it's] like, 'Oh well, yeah you have experience as an assistant manager but we don't need an assistant, we need a cashier.' So you go down again and it's like, I wouldn't."

At $9 per hour this woman was among the very highest paid TANF leavers. Her husband also had a job delivering pizzas, and they shared a home with in-laws but were still barely making ends meet. As a result of her earnings, her food stamps had been cut, "because $600 every two weeks is *too* much [*her emphasis*]," as had her Medicaid. Worse yet, she had been informed that Medicaid for her daughters, one of whom had Turner's Syndrome and needed years of costly hormone treatments, was about to be terminated.

Such employer practices created specific problems for women seeking work under welfare reform. It was common for small employers, many of whom were from Mexico and practiced Mexican customs, to hire one or two persons on the books and complement them with others hired under the table. Working off the books was not commonly credited by the TDHS as fulfilling work requirements (except when it met administrator needs, as in the case of "Maria" cited above) and, perhaps more important, did not allow respondents to access the EITC, the most generous program serving the working poor today. As one woman stated: "*Pues* [Well], I was working in that motel right here in Del Rio [Boulevard]. They were paying me [*laughs*] $2 a room. . . . [H]e didn't wanna pay me check, he wanted to pay me cash and I told him I wanted check because I wanted to make income tax. He said no. So I said, well I'm gonna try at least. Because with the kids you get all your income tax."

Although the jobs obtained by most TANF leavers were insufficient to support a family and resulted in reduced access to food stamps and Medicaid, every former participant who was working stated that they were "better off" than they had been on TANF. There were three main reasons. First, even working only part time at minimum wage provided much more money than the approximately $160–$200 per month TANF offered; second, they were paid every two weeks rather than once a month; and third, they were no longer subject to abuse and humiliation by their caseworkers.

The Unofficial Labor Market

According to workforce board executives, the "black market on jobs" along the border is "huge." One Maverick County administrator estimated that 60 percent of the initial (1997) TANF caseload had been working outside the formal labor market and explained the decline as the result of the fact that all those with "any other options" left the program. This was echoed by some TANF leavers, who described how TANF requirements interfered with the ability of family members to pursue more important economic activities. The following statement represents the experiences of families headed by married couples, who were more likely than families headed by single females to engage in significant amounts of informal work: "Sometimes we need to get TANF, right, but sometimes my husband goes out and finds something, like say, . . . he goes out and he'll throw out some garbage. They'll pay him like thirty dollars a day. But . . . if we get TANF we have to be there like for a week, going to 'Choices-thing' [*stated with disdain*] when he can be getting like, at least sometimes $100 a week."

Married couples, as well as single women with strong networks, were better able to carry out informal work than single mothers with weak supports. The most frequently cited sources of unreported income were day labor in local fields, cleaning yards and houses, making food or "plates" to sell, and the sale of all kinds of goods from used clothes to candy purchased in Mexico. One man described day labor in the fields. In some cases this work was reported by employers, in others it was not, and still others left it up to the worker to decide. He stated: "When I work, some days I get seventy-five, ninety dollars a day. . . . [W]e go over here to the bridge, over there, it's a big parking lot. We go in the morning [five a.m.], and a lot of vans get there. [They] say, 'I'm gonna need four people.' Ok, go, four people. And then go, five more. And three. . . . Sometimes we get work there . . . [but] like today, I go to work but I don't get a work so I come back. [INTER-VIEWER: And they pay you by contract?] Yeah, by contract . . . sixty cents a sack, onions, they're two buckets. But it's a lot of work for the sixty cents they give you . . . because they sell the sack about ten, fifteen dollars. [INTERVIEWER: And so about how many days a week do you get picked up?] Some weeks all week. . . . But some weeks two or three days a week. But with two or three days a week I still make more money than the [TANF] check."

Some women reported earning twenty to forty dollars per week cleaning houses for a neighbor or two. In some cases this was steady work, in others it was "just once in a while." Another very common activity among women was "making plates," that is, plates of food to sell at offices and schools around the county where many people worked. This was often a highly organized activity. The women tended to have regular customers who called in advance to place orders. They sold for four dollars each, and a large "batch" comprised about fifty plates.

One woman explained how she fit plate making into her daily routine. In response to the question, "If you didn't have money for rent, what would you do?" she replied: "I would try to obtain it—even if I can sleep only two hours per night I have to get the money. Sometimes . . . I make tamales for [my son] to sell at school." She noted that the last time she did it, her son forgot to inform her of the order until the night before: "I went to buy the things from 7 p.m. to 8 p.m. and then I cooked from 8 p.m. to 12 a.m. and then did the tamales from 12 a.m. to 3:30 a.m. And then I got up at 6:30 a.m. to warm them up and take them to the coaches [at school]." She added that she had also "made a Bingo" the following day because it was her son's birthday and "I can get some money through there." She continued: "I had to go to make a Bingo, so I'm running around to clean [up the mess from the tamales] and leave to do Bingo." These activities were carried out in addition to attending six hours of class, babysitting, and selling beauty products door to door. She concluded, "That's just an example of how much I have to struggle every day. I have to create something because I would not allow them to cut the light. If I can't they will cut it. But I will struggle. . . . I will fight to the end."

Such activities were carried out as needed by some and regularly by others. Food stamps were invested by some in these activities in order to parlay them into cash. For example, a woman might use fifty dollars in food stamps to make two hundred in cash through the sale of plates. Some TDHS officials were aware of this practice and appreciated their entrepreneurial skills. In most case, the cash raised through such activities was small and used to meet immediate needs. No one was getting rich through working on the side.

Finally, our discussion of the informal economy would be incomplete were we to fail to mention the enormous impact of the drug trade. Being located at the border, the drug trade played a huge, albeit unmeasurable, role in the unofficial economies of these counties. This is particularly true in Starr, where Maril (1989), among others, cites drug smuggling as an alternative economic "institution" (Maril 1989, 87). Maril captures economic conditions in Starr well when he writes: "There is money in [Rio Grande City], and there is not; there is a vital economy at work, as reflected in the homes and material possessions of the residents and there is too, a poverty common to the Valley" (Maril 1989, 87).

Both counties contained significant "export industries" unaccounted for in the official statistics presented in Chapter 2. Anyone who visited them could see that there was far more cash flowing through these communities than census data on income and poverty rates indicated. This was common knowledge to residents of South Texas, and our analysis of household survival would lack any validity were we to overlook it (Richardson and Pagán 2002, 24–25; Blakeslee 2001). At the same time, however, the role of the drug trade must not be overestimated or understood to function as a substitute for a strong formal economy. While it is impossible to estimate its impact on low-income families, it is reasonable to believe that most profits from the trade are concentrated among elites and only some small fraction trickles down to the poor through various channels. Because respondents could not be expected to admit participation in such channels, we cannot ascertain the role of drug money in household survival strategies.

The Family Side of the Everyday Economy

Much of the activity carried out through the everyday economy in the Valley was grounded in extraordinarily strong family networks that transcended the geographic boundaries of the areas, extending as far south as Central America and at least as far north as Montana. The local elements of these networks provided access to jobs, transportation, child care, housing, and food assistance. The extralocal elements largely provided cash on a regular or emergency basis. The overwhelming majority of respondents in both counties reported that someone was "always" there for them in an emergency and in most cases it was a family member. While such assistance often involved reciprocity on the part of the recipient, arrangements were flexible and "payments" could be made far in the future. In some cases, particularly those in which the respondent was young and still living with her parents, payback was not expected at all.

The most important need met through family networks was housing. As noted above, the *colonias* greatly facilitated homeownership among low-income families, and many respondents or their parents or relatives owned their own homes. Homeownership allowed families to take in relatives who hit hard times, and fifteen of the sixty-two families interviewed were living as "subfamilies" in the households of parents, siblings, or other relatives. In many cases, this arrangement was of benefit not only to the subfamily but also to the householder. For example, one woman's family was living in her father's house with her father, her brother and his wife, and her husband and two children. Her father relied on her for money, and the three families pooled their resources to cover utilities and food expenses. Because her father owned the house, rent was, in her words, "a non-issue." She explained: "For rent, at first we would give, well I would give, $150 a month, *pero* [but] that would include bills and stuff. . . . But now it's like I just, I either pay the light or I pay the water depending on when we get the bill and when I get paid and what I have to pay that week."

On the other hand, living conditions for subfamilies were often over-crowded, especially in households such as hers where there was more than one subfamily: "[When] it was just us it was okay and we were making it with the food that we would get. And now [my brother and sister-in-law], they come along and everything changes, you know, fights and it just being too crowded. . . . [There's] four of us living in my old bedroom, sleeping there. You know, there's mess everywhere. I don't have anywhere to put it."

As in the other regions in this study, funding for official childcare services was limited, and quality childcare placements were scarce. Thus, the role of the family was critical. In response to the question, "Who provides your child care?" one woman responded, "Well, right now my sister-in-law." When asked, "And how much do you pay her?" she stated, "Ah, no, I cannot, I don't have the money. . . . When she leaves or has an appointment, I take care of her kids or do things in the house. But I don't pay her with money."

It is important to note that while family members were often the preferred givers of care, they were not always reliable or quality sources of care. In some cases parents became too ill to watch children. In others, family conflict resulted in the provider cutting off assistance. One respondent with an infant had recently missed her volunteer work and was facing sanction for just this reason. She stated: "Well, when I had to make up the hours I didn't have a babysitter so I had to quit making my hours." Others complained that their network providers, particularly their own parents or grandparents, did not provide the kind of quality care, including educational activities, which children received in formal placements such as Head Start. Family was also the main source of transportation for those lacking cars. While most respondents had at least one car in their household, it was usually shared with at least one other adult and not technically theirs. Difficulties with transportation were highly variable. Some stated that it was not a problem at all; others endured huge problems because of the complete absence of public transportation systems in these counties. One respondent related that merely having to constantly ask friends, neighbors, and relatives for rides was difficult. Rides also came at a financial cost. The rate for a trip to the grocery store or welfare office ranged from five to ten dollars, depending on the distance. One woman who had formerly depended on her father to drive her to work stated: "Actually, when I didn't have a car . . . I had to pay my *own* [*her emphasis*] family just to take me to work wherever I was working. I had to pay my father every week. It was ten dollars [a week] for him to take me and get me back." Another respondent's neighbor drove her to our interview. She stated that in exchange for the ride, she was helping her make tamales for sale.

A few respondents had extraordinarily strong family supports that provided child care, transportation, and even allowed them to quit TANF and continue to pursue their education. One woman stated: "I was all fed up with [my caseworker] so I just [said], 'Ok, keep your money' [and quit]." At the time of the interview she was attending college and living with her mother, who provided child care among other things: "My mother pays all the bills. I only pay twenty dollars for the water and forty dollars for the cable [TV] and then my gasoline in the car. [INTERVIEWER: Do you pay any rent?] No, my mom, she owns her house." While most family networks were strong, few respondents enjoyed such extensive supports. In sum, the strong family supports and extensive unofficial economic activities that comprised the unreported side of the everyday economy cushioned the impacts of welfare reform for most respondents. But heavier reliance on these institutions was no panacea. Cash earnings in the unofficial economy were meager and irregular, and reliance upon assistance from family and kin often came at a price. The family networks upon which many depended were stretched thin to begin with, and some were fragile. Among those living with parents or other relatives, TANF cash and food stamps functioned as key sources of reciprocity. Any reduction in these benefits created problems that went beyond the loss of the benefit itself. Additionally, when a parent became ill or a family feud erupted, access to assistance could be cut off and precipitate the collapse of a household's entire survival strategy.

We have repeated a number of times here that welfare reform produced neither widespread negative impacts on the well-being of most respondents nor widespread positive ones. We have argued that this was due to the minor role played by TANF in household survival strategies centered around work and family. We conclude with a description of the significant material hardships that did occur as effects of welfare reform. These impacts were concentrated among a small group of interviewees who were the worst off to begin with—families headed by younger, single women with little formal education and work experience. The key factor differentiating them from the others was their lack of strong and reliable networks to turn to in times of crisis. As such, these families lacked the network support needed to meet TANF requirements. They could not simply quit TANF, nor could they afford even the $78 per month sanction for failing to complete work requirements. Yet they were the most likely to have been sanctioned or to be under the threat of sanction. In the absence of strong, state-provided support services they were the least able to negotiate the requirements of the job search and community service. The public safety net was their only safety net, and its failure resulted in hunger, exposure, keeping children out of school and school activities, and homelessness.

Respondents were understandably hesitant to speak of the hardships experienced by their children, and there is good reason to believe that they underreported them. Like all parents, they sought to provide for and protect their children. Many expressed feelings of regret over "the little things," for example, not being able to buy their kids the occasional toy or treat. When it came to answering questions about serious hardships such as child hunger, respondents usually stated, flatly, "No. Never." This was probably true in most cases, but it was also quite likely a reaction by some to a deeply intrusive question. Obviously, most people would not share such details with a stranger.

Nonetheless, a few respondents stated that their children had in fact gone hungry, usually because they had been cut off from what is perhaps the most important of public assistance programs—food stamps. When asked, "What happened?" one respondent stated: "That I really don't have some money. And I really, I mean, it was embarrassing to go to a neighbor's house. [INTERVIEWER: And did your kids ever have to skip meals or go hungry?] Yes, one time." She began to cry and turned to our interview assistant, who was her friend, and stated, "I didn't tell you that."

While such reports were few, accounts of parents going hungry so children could eat were common, and cases of near hunger and malnutrition were even more ubiquitous among parents. One mother who had Type II diabetes reported subsisting on potatoes near the end of every month. Others cited bananas, beans, drinking lots of water, and "going to sleep" as their defenses against hunger near the end of the month.

While many families regularly experienced food hardship near the end of the month, in most cases hunger was prevented by network assistance. Incidents of extreme food hardship and hunger stemmed almost entirely from loss of food stamps. Loss of food stamps resulted from a number of causes, including changes in administrative rules, caseworker errors, and respondents failing to file necessary paperwork on time.

Loss of access to food stamps represented a very serious threat to family well-being for all families in this study. In 2002, this became even more likely when the state changed the way it implemented the federal Food Stamps Employment and Training program (FSE&T), allowing workforce boards to sanction a family's full food stamps grant for noncompliance with TANF work activities.

Evidence of the potential impacts of this policy was gleaned from the experiences of respondents whose food stamps were cut off. When asked, "What would you do if you had no money for food?" one young woman replied:

> Just look for work somewhere. . . . I won't let my children die without eating. [INTERVIEWER: Have you or your children ever gone hungry?] [*Deep breath*] Yes. When I came back from Illinois we didn't have enough food for my family and my sister's. I had to ask a neighbor of mine if she had anything she could give me so I could give my kids. [INTERVIEWER: And you had no food stamps?] No, because at that time I went to [Illinois], I closed the case and I didn't have enough time to come and reopen it again. And they took like a month to finish the case. . . . I barely get enough and I don't have enough to buy the kids clothes for winter . . . . [When it was AFDC] I had enough money to buy for the food and everything,

I had [money] for blankets, even for blankets! I don't have right
now blankets for my kids.

Another woman who had recently moved in with her sister in Eagle Pass
answered the question: "Did you ever have your food stamps cut off acci-
dentally because you did not receive a letter to recertify?" as follows: "Yes,
yes, yes. [INTERVIEWER: What happened?] Like, I didn't take some papers in
that needed to be taken in at the same time so they cut me off . . . for a
month. . . . That's what messed me all up. And that's why I'm here [in Eagle
Pass] now. [INTERVIEWER: That's what led to you losing the house?] Yeah,
everything. I had to spend that money to leave. I got evicted, nowhere to
go, I didn't wanna go to a shelter, and I just came over here with my sister."
The sanctioning of food stamps presented an extremely serious threat to
the well-being of the most vulnerable Valley families, who, despite their efforts,
could not meet the work requirements of PRWORA. For example, a young
single mother whose own mother and main network support had died was
mandated to perform thirty-three hours per week of community service.
She was living with her elderly grandmother, her three children, and her five
younger siblings her grandmother had taken in. A total of ten individuals
lived in the house. In describing her difficulties in meeting her work requirement, she explained that upon returning home from her first night of work
cleaning a public building she found that her youngest children had not
been bathed and the older ones had not done their homework. She stated
that her grandmother could not adequately care for her kids, adding:

> Since that day when I went [to work] from the morning to ten p.m.
> at night I told [my caseworker] that I didn't wanna go anymore. So
> that man told me, "Well, if you're not gonna do the hours then
> we're gonna cut your food stamps." I said, "What does food stamps
> have to do with Choices? That's for TANF." And he said, "Well,
> that's a new law right now over there in the Food Stamp office. If
> you don't do the hours they're gonna cut your food stamps and cut
> your TANF." I said, "Well, how do you expect my kids to eat if we
> don't have food stamps?" And he said he didn't care, that we just
> had to do everything they asked [us] to do. . . . I really need the
> food stamps for my kids.

While welfare reform did directly cause some hardships, it was more often
the case that it lessened the ability of families to access resources to deal with
the broader difficulties of life on the edge. One widely reported hardship

with respect to children was that parents often could not afford the fees required to allow them to participate in school activities such as field trips and sports. As one single mother related in regards to such activities: "*Pues* [Well], sometimes I have told my kids that if I don't have the money, tough, I don't have it. I can't do nothing about it because it's kind of hard to pay all the bills and then give them money to go to field trips but sometimes, *pues*, they're kids, we have to look for a way how to do it because we were kids once."

Others stated the work requirements of TANF in particular cut into the amount of time they had to assist their children with school work: "To me, it's hard because one of my daughters . . . she's in second grade now . . . the only problem is that she's below [grade] level in reading so they put her in special-ed so she can get extra help. So it's hard because I don't have time for her."

If we expand our definition of the "impacts" of reform, as we should, to include its effects on access to opportunities to pursue education and training, the negative impacts of reform in these counties were quite widespread. According to caseworkers and board executives, the rules regarding education and training under welfare reform significantly restricted their ability to place participants in remedial education. It also curbed their ability to serve participants who sought various forms of postsecondary education. One administrator explained that under the old AFDC-JTPA model, he had helped many recipients, "in some cases entire families," go to college by combining JTPA funds and Pell grants with their public assistance. He stated that the new TANF-WIA model reduced his ability to assist participants with education and left them "shackled" in community service placements or low-wage jobs.

Conclusion

The rhetorical promise of welfare reform in Texas was: "Get a job, Get a better job, Get a career" (TDHS 1996). A more empirically informed statement of that promise as it was translated into practice in the Valley would be: "Accept the first low-wage part-time job you can find or we'll warehouse you in community service. If we have the money, though we often do not, we might help you with some basic education or training. If you get a caseworker who is not overburdened or uncaring, you may be informed of more specific opportunities and resources. Best of luck."

TANF cases in these counties declined so rapidly upon the implementation of work requirements because the services offered by the program were of little substance and the cost of participation was high. Moreover, rates of sanction were also high because the support services necessary to facilitate participation among those who lacked the private network supports needed to meet work requirements were not in place.

The Maverick caseload declined earlier than Starr's because in Maverick County work requirements, time limits, and a culture of deterrence among caseworkers were put in place about three years earlier. Because labor market conditions and support services in the counties were equally weak, their differential treatment was explained by their structural position in their respective local workforce board areas. Punitive welfare policy drove caseload declines, and the implementation of that policy was based on the political and economic calculus of local elites who directed service organizations and held key positions on or over the workforce boards. Each county, in its own way, represented the nightmare of devolution for TANF participants, particularly the weakest among them.

Despite the enormous shortcomings of welfare reform in the Valley, the great majority of respondents who had left TANF reported they were better off for it, regardless of where they were working or whether or not they were working at all. A huge factor in their feeling better off was that they were no longer subject to what many described as the "humiliation" and "hassle" of receiving TANF. The nature of poverty in the *colonias* and the everyday economy explains why significant material hardships stemming directly from welfare reform were not widespread.

The Valley families interviewed for this study were headed by women best described as survivors. They wanted to work and held high aspirations for their children and what remained of their own lives. They believed in the "American Dream" as strongly as anyone as they carried on their daily struggles to "find a way." Their extensive work and their limited reliance on welfare expose the notion of "welfare dependency" as a baseless ideological construct created to fuel the "reform" movement. They also indicate that the punitive policy tools of time limits and mandatory work hours are unnecessary because TANF participants have never desired to live their lives on welfare.

In sum, welfare reform disrupted household survival by impinging on women's ability to participate in the everyday economy. A Starr County migrant farmworker and single mother of three captured the essence of the struggle to survive in the everyday economy of the Valley under reform as follows: "The lady started growling at me there in the Tex Force [the

Workforce office], saying that this was, 'temporarily needed' [and] it was, 'not to stay on it.' And I told her, 'I know, because if I was to stay on it, I wouldn't leave a million miles to go and work over there at Chicago, Illinois, to try to get what I can to my kids. I would stay here, [and] keep on going with what you give us. And what you give us, we barely make it. . . . We don't. We have to look for a way, how to do it.'"

EIGHT

Welform Reform in the Misissippi Delta, Mississippi

The Mississippi Delta is the most Southern place on earth.
—James C. Cobb

Holmes and Sunflower counties lie at the heart of the Mississippi Delta, a region referred to by historian James C. Cobb as "the most Southern place on earth" (Cobb 1992). The Mississippi Delta has been the domain of wealthy white planters from settlement to the present. The economic, political, and social institutions of the region were created to serve the planters' economic needs and to sustain the style of living to which they were accustomed. This small but powerful planter class has always governed the affairs of the Mississippi Delta. Throughout the era of the New Deal reforms during the 1930s, and the civil rights movement in the 1960s, Holmes, Sunflower, and surrounding counties were the locus of the strongest resistance to agricultural, political, and social reforms in the Mississippi Delta, led by wealthy elites like U.S. Senator James O. Eastland, a prominent Sunflower County planter. Even though their economic interests and investments have gone beyond agriculture, they still maintain a powerful influence on life in the Mississippi Delta through the inertia of established institutions and by active participation in the affairs of the region. Given this history, welfare reform in these counties faced a very special set of circumstances.

With the advent of PRWORA, Mississippi was once again at the forefront of limiting the resources available to poor, predominantly African American households. In a state that never provided general assistance, emergency assistance, or a state SSI supplement, and made minimal investments in human services, national welfare reform to reduce caseloads was simply another page from the same book. The opportunity for devolution further enhanced an already existing strategy to rely on private organizations, charities, and other federal monies to meet the needs of the state's poor. In sharp contrast to the approach in Kentucky, education for the poor has been a struggle in

Mississippi. In this context of stringency and minimal support, the everyday economy in the Mississippi Delta is both extensive and essential.

This chapter represents the results of a series of interviews conducted in Holmes and Sunflower counties between April and May 1999 and between September and December 2002. Directors and personnel within county, state, and federal agencies; private businesses; and nonprofit organizations were interviewed about their involvement with, observations of, and responses to TANF. In addition, a total of sixty current and former participants of TANF were interviewed about their experiences with and reactions to the requirements of TANF, twenty-nine in Holmes and thirty-one in Sunflower (for general characteristics of participants, see Appendix A, Tables 11–14).

Bad Timing for Welfare Reform

Throughout the Mississippi Delta rural industrialization has been a high priority of public policy and government action. Holmes County is no exception, and there was noticeable success in the opening of several small manufacturing plants. The jobs were mostly semi-skilled, but that was a reasonable match for the labor skills and educational attainment of many potential workers. At the very least, they provided steady employment, a regular paycheck, and some employee benefits for more than a thousand Holmes County families. At the time of the 2000 census, Holmes County had several manufacturing plants in the hill country around the county seat of Lexington. These employment opportunities gave Holmes the second-highest percentage of employment in export industries among our study counties (33.9 percent), with the second-highest percentage of people employed in manufacturing industries (24.6 percent). However, it should be noted that some of the Holmes County workers commuted to neighboring counties to work in manufacturing plants.

The announcement of welfare reform in 1996 preceded a series of plant closures between 1999 and 2001, which dealt a severe blow to the region's substantial manufacturing sector. Shortly after the data for the 2000 census were collected, the availability of these reasonably good manufacturing jobs declined dramatically. Holmes County experienced the largest decline in overall employment among all the counties in our study (19.2 percent), mostly in manufacturing employment (53 percent). Welfare reform could not have come at a worse time for Holmes County. Shortly after the "work first" require-ments of TANF hit low-income residents, six manufacturing plants closed their doors. Those six employers accounted for nearly half the jobs in the county. The closures left approximately 1,200 workers without employment and in need of education, job training, and new employment. It also placed them in direct competition with TANF participants for very limited social service resources and job opportunities.

According to the director of the Mississippi Department of Human Services in Holmes County, "We have lost almost every employment in the county. Fleetwood had three plants here. They closed all three of them. We had two electric appliance manufacturing plants. They both closed. Another small manufacturing plant closed. We just had tremendous amounts of closing in the county, and it has really impacted our caseload. And it also makes welfare reform hard for this county because there is no public transportation. There's just nothing here for them to do. They have to go to Greenwood, Kosciusko, Jackson, Madison, and Canton [commutes of 40–60 miles]."

To make matters even worse, neighboring counties were also the victims of plant closures brought on, in part, by the North American Free Trade Agreement (NAFTA). Some of the plants that closed reopened "off shore" in Mexico and elsewhere, or the work was transferred to existing "off shore" plants. Thus, while one federal policy was demanding that low-income single mothers go to work, another federal policy was effectively removing employment opportunities.

Devolution and the Private Sector

There was some indication that TANF participants who were not job ready were not being made job ready. According to the executive director of the Sunflower County Economic Development Corporation, "Welfare reform has put a lot of people into the labor market who have remedial problems." He also felt that a significant segment of the TANF labor force had never worked outside the home, had no job skills, and sometimes suffered from drug and alcohol abuse, and other disabilities. "The numbers are in the thousands for the four-county area of Sunflower, Washington, Bolivar, and Leflore counties." He claimed that because he is forced by welfare reform to work on these "remedial problems," he has less time to identify and assist firms capable of creating the kinds of jobs that would provide higher wages. Rather than attach this hard core, unemployable group of people so immediately to the workforce, he suggested that MDHS, "work with them [TANF participants] to identify and resolve underlying problems before shifting responsibility for them over to economic development. There also should be an emphasis on improving employment, as well as securing employment in the first place."

Given the limited number of employment opportunities, many TANF participants met their work requirements by serving as volunteers in government agencies, schools, and nonprofit organizations. At least some of the TANF interviewees viewed such participation as beneficial. One mother said, "Life has improved for my family. I am learning a skill that may help me reach some of my goals." Another voiced a similar sentiment, "I am better off because I am learning a skill in child care." In spite of the general economic downturn, nearly half of the fifty-nine mothers we interviewed felt they were better off than they were five years previously because of the work requirements of TANF. Only four felt they were worse off, usually because of reduced benefits or their preference for staying at home with their children.

For public agencies and organizations, TANF volunteers became a key source of personnel able to partially fill staffing shortfalls. For example, TANF volunteers were working as teacher aides in the public schools, as well as providing assistance in understaffed school offices. According to school administrators and teachers the volunteers were a welcome resource for the schools.

The Crisis Accompanying Privatization

When welfare reform was implemented in 1996, it followed Governor Kirk Fordice's strategy of relying on private sector and other organizations outside state government for the delivery of case management and job placement services. According to a report published by the Rockefeller Institute (Breaux et al. 2000), the privatization that accompanied welfare reform in Mississippi resulted in a lack of administrative accountability and grossly inadequate service provision.

There were three facets of welfare-to-work administration in Mississippi. County MDHS offices continued to determine eligibility for welfare. Case management could be subcontracted to private organizations known as Case Management Entities (CMEs). Job placement services also could be subcontracted to private organizations known as Job Placement Contractors (JPCs). CMEs were responsible for conducting orientations to the Work-first program, assessing the employability of participants and assigning them a work status (mandatory or exempt), and assisting clients in preparing a personal "Employment Development Plan" that addressed childcare and transportation issues, including payments, among other things. The CMEs were also responsible for initiating the sanctioning process for noncompliant participants (Breaux et al. 2000, 2; Brister, Beeler, and Chambry 1997, 12). The JPCs administered the four-week Job Readiness / Job Club component of the

Work-first program and were also responsible for recruiting employers to hire participants (Brister, Beeler, and Chambry 1997, 12). Participants not placed with private employers by the JPCS were referred back to the CMES for placement in community service work, "alternative work experience," or additional training programs.

When the state's "New Directions" work-first welfare waiver went statewide as the TANF program in 1997, state contracts were awarded on a competitive basis to the lowest bidders. It was expected that the experienced Planning and Development Districts (PDDS) and Community Action Agencies (CAAS), which had administered and delivered welfare to work services under the JOBS program, would win the contracts. As it happened, these entities were underbid by private for-profit corporations, including Lockheed IMS and Green Thumb, organizations with little to no experience with work-force development programming or providing such services in the state and, according to the Rockefeller Institute, "ill prepared for their role." In many areas, programs were "hastily put together," resulting in much "difficulty placing the hard to serve." Case management effectiveness was also cited as varying "too widely from district to district, compromising the entire pro-gram" (Breaux et al. 2000, 5). One participant testified in a state hearing that she had had four different case managers in eleven months, noting, "I think that's a lot of the reason why my case is so messed up" (Breaux et al. 2000, 5).

Case management problems were compounded by the performance-based contracts made with the JPCS. According to the Rockefeller Institute, the pay structure provided an incentive for JPCS "simply to move clients through their component so they could get paid" (Breaux et al. 2000, 5). After moving the initial "mass of work ready" participants who required little assistance through their programs, JPCS began "shirking." As a result, "the greatest number of those leaving the rolls were not entering and completing the work programs but were leaving voluntarily at the point of entry" (Breaux et al. 2000, 4–5). Problems with the JPCS were articulated by participants, who reported being put in a room and told simply to "play with the computers" (Breaux et al. 2000, 5).

In sum, the administrative structure of the program lacked accountability because it required local MDHS offices to work with private agencies over which they had no direct control (Breaux et al. 2000, 4). Eventually MDHS reasserted control over TANF case management and services, and by 1998 all the private JPC contracts were retired. By September 1998, MDHS was providing eligibility determination, case management, and job services for the Work-first program for the majority of the state. However, MDHS continued to lack the staff needed to carry out these functions and thus had reverted in some counties to "personal services contracts" with private individuals to do job readiness. These contracts were awarded mainly to former MDHS employees, renewed monthly, and paid according to a flat fee.

The decline in caseloads was accompanied by a freeze on hiring, and county MDHS offices were unable to fill case manager vacancies. The Holmes County MDHS office had two vacant positions for over two years, and TANF participants suffered as a result. The following is typical of the complaints we heard: "They don't process your papers on time and then they close your case. If you bring in your papers and they misplace them, then they'll tell you your case is closed. If you leave them [papers] at the front desk and just because someone misplaces them, they'll tell you your case is closed. Then you have to go through the whole [re-applying] process again." Another TANF participant had this to say, "They're very rude to you. It's their way or no way at all. They don't process your papers on time, or misplace them. Then they close your case for their mistake." According to the supervisor these unfortunate and undesirable situations occur because they are understaffed.

Other Private Efforts

Following its privatization debacle, Mississippi looked to a variety of organizations, including governmental, nongovernmental, for-profit, and nonprofit entities; employers and community leaders; and religious organizations for help in serving low-income families, but MDHS remained the sole agency responsible for administering TANF funds (Mississippi Department of Human Services 2003).

One consequence of the financial independence of the other, non-TANF, federal programs being administered by the nonprofit sector was limited program coordination with state and local government agencies. TANF participants whom we interviewed found this lack of coordination frustrating. One wonders if this was not an unofficial policy on the part of the state, which said, "If we can't control it, don't cooperate." These are also examples of how Mississippi succeeded in shifting the financial burden of human services provision to private organizations and the federal government.

There were, however, some examples of greater interorganizational cooperation stimulated by welfare reform. MDHS job placement coordinators were working closely with at least some employers to increase the flow of information about employment opportunities. School administrators and teachers also reported new instances of cooperation with local employers. For example, the Sunflower County Economic Development Authority staff was holding meetings in the schools with students to inform them of work opportunities and the importance of completing high school before entering the labor market. However, these efforts were not designed specifically for TANF participants, although some did participate. Cooperation was mostly bilateral, involving pairs of organizations, rather than all-inclusive and coordinated.

The various welfare-to-work related assistance programs appeared to be minimal and fractionated. They were also underfunded, in part because the state left over $12 million dollars available through the U.S. Department of Labor's Welfare to Work program for hard-to-serve TANF participants on the table in Washington, D.C., in 1998. Most of the nongovernmental organizations engaged in the process were also underfunded, understaffed, and struggling for their own organizational survival. Thus, interorganizational cooperation to assist TANF participants suffered from limited resources as well as divergent philosophies and diverse organizational rules and regulations. As TANF and former TANF participants tried to navigate the changes brought by welfare reform, the organizations upon which they relied for services struggled under increased demand for services and changes in scope and strategy.

For example, nonprofit programs to combat food insecurity are extremely important in the Delta. After the implementation of welfare reform, the number of persons receiving food stamps declined in both counties, although not as sharply as the number of TANF cases. By May 2000 there had been a 37.7 percent drop in food stamp recipients in Sunflower and 36.2 percent in Holmes. While MDHS staff attributed the decline to good economic conditions in the late 1990s, county food banks and food pantries appeared to have picked up many of the families that had formerly received food stamps.

Grace Community Church operated one of these food pantries. It is located in Tchula in the Delta portion of Holmes County and receives referrals from MDHS. The food pantry was part of the Mississippi River Ministries, and was provided with food through the Mississippi Food Network as part of "Second Harvest," a national clearinghouse for hunger relief. The food boxes were said to contain enough food to feed a family of four for about one week. Participants paid $1 to get a card which entitled them to one visit to the food pantry every thirty days. Food pantry workers reported that most of the families served were TANF participants. According to workers at the church, they served a monthly average of approximately 250 clients, a noticeable increase since the implementation of TANF. The church also operated a "clothing closet" for those using the food pantry. According to the pastor, "the pantry serves as a recruiting tool for encouraging participants to become involved with other available services."

In Sunflower County, Sunflower-Humphreys Counties Progress, Incorporated, was providing a variety of emergency services, including short-term food and housing. These services were available prior to TANF, but the people served were reported to include an increasing number of TANF participants whose cash benefits had been reduced, or who had dropped out of TANF. Their services were funded largely through the federal government, with a small role played by the state of Mississippi. There was also a local food pantry providing emergency food services in Sunflower; however, their focus was primarily on the low-income elderly residents of Indianola. When asked directly if TANF participants visit the food pantry, the director said, "We don't get very many of them."

Stringency, Gender Burdens, and Household Hardships

To a degree greater than most counties throughout the United States, the number of TANF cases in Holmes County plummeted following the implementation of welfare reform. In 1996, the monthly average caseload was 1,253. During the first ten months of 1999 it averaged 564 cases. In October 1999 the number of cases was 504, representing a decline of 60 percent over the first three years of TANF.

It is important to note that caseload decline began prior to the implementation of TANF. By 1992 the average monthly number of cases in AFDC was 1,474. Each year from 1992 to 1996 the average declined between 30 and 50 cases from the previous year. With the start of TANF, however, the rate of decline increased with the caseload dropping by between 250 and 300 each year. It is also worthy of note that after the plant closures there was an increase in the number of TANF cases. By October 2002 the number of cases was back up to 798. In Sunflower County the TANF caseload trend was similar to that in Holmes County. The monthly average of AFDC cases in 1992 was 1,442. In 1997, the first full year of the initial reform regime, average monthly participation was 1,205. Over one year, participation had dropped precipitously to 773 cases. In 2002 the number of TANF cases had fallen to a monthly average of 639.

Stringency

According to Sunflower County MDHS staff and others interviewed, the size of the monthly TANF cash benefit, a mere $170 a month for a woman with two children, contributed to the decline in participation. As in the Texas counties, when the amount of benefits offered were compared to the responsibilities associated with participation, some persons who qualified for assistance decided the benefits were not "worth the hassle" and elected to "opt out of the welfare system." Others who were sanctioned decided to leave the program rather than attempt to fulfill the requirements of participation and by doing so forfeited the cash benefits they might have received.

Mississippi's TANF plan was essentially its "New Directions" waiver, a program the Urban Institute cited as enforcing "the toughest sanctions in the country," including "loss of the entire AFDC and Food Stamp benefit for the entire family" (Kirby et al. 1998, 5). As modified under TANF, sanctions were less severe but became progressively more stringent with each violation. The first violation resulted in the sanctioning of only the noncompliant adult's portion of the TANF grant and her or his Medicaid coverage (but not Food Stamps benefit) for at least two months and until compliance. The second violation imposed these sanctions for a minimum of six months, and the third for one year. The fourth violation resulted in permanent termination of benefits (Brister, Beeler, and Chambry 1997, 4).

Additionally, Mississippi enforced a "family benefit cap," first instituted under the state waiver in 1995, which prohibited an increase in a family's TANF benefits following the birth of a child after the family unit had received benefits for ten months, with some exceptions (Kirby et al. 1998, 18; Mississippi Department of Human Services 2003).

More progressive elements of the policy included child support reforms allowing the "pass through" of all funds collected from the noncustodial parent. Participation in JOBS was made mandatory for absent fathers who were not meeting child support obligations, and the Unemployed Parent family work rules were rescinded (Kirby et al. 1998, 19). In cases of hardship, such as someone in need of alcohol or drug abuse treatment, or in a domestic violence situation, the lifetime limit of five years could be extended. However, women with a documented history of domestic violence could only be exempted from participation in work-related activity for up to twelve months (Brister, Beeler, and Chambry 1997, 11).

Gender Burdens

The unavailability of child care was also identified as a barrier to labor force participation. MDHS staff acknowledged that the long commutes make child care a problem, especially when the job required night work. Just finding a reliable childcare provider was problematic. And even though MDHS provided subsidized child care, problems, including delays in payments to providers, created hardships for participants. One mother reported, "I had to quit my job because the state was several months behind in paying [the childcare provider]. She refused to keep my kids without getting paid on time."

Child care was a major problem for those who left TANF, marked by waiting lists and heavy competition to access official care. When funds were available, families with an income below 85 percent of the state's median income level and who were deemed at risk of going on TANF were eligible to receive childcare services. Estimates by the Mississippi Forum for Children and Families suggested that even if the state's childcare system functioned at its most efficient level, it could have met the needs of only 10 percent of the eligible population (Kirby et al. 1998, 24–25).

Household Hardships

Arguably, medical insurance is more important to TANF eligible families than the cash grant. While families may be able to overcome the loss of $150 to $200 a month, a single visit to the doctor's office and pharmacy may cost many times that amount. Therefore, it is important to examine the impacts of welfare reform on medical insurance eligibility through Medicaid and the State Children's Health Insurance Program (SCHIP).

The availability of health care was also a major problem. Medicaid was the only health insurance program available to low-income families, and the state suffered from a "substantial shortage" of healthcare professionals. "Community health centers," which are important sources of health care for low-income individuals and the uninsured, were found to be serving three times the number of persons as they did in other states (Kirby et al. 1998, 7–8).

When TANF participants in Mississippi found work and were no longer eligible for TANF, they could continue to receive Medicaid for up to one year. After that time, however, they were solely dependent upon their employers for medical insurance. As in the other states, children continued to qualify for medical insurance through SCHIP, regardless of how the parent left TANF (e.g., for work, sanctioned, timed out). Therefore, one would expect the trend in Medicaid cases to decline in association with the trends in TANF participation, as would other programs that are tied to family income. However, the number of SCHIP cases would be expected to rise as decanted TANF participants enroll their children in the program. The experiences in Holmes and Sunflower counties were consistent with those expectations.

The annual data series from 1992 through 2002 indicates a steady decline in Medicaid cases for both counties from 1992 to 1999. However, this decline reversed in 2000. In that year, and each of the following two years, the number of Medicaid cases increased. Indeed, the increases in those three years were large enough to more than offset the decreases in the previous seven years; the number of cases in 2002 was greater than in 1992 for both counties. At the beginning of 1992, the caseload in Holmes County was 9,933. This decreased to 8,963 cases in 2000 and rose to 10,787 cases in 2002. Similarly, Sunflower County had 10,895 cases in 1992, 10,220 in 2000, and 12,113 cases in 2002. These trends were consistent with the declines in TANF participation followed by increases in the years just prior to 2002. The decline in Medicaid cases is said to be related to the inauguration of SCHIP. According to a case manager in Holmes County, "We're moving [children] from Medicaid to SCHIP. Almost everyone not eligible for Medicaid is eligible for SCHIP."

Yet medical care continued to be a serious problem for some of the adult TANF participants and former participants. Parents who found work but were not insured by their employers were perhaps the most vulnerable. As one mother said, "I don't go to the doctor because I don't have the money really." Another mother told us, "I take blood pressure pills and thyroid pills when I can afford it. A lot of times I can't afford it." She had no medical insurance. Others told us of not having prescriptions filled because they did not have the money to make the co-payment. Thus, it appears that limited access to transitional Medicaid and employer-provided insurance left some families with no medical insurance and inadequate health care.

Transportation problems also created hardships for families. When TANF participants in Holmes and Sunflower counties found employment, they often were confronted with long commutes, up to a hundred miles from home to work. Given that commuting is also a requirement of participation in voluntary service placements, inadequate transportation was a major hardship for respondents. There were no public transportation systems in either county. Although there are some "taxi" services, these are too expensive for most low-income people. Moreover, many low-income families, especially African American families, live in remote rural neighborhoods and unincorporated settlements. For them, the lack of reliable and affordable transportation creates an even greater barrier. It also limits their access to health care and social services. It is not surprising that TANF participants and community leaders both report that lack of transportation is a significant barrier to participation in the labor markets within the county and neighboring counties.

The Holmes County MDHS staff described the interaction between deficits in local labor market and inadequate transportation as follows,

We have a lot of people who work at Carthage at the chicken factory. That's hard work. A lot of night work that makes a problem for people with children. There are buses that run from here [Lexington]. The chicken factory contracts with them [the bus company] and they take so much out of the [worker's] check each week. I believe it is twenty-five dollars per week to ride the buses. But they're still gone so long, twelve hours or more, and it makes a problem in child care. And then we have some catfish factories over in the Delta. We do take some over to Belzoni and Isola.

This was confirmed by TANF participants whom we interviewed. As one mother said, "On the chicken factory bus you have to pay the driver twenty-five dollars a week. You're gone from home nine to twelve hours a day. And you get minimum wage and no benefits."

The transportation problem was exacerbated by the fact that many TANF participants had no vehicle and thus were dependent on the contracted bus service, which they claimed was not always reliable. Some people car pooled, which was only a partially successful solution, as the cost to riders was reportedly high and, moreover, in cases where drivers quit or lost their jobs, the riders also lost their transportation, and possibly their jobs as well, if they couldn't find another way to work.

When respondents who were working were asked what had been most helpful to them in keeping a job, transportation loomed large. "Reliable transportation" or "dependable transportation" was mentioned by nearly half of the participants interviewed. Transportation surfaced again when we asked participants for their suggestions for ways to help people make the transition from welfare to work. Their answers included: "The town needs public transportation," "I need transportation," "Donate me a car," "Provide better transportation service," and "[Develop] public transportation."

The Everyday Economy in the Delta

Wage Work

To make the transition from welfare to work, employment opportunities are obviously critical. But jobs are scarce in the Mississippi Delta, especially those that offer full-time, year-round employment. Holmes and Sunflower counties are no exception, both being surrounded by other persistently poor counties with limited employment opportunities. When we asked a leader in the African American community what was the most important thing that could be done to improve the situation in Holmes County, he said emphatically, "Jobs. We need jobs. Good-paying jobs."

After a century of extreme dependence on agriculture for employment, Sunflower County has struggled to create employment opportunities for the thousands of workers forced out of agriculture since the end of World War II. The Mississippi Delta was a low-wage, unskilled labor market area long before the era of globalization. Indeed, it specialized in attracting employers who offered wage and benefit packages below the poverty line for many families and jobs that proved vulnerable to international free trade agreements, such as NAFTA. The manufacturing plant closures and layoffs demonstrated the problem.

The Sunflower County Economic Development Corporation's executive director stated that he had "never been in the business of selling minimum wage jobs, but welfare reform [had] expanded the labor force and exerted downward pressure on wages." He continued: "To raise employees above the poverty line, employers need to offer jobs for eight to nine dollars an hour, plus benefits." According to the executive director, TANF participants were "no longer the problem of the state but of the economy [private sector], and therefore economic development officials."

Labor markets in the Delta are also starkly segmented by race. One TANF participant's assessment of hiring practices in her community was as follows: "There ain't no discrimination because only African Americans apply for the jobs African American people get. But if they applied for better jobs, they wouldn't get hired." Race remained a decisive factor in securing employment. As indicated by the respondent, it operated though the network-based hiring preferred by employers. Most of the business establishments in each county were small and family owned; the majority of the owners white. Most of their employees were either family members, kin, or family friends, virtually all of whom were white. African Americans seeking work were seldom within the "labor pool" to which white employers turned. And when employers did turn to the African American labor pool, it was often to fill less desirable jobs which paid low wages, were often part time or seasonal, provided no benefits, sometimes paid "in-kind" services, and were often "off the books."

Two points are noteworthy. First, the hiring practices of small family-owned businesses in Holmes and Sunflower counties differ very little, if at all, from those of small businesses elsewhere in the United States. However, because of the history of race relations throughout the Delta, the African American labor pool frequently is used as a source of labor only for the least desirable jobs, even though many of the African American workers have the skills needed to perform the tasks involved in the better jobs.

Second, small business establishments everywhere escape the enforcement of equal employment opportunity laws and regulations by either one of two ways. Either their small size exempts them from laws and regulations intended to eliminate discrimination in labor markets or the laws and regulations that do apply are simply not enforced. Because most business establishments in Holmes and Sunflower counties are small, the legal approach to reducing discriminatory practices has limited impact on local labor market dynamics. Race continues to be a critical factor in determining the outcomes of labor market transactions.

It is important to note that the "small-size loophole" does not provide an easy escape from the antidiscriminatory hiring regulations in larger firms and government agencies, including school districts. In these labor markets African American workers are hired in significant numbers. Yet the targeting of jobs by race or gender continues to operate to a measurable extent. That is, certain jobs are regarded as "black jobs" or "women's work." Thus it is not surprising to find that the employment opportunities in these counties available to African American women pushed off welfare were quite limited.

Entrepreneurship and Unreported Activities

Based on interviews with local leaders and TANF participants, nearly everyone was aware of people doing various economic activities outside formal wage work. As one community leader said, "There's a lot of informal work here. The activities range widely, but most of them are service activities and some selling of products—used cars, Avon products, crafts, food." TANF participants engaged regularly in activities outside wage work to help make ends meet and knew many family and friends who were doing the same. The activities included housecleaning, babysitting, providing elder care, doing hair, cutting grass, doing car repairs, house painting, home repairs, cutting fire wood, and giving rides for payment.

In the course of our fieldwork we became aware of women running "restaurants" in their homes. They did no advertising, but local clientele knew of their existence and at noon every day people stopped by for lunch. There was no printed menu or listing of prices, "guests" simply ate what was offered that day and put money on the table as they left. As in the Texas counties, some women made lunches in their homes and delivered them to regular customers at job sites, at work, or at their homes. As one women told us, "You gotta have a hustle if you gonna make it." A project of the Christian Women's Job Corps at the Grace Community Church was working on helping women develop cottage industries, like restaurants, repair shops, and crafts as a way out of poverty.

We also learned of people who "ran cards" in their home; they hosted card playing in which bets were made and the host took a small percentage of the winnings. Other illegal activities included copying and selling video tapes, selling drinks and package goods without a liquor license, dealing drugs, and prostitution.

Education

The underemphasis on education in the Mississippi TANF plan was not surprising, given the state's history of underfunding its public schools, which in the Delta, serve an almost exclusively African American student body. The legacy of the plantation and sharecropper systems of agriculture contribute directly to underinvestment in public education. Communities throughout the Mississippi Delta have always operated and continue to operate dual school systems in which African American children attend one set of schools and white children attend another. The 1954 U.S. Supreme Court ruling in *Brown v. Board of Education,* which found the "separate but equal doctrine" unconstitutional, did little to change the Mississippi system. A system of private academies supported by private funds grew dramatically in direct response to *Brown,* and being private, they were (and are) exempt from court-ordered desegregation. Extensive poverty is related to low levels of education. The 1990 census showed that in Mississippi 36 percent of adults twenty-five and older had less than a high school education, and 15.6 percent had less than a ninth grade education. When these data are disaggregated by race, we see that the statistics for African Americans are far worse than the aggregate data while those for whites are far superior. For example, in Sunflower County in 2000, 36.2 percent of adults had less than a high school diploma; however, 48.6 percent of African Americans lacked this credential compared to 26.1 percent of whites.

The school districts are faced with a number of challenges. Because of the racial segregation of public and private schools, public school students come largely from low-income families. Because most white families pay tuition to send their children to the private academies they are resistant to property tax increases to support schools. This means that public schools often do not have the money to pay for materials and other resources, which the academies are able to provide to their students. This is compounded by the fact that significantly higher rates of poverty among African American families means that they often cannot afford basic school supplies. There is also a shortage of certified teachers in the public schools, no doubt tied to the schools' insufficient resources, and low pay scales.

There were some private nonprofit efforts in Holmes County directed at helping students "at-risk" by compensating for the insufficient resources of the public schools. One that had achieved national recognition and praise was operated by the Community Culture and Resource Center (CCRC) located in Lexington, a nonprofit communitybased organization promoting education, leadership, and community development primarily in the African American community. During the school year, a core group of thirty to forty students worked on CCRC activities, while double that number participated during the summer. Oral history has been their major technique for youth leadership development. The students decided they wanted to go into the community and talk to elderly residents to learn from them what life was like when they were growing up. "The project strengthened their self-esteem and was truly empowering," according to the CCRC executive director. Their project on the Civil Rights Movement in Holmes County, "Minds Stayed on Freedom," was published in 1991 by the Rural Organizing and Cultural Center, and appeared on the CBS Sunday morning show with Charles Karault on July 15, 1992. CCRC staff and students have traveled across the country to conduct workshops on their oral history project, most of which have been run by the students themselves.

There were also programs in Sunflower County to prevent children from continuing the cycle of poverty. Sunflower-Humphreys County Progress, Incorporated, offered a Summer Youth Employment Training Program. Head Start was very active in the community. Many of these nonprofit community organizations also provided placements for TANF participants where they did volunteer work to qualify for their cash benefits.

In the area of adult education, the state was similarly tight-fisted, and as a result, the private nonprofits and charitable organizations were expected to step in. TANF participants were generally not offered skills training or education beyond GED (Kirby et al. 1998, 22). The Holmes County Community College was providing funds to local organizations that offered GED classes for welfare participants, and the Grace Church offered a GED program that met three times per week. Most students were between the ages of sixteen and thirty-five with very low educational performance scores; none scored above the sixth grade.

Local leaders in Sunflower County also were well aware of the human capital deficiencies caused and perpetuated by the bifurcated educational system. The executive director of Sunflower County Economic Development Corporation was devoted to creating jobs and improving incomes. He noted that his economic development efforts were influenced greatly by the human capital deficiencies. "If you don't do intervention work, then you lose in the process." As a result, he was involved with a number of key social groups, including youth. He visited schools to give presentations dealing with job performance, interviewing skills, and career planning. "If I can go and get some good, sharp high school students to play the game I'm talking about playing, then I've got something to offer a company that comes in."

The Center for Career and Workforce Development was an outreach arm of Mississippi Delta Community College, which offered services to individuals, businesses, and industries in their seven-county district. The majority of their funding came from the state and federal governments and local employers. The services included everything from literacy programs to career counseling and job-specific industry training. According to the director, many local employers realized that some of their new employees were making the transition from welfare to work and needed help coping with this change. The center was receiving an increasing number of requests from business and industry to do basic job skills training programs, including orientation to the workplace and workforce readiness skills. For example, nine employers in the college's service area requested Life Skills and Basic Skills training sessions for a total of 315 participants during the 1998/99 fiscal year. An additional 173 people were served through Adult Basic Education / GED training provided at a number of locations in Sunflower County, including schools, Head Start centers, and the county jail.

Career Centers were created to meet the demands of local businesses for labor, and all training programs were geared toward developing skills for "in-demand occupations." Services were directed toward low-income workers and were quite extensive, including "recruitment, skills assessment, counseling and referral services for training and job placement, pre-employment training for those with no work experience, basic literary skills training and GED, vocational and technical training, and short-term skills training for JTPA participants." The centers were supported by state and corporate funds and were administered by community colleges. They were largely independent of the federally funded JTPA and JOBS programs, and therefore were not integrated with the One Stop Shops for TANF participants (Kirby et al. 1998, 21).

According to one Mississippi administrator, the Career Centers were "wildly successful" because of the partnerships they create between community colleges and private enterprise; however, TANF participants were not directed to the Career Centers by caseworkers, who, they reported, "tend to believe" that community colleges were not interested in serving the welfare population. "At times," however, TANF participants "seek them out on their own" (Kirby et al. 1998, 23). Thus, a two-tier employment services system developed in which TANF participants were referred to the more limited services provided at the One Stop Shops.

There were other organizations and programs in the county working to increase levels of human capital among adults. The parent centers in Indianola public schools worked to involve parents in the schools. During the 2001–2 school year they offered computer training courses for interested parents. The centers also worked with teen parents. For example, the local extension agent visited the schools twice a month to provide information and counseling for teen parents. The utility of all of the services just described was limited, however, by the state's general unwillingness to invest state money in education, workforce training for the "hard to serve," and the crucial supportive service of child care.

Conclusion

The task of moving hundreds of families from welfare to work in labor markets with extremely limited employment opportunities, double digit unemployment, and segregated labor markets is daunting. Moreover, Holmes and Sunflower counties are surrounded by other counties faced with similar challenges. It is frustrating and stressful for all involved: MDHS staff, other service providers, and most of all, TANF participants, the vast majority of whom want nothing more than to leave welfare for full-time work.

Initially, devolution resulted in a lack of accountability and failure to provide some services to those who needed them most. Even now, Mississippi continues its tradition of leaving the responsibilities for the poor largely to charities and other federal programs, rather than to the state revenue system. An important consequence of welfare reform is the increased demand placed on community groups to provide the urgent care required by former TANF participants and their families. These are mostly nonprofit, charitable organizations with limited resources, which are being stretched to their limit, and perhaps beyond. They were making valiant efforts to address the needs, but they were incapable of replacing government agencies as a provider of human services for more than a very short time.

The caseload declines, despite worsening economic conditions, also reflect the stringency of Mississippi's TANF policies. This inflexibility created additional hardships for women in particular, and households generally, struggling to leave poverty. As in other pockets of persistent poverty, the everyday economy in the Delta finds households engaged in a broad array of formal wage work, albeit for low pay, and a variety of home-based enterprises.

Education, the logical starting point for Mississippi, has not been given the state support we found in Kentucky. One of the most salient and positive impacts of welfare reform in the Mississippi Delta was the increased awareness and attention to human capital and labor demand deficiencies. The leaders who are addressing these needs face a daunting challenge, inherited through a local society burdened by the weight of institutional racism, a legacy of underinvestment in human capital, and an economy which remains led by a planter class who no longer demands labor.

NINE

Welfare Reform in Persistent Rural Poverty

Despite chronically high levels of poverty and unemployment, the pockets of persistent poverty we studied experienced significant declines in welfare caseloads over the last decade. South Dakota, Texas, and Mississippi all received waivers for their AFDC programs and began implementing work requirements and other reforms in some locales before the federal PRWORA reforms were enacted. All four states had declining welfare rolls between 1992 and 1996, including Kentucky, although among our focus counties Todd and Starr had increases over that period. Following the passage of PRWORA, all of our focus counties exhibited significant caseload declines, some of which approached the 60 percent decline nationally. At first glance, this fact seemed astonishing, given their poor overall economic conditions and extreme labor demand deficiencies. It became less surprising as we began to understand the complex institutional factors underlying household survival in these areas and the limited role of cash welfare assistance.

Economic Conditions

There is little evidence that the dramatic declines in welfare participation are attributable to significantly improved economic conditions. Leaders of the counties in our study universally identified the need for greater and broader economic development in their regions before welfare reform's stated goal of decreasing welfare "dependency" could be realized. While poverty rates in the focus counties declined during the 1990s, they remained astronomical in 2000 compared to the U.S. rate and were only slightly better in most of the counties than they were in 1980. Per capita income in the counties remained approximately one-half the per capita income for their respective states, and their economies remained undiversified and highly vulnerable to single-sector job loss and declines in government jobs and spending. While there were some increases in employment in every county except Holmes, Mississippi, these increases were in lower-paying, less stable service sectors, with ongoing losses in manufacturing jobs for most of the counties.

It is also evident that although these places are remote, they are nevertheless strongly affected by changing global economic forces. This is not surprising when one considers the integral roles played by the Delta, the Valley, and Appalachia historically in the development of the national economy. Nor is it surprising when we realize that the present movement of manufacturing off shore is the result of a process which began in the 1960s with the movement of manufacturing processes from the unionized North to the rural South. Losses in manufacturing in Mississippi, Texas, and Kentucky were all associated with the implementation of NAFTA and the broader movement of capital investments in manufacturing to foreign countries with even lower labor costs. On the other hand, the location of the Texas counties at the Mexico border allowed them alone to reap some benefits from increased internationalization through their retail and service sectors.

Full Employment

It is readily apparent that people were not leaving welfare for full-time, year-round employment. The nature of these rural labor markets increases the likelihood that whatever formal employment is found will be for low pay, no benefits, and limited duration. For example, of those people employed in these counties in 2000, between 75 percent and 85 percent were employed full time, but only between 25 percent and 50 percent were employed year-round, full time. In several counties, the concern was expressed that TANF participants were competing with other poor families looking for work, especially where manufacturing jobs had declined significantly. Overall, the job trend is toward lower-end, minimum-wage, service sector work. Among the former participants interviewed who were working, most were making minimum wage or slightly above minimum wage. However, the self-sufficiency standards for these counties indicate that something between $11 and $15 an hour is needed to meet the needs of a single parent with two school-aged children (Pearce 1997, 2000a, 2000b, 2003).

Reliance on Social Networks and the Everyday Economy

All the regions in this study demonstrated the tremendous role of extended family and friends in covering shortfalls created by underemployment and lost welfare benefits. It is also apparent, however, that family supports are limited, vulnerable, and fragile. There are also potential problems within these networks, including unresolved conflicts and substance abuse. Nonetheless, these social networks form the foundation of what we have termed the everyday economy.

All these pockets of persistent rural poverty shared the phenomenon of families making ends meet within an "everyday economy," which encompasses both formal market employment and access to public assistance benefits but is grounded in a broad set of alternative and socially based relationships. The model of the economic world employed by many leading academics and policymakers, which rigidly distinguishes between formal markets, on the one hand, and informal activities and social relations, on the other, is of little use in understanding the economic behavior of families in these regions who merge both into complex household survival strategies. The experiences of TANF participants in these counties demonstrate that the bright line drawn by the authors of PRWORA between the morally deserving "working" poor" and the undeserving "welfare dependent" is a fiction. These households move fluidly and dynamically across an array of activities and social relationships as opportunities to work appear and disappear as needs dictate. Patterns of cycling off and onto welfare were apparent in all of these areas, probably exceeding the 10 to 15 percent of the national caseload estimated to be constituted by such churners at any point in time. As social networks are strained and alternative economic possibilities exhausted, it is reasonable to expect that caseloads will increase again.

It is also apparent that the greatest labor of all is managing the constant uncertainty about where to find the next meal, the next dollar, the next ride, the means to deal with the next emergency, and, above all, someone to care for one's children while attempting to address these concerns. Far from leisurely, life within these extremely marginal market economies demands a level of managerial, entrepreneurial, social, fiscal, and emotional genius that would severely challenge any middle-class family. This constant stress plays a role in other common features among these communities, such as domestic violence, substance abuse, poor health, and internal conflict.

Diversion to Other Programs

In some areas, caseload declines might simply result from a shift or diversion of families from welfare support to other types of public programs. In Pine Ridge, there was a 15 percent increase in child-only TANF cases, amounting to two-fifths of the remaining caseload. In Starr County, SSI cases increased by more than 70 percent over the early years of welfare reform. In Mississippi, nonprofit charitable and private sector food pantries, support programs, and emergency services were being strained. Programs of diversion were explicit among some of the TANF offices in this study, pointing to the potential influence of administration on caseload declines.

State Policy and Local Administration

State policy and administration, on the other hand, seems to have played an increasingly vigorous role in moving people off welfare in these areas, although not necessarily into work. With the exception of Kentucky, the enforcement of administrative rules and the stringency of sanctions increased in all counties over the period from 1996 to 2002, and increasingly focused on administrative requirements rather than work-related failures. In Kentucky, sanctions were not imposed for failure to meet administrative requirements such as a missed appointment. In contrast, Mississippi imposed the toughest sanctions for failing to fulfill any TANF participation requirements, terminating all welfare benefits and food stamps for the entire family, and making termination permanent after a fourth compliance failure. Mississippi was also the only state in this study to impose a "family cap" on benefits such that families who had additional children after they began receiving TANF could not receive additional benefits for the new child.

Among those who did not or could not afford to quit the program, the overwhelming majority were placed in "voluntary community service" positions. Although some participants derived some benefits from participation in community service, such as establishing new network connections, there were many problems associated with such heavy administrative dependence on this work activity. Additionally, participants in both South Dakota and Texas described their TANF community service placements as more stringent than those of a real job. In South Dakota and Texas, rates of sanction increased over time. By 2002 most TANF participants in South Dakota had been sanctioned, indicating an overall decline in morale among participants since 1999. Rates of sanctions had also skyrocketed across Texas. Sanctions were often imposed for failure to fulfill work requirements. While Kentucky and South Dakota imposed a fixed thirty-hour-per-week requirement for a single parent with children six years or older, Texas and Mississippi calculated the number of work hours required by dividing the family's total amount of TANF and Food Stamps benefit by the federal minimum wage. In Texas, the median number of work hours per week mandated for the single female–headed families we interviewed was thirty-five. Some respondents reported accepting a sanction in order to avoid these requirements. Others reported having quit the program because the burden of the work hours far exceeded the benefits received. The weakest families were sanctioned in spite of their efforts to fulfill the requirements.

The specific features of TANF implementation in these areas also contribute to the conclusion that caseload declines were not due to leavers finding full-time, year-round employment. Apart from Kentucky, none of the regions were encouraging higher education as a means of leaving poverty. Limited funds, infrastructure, and politics severely curtailed access to available training programs such as WIA-funded On the Job Training. Importantly, the transitional and postemployment supports also promised by PRWORA were disbursed parsimoniously, if at all. As TANF participants entered the labor force, they were not accessing programs established for working-poor families, like the EITC, subsidized child care and other transitional work supports, and transitional adult Medicaid to the extent that policymakers anticipated. This was due to a number of factors: first, the many leavers who simply quit TANF to look for jobs on their own did not technically leave welfare for work and thus were ineligible for most transitional services. Second, funds for transitional programs, particularly child care, were extremely limited and conserved by caseworkers for TANF participants. Third, many participants were never informed about such benefits. Fourth, poor treatment at the welfare office discouraged many from applying for postemployment services. And last, employer preferences to hire workers under the table also limited access to work-related benefits. The one exception to all of this was the success of the SCHIP program in picking up almost all of the children of TANF leavers.

Perhaps the ultimate irony of welfare reform is that several participants from each of these regions commented on how AFDC had been more supportive of their efforts to find work than TANF. Some participants observed that job opportunities would be greater under AFDC because it allowed them to pursue all levels of education. With more education, the participants would be more likely to find jobs. Participants also expressed the belief that AFDC rules had provided better transportation and childcare opportunities.

Family Well-Being

While more difficult to quantify, the participant interviews convey a combination of hope and concern about their family well-being because of the
work requirements and sanctions associated with TANF. Across all counties,
people consistently had a positive attitude about work. They supported the
notion of work requirements and were drawn to the promise that welfare
reform would result in their finding permanent employment. In short, people
wanted to work. And while participants embraced the employment goals of
PRWORA, the reality of TANF was far different. Because of the poor labor
markets and inadequate supports for education or training, many became
discouraged as the additional time constraints and other costs of participation in TANF imposed on their limited household funds while offering them
almost no chance of getting real jobs. Child care was a particularly significant
issue. While all working parents struggle with leaving their children in day care,
the parents in these communities were particularly suspicious of professional
day care, and some had good reason to be. Across all counties, access to quality
licensed child care was limited. In Texas and South Dakota, for example, a
number of respondents reported children suffering injuries while in child care.
Others who had worked in commercial childcare centers or were required
to perform their volunteer hours in childcare settings complained of overcrowding and a lack of attentiveness to individual children. This reinforced an
already strong preference among most respondents for family-provided care.

The additional burdens created by TANF must be placed in the real
context of the already tremendous stress and hardship associated with life
in the everyday economies of these regions. The demands imposed by TANF
without adequate compensation or supports sapped participants' abilities to
pursue other activities to generate and access resources. For this reason, life
seemed harder from the perspective of many of the participants, economically as well as socially and emotionally.

Among the most extreme hardships, hunger was an issue for many of
the participants interviewed. Interestingly, in Rosebud, for example, it was
the households who were working and no longer on TANF that were most
likely to report problems of hunger, highlighting the hardships experienced
by the working poor. In Texas, administrative errors stemming from policy
changes and massive bureaucratic restructuring resulted in numerous respondent families being cut off from food stamps for one to two months. While
families with access to very strong network supports were able to weather
these incidents, those without such connections experienced the most severe
material hardships, including child hunger. In both Texas and Mississippi,

the implementation of the Food Stamps Employment and Training Program allowed the states to sanction a family's entire Food Stamps grant in addition to their TANF grant. This caused great concern among families over how to feed their children.

There was a broad array of attitudes about women and work across these regions. While the counties in Kentucky and Texas seemed to express the greatest paternalism over women, women from all the counties mentioned the tensions created within a relationship when the woman makes more money than the man. Because these were areas of high unemployment, some felt that TANF's insistence that women work while men were without jobs was increasing family frictions and domestic violence. The prevalence of *machismo* combined with significant populations of undocumented women immigrants in the Texas counties complicated women's moving to work and exacerbated the problem of domestic abuse. At the same time, many participants observed that women felt better about themselves when they were working.

Implications of Devolution

While "devolution," understood as the notion that local people know how to best solve local problems, seems like a good idea to most people, when employed in a facile manner ignorant of history and contemporary power relations, it can be harmful to some groups, especially members of nonwhite racial and ethnic communities. Among the explanations for why there is such stringency in the welfare rules in Texas, Mississippi, and South Dakota, and so little in Kentucky is the role of race and ethnicity in formulating state and local policy. The three regions in this study with the most stringent TANF policies each have significant populations of ethnic minorities heavily concentrated in specific geographic regions in which they constitute the majority. In 2000, Mississippi as a whole was 61.4 percent white and 36.3 percent African American, whereas Holmes and Sunflower counties were 78.7 percent and 69.9 percent African American respectively. Overall, the population of Texas is 71 percent white and 32 percent Hispanic, while Starr and Maverick counties are 97.5 percent and 95 percent Hispanic respectively. South Dakota is 88.7 percent white, with 8.3 percent Native American, but Shannon County is 94.2 percent Native American, and Todd county is 85.6 percent Native American.

In contrast, Kentucky is 90 percent white, and the focus counties of McCreary and Owsley were 98 percent and 99.2 percent white respectively. It is interesting to note that the Cumberland Plateau was the only region in this study where there was consistent cooperation, coordination, and proactive support to improve the conditions and opportunities for TANF participants. Theoretically, social exclusion based on race, over time, can create an economic underclass that would fit the descriptions of poverty and lack of opportunity for Native Americans, Hispanics, and African Americans in these regions. All of these regions, apart from Kentucky, have long histories of deliberately excluding these racially defined communities from the social, political, and economic opportunities of their states.

Devolution also highlights concerns over the potential for favoritism, lack of accountability, and poor administration and oversight at the state and local levels. These case studies reveal the strong role of local political apparatuses, even those working within a group viewed as ethnically homogenous from the national perspective. Within Native American communities, tribal government represents both the best hope for self-determination and the worst aspects of political factionalism, nepotism, and discrimination based on family relationships and degree of native ancestry. Political patronage systems, both long-standing and newly emergent, along the Texas-Mexico border systematically reproduce relations of privilege and exclusion along informal lines. The mismanagement and politicization of program funds that occurred in Starr County, the abusive treatment dispensed by some caseworkers in Maverick County, and the appearance of favoritism in both places all represent components of a system. Moreover, these local systems do not exist in isolation but, rather, in relation to broader systems. It is therefore important to recognize that the problems associated with devolution were not limited to the local level. The orientation of the state of South Dakota toward social programs affecting the tribes within its boundaries clearly affected welfare reform and exacerbated the negative aspects of it in Pine Ridge. In Texas, state use of so-called surplus TANF funds for other non-TANF related programs, among other things, exacerbated the general ineffectiveness of its Choices program. Similarly, the rush to privatization in Mississippi without accountability, experience, or coordination resulted in inadequate services for the African American families struggling to create better lives. All of these manifestations of problems with devolution at the state and local levels point to the need for a better balance between local flexibility and national oversight.

Conclusion

The promise of integration into labor markets embodied in welfare reform was consonant with the dreams of the impoverished families in these regions that they might one day find steady employment and make progress toward the universal goal of providing better futures for their children. The ideal articulated in Texas of "Get a job, Get a better job, Get a career" appealed to almost every TANF respondent. This ideal depends, however, on access to education, training, and other work supports. Among the states included in this study, Kentucky stands alone in having implemented policies where that dream has the potential to become reality for more than a handful of select participants. For most participants, the greatest areas of disenchantment centered around inadequate provision of support for their transition to work, including education, training, child care, and transportation. While no one thought of AFDC as a work-support program, several respondents who had received AFDC mentioned that it had offered more support for the transition to work than TANF. Even among those who left TANF for work, disenchantment came with remaining in poverty despite finding a job, because of a combination of low wages, poor benefits, and too few hours of work.

The hopes of community leaders and welfare administrators associated with what they had originally perceived as the opportunity of devolution to customize services to meet the specific needs of the area were also unfulfilled. Contrary to PRWORA's rhetoric of "local control," administrators continued to struggle with a lack of real flexibility to respond to local conditions of extreme and persistent poverty and extreme educational deficits. The lifetime limits on assistance and federal participation rates put incredible pressures on administrators in these communities where participants wanted desperately to find jobs and get off of welfare, but job creation needed to happen first. Like the participants themselves, however, administrators were bound to comply with federal and state mandates. While some found room to maneuver and provide more supportive services under their state waivers, those loopholes became smaller over time and eventually closed with the expiration of those waivers. Kentucky, again, was notable in that its policies toward education became more progressive over time.

Respondents were not the only ones who complained about the stringency of program rules. Administrators too complained of contradictions and irrational provisions in the new policies that undermined their abilities to meet client needs. Some reported regularly traveling to their state capitals to contest administrative rules they perceived as harmful. For example, one Texas administrator was incredulous that the rules precluded him from providing childcare assistance to TANF participants who were attending school at night "to try to improve themselves."

Other problems with devolution arose from the resources of welfare reform becoming the object of competition among regional and local elites within the states, reinforcing and enriching preexisting forms of patronage, nepotism, and favoritism. This was most evident in the problems experienced in Starr County, which stemmed from the history of machine politics in the county itself and throughout the Lower Rio Grande Valley, as well as the status of the Valley and its overwhelmingly Hispanic population in the eyes of the state. Similarly, the problems in Pine Ridge were centered on inequalities that may be traced to the origins of the federal creation of tribal government. It was also evident in Mississippi around the process of bid selection for privatization of welfare services.

One striking general finding of this study is the similarity that obtained among these counties, with the exception of Kentucky, in the way that welfare reform was implemented and experienced by participants. Devolution might reasonably have been expected to lead to an incredible diversity of policies, specific regulations, and timing on when, where, and how welfare reform would be experienced. Poor areas such as the ones examined in this study and which among themselves are very different, might reasonably have been exempted from the work mandates and time limits of PRWORA or been targeted for extra funding from state block grants to address job development, training, and the enormously problematic issues of education and transportation. This did not occur. Rather, temporary exemptions quickly gave way to the full imposition of participation requirements. As regards participation mandates, the states treated TANF participants in these counties in the same manner as they treated them in Dallas, Jackson, Lexington, and Rapid City.

There was also, however, tremendous diversity in how welfare reform was implemented among a set of counties that objectively share similar rates of poverty and underemployment. For example, the South Dakota and Texas chapters present myriad and very significant points of difference between the two counties in their experiences of welfare reform. Moreover, the constant flux in state welfare laws, budgets, administrative rules, program personnel, and supports over time functions to amplify such differences. In no small sense, the diversity we uncovered in welfare implementation appears to be the result of ad hoc responses to politically driven but empirically vacuous perceptions of what was required to turn so-called social dependents into working families. Because the economic, political, and social conditions were not in place at either the local or the state level (see Mead 2004) for the changes welfare reformers imagined, the results of reform in these regions of persistent poverty were largely to reduce access to assistance without any significant improvements in employment, employability, or poverty relief.

Another striking similarity was the way in which families in all of these areas navigated the changes brought by welfare reform. As they had prior to reform, they worked, they relied on family and friends for regular and emergency assistance, they accessed other public programs, and usually after all else failed, they sought help from outside organizations. In each area, they faced similar conditions, including downgraded labor markets where the best they could find was part-time or seasonal minimum wage or "under the table" work. Close-knit families were usually willing to help, but often at a price. Unpredictable third-sector organizations helped them one month, but had no funds the next.

At the same time, while all of these regions exhibited a strong reliance on social networks, the nature and structure of those relationships varied, particularly in relation to gender expectations. Similarly, while these communities shared an experience with the everyday economy, the specific components, alternatives, and balances within that economy varied widely from region to region.

Perhaps the greatest disservice to emanate from the broad brush of welfare reform is the perception that life in extreme poverty results from a shortcoming in the values and attitudes of individuals. This prejudice, colored by ideology, functions to obscure the historical, geographic, economic, political, and social factors that continue to exclude most residents of these areas from the investments and interactions that generate prosperity elsewhere in the United States.

APPENDIX A:
TANF PARTICIPANT RESPONDENT CHARACTERISTICS

South Dakota Respondents

Table 1 Pine Ridge TANF Participants (1999)

	Mean	Range
Age	35.00	20 to 56
Number of children	3.76	1 to 6
Household size	6.20	2 to 10
Educational grade level	12.10	10 to B.S.
Years of work experience	2.20	0 to 9

NOTE: N = 13.

Table 2 Pine Ridge TANF Participants (2002)

	Mean	Range
Age	38.6	20 to 68
Number of children	3.9	1 to 13
Household size	6.9	3 to 20
Educational grade level	11.7	8 to B.S.
Years of welfare support	8.6	0.5 to 18
Years of work experience	3.8	0 to 24
	Number	Percent
Currently on TANF	16	73
Obtained a job	1	4
Sanctioned off / left TANF without a job	5	23

NOTE: N = 22.

Table 3   Rosebud TANF Participants (1999)

	Mean	Range
Age	28.0	18 to 47
Number of children	2.0	1 to 4
Household size	3.8	2 to 6
Educational grade level	12.4	9 to B.A.
Years of work experience	3.8	0 to 15

NOTE: *N* = 10.

Table 4   Rosebud TANF Participants (2002)

	Mean	Range
Age	36.0	19 to 61
Number of children	3.3	1 to 9
Household size	4.3	2 to 7
Educational grade level	11.9	8 to last year before B.A.
Years of welfare support	6.6	0.5 to 19.5
Years of work experience	5.9	0 to 18

	Number	Percent
Currently on TANF	9	45
Obtained a job	9	45
Sanctioned off / left TANF without a job	2	10

NOTE: *N* = 20.

Kentucky Respondents

Table 5   Owsley County TANF Participants (1999)

	Mean	Range
Age	30.8	20 to 53
Number of children	1.8	1 to 3
Household size	3.9	3 to 6
Educational grade level	9.7	6 to 12

	Number	Percent
Currently on TANF	6	60
Obtained a job	4	40
Sanctioned off / left TANF without a job	0	0

NOTE: *N* = 10.

Table 6   Owsley County TANF Participants (2002)

	Mean	Range
Age	32.7	21 to 52
Number of children	1.7	1 to 4
Household size	3.0	2 to 5
Educational grade level	10.5	6 to 12
	Number	Percent
Currently on TANF	7	63.6
Obtained a job	3	27.3
Sanctioned off / left TANF without a job	0	0

NOTE: $N = 11$.

Table 7   McCreary County TANF Participants (1999)

	Mean	Range
Age	29.9	21 to 38
Number of children	2.3	1 to 4
Household size	4.4	1 to 6
Educational grade level	9.8	6 to 12
	Number	Percent
Currently on TANF	1	10
Obtained a job	2	20
Sanctioned off / left TANF without a job	1	10

NOTE: $N = 12$.

Table 8   McCreary County TANF Participants (2002)

	Mean	Range
Age	30.3	19 to 46
Number of children	2.95	1 to 5
Household size	4.8	2 to 10
Educational grade level	9.9	6 to A.A.
	Number	Percent
Currently on TANF	6	33.3
Obtained a job	3	16.7
Sanctioned off / left TANF without a job	2	11.1

NOTE: $N = 18$.

Texas Respondents

Table 9 Starr County TANF Participants (2002–2003)

	Mean	Range
Age	30.0	20 to 50
Number of children	3.0	1 to 5
Household size	5.0	3 to 11
Educational grade level	9.6	4 to some college
Years of welfare support	2.43	2 months to 10 years
Years of work experience	No data	No data
	Number	Percentage
Currently on TANF	16	48
Obtained a job	11	33
Sanctioned off / left TANF without a job	6	18

NOTE: $N = 33$.

Table 10 Maverick County TANF Participants (2003)

	Mean	Range
Age	29	19 to 48
Number of children	2	1 to 4
Household size	5	2 to 11
Educational grade level	10.12	6 to some college
Years of welfare support	.5	3 months to 13 years
Years of work experience	No data	No data
	Number	Percentage
Currently on TANF	14	48
Obtained a job	4	13
Sanctioned off / left TANF without a job	11	37

NOTE: $N = 29$.

Mississippi Respondents

Table 11 Holmes County TANF Participants (1999)

	Mean	Range
Age	29.1	21 to 46
Number of children	2.9	1 to 5
Household size	4.4	3 to 6
Educational grade level	11.1	9 to some college
	Number	**Percent**
Currently on TANF	8	80
Obtained a job	1	10
Sanctioned off / left TANF without a job	2	20

NOTE: *N* = 10.

Table 12 Holmes County TANF Participants (2002)

	Mean	Range
Age	34.4	22 to 49
Number of children	1.6	0 to 5
Household size	3.3	1 to 7
Educational grade level	11.7	8 to B.S.
	Number	**Percent**
Currently on TANF	9	47.4
Obtained a job	6	31.6
Sanctioned off / left TANF without a job	0	0

NOTE: *N* = 19.

Table 13 Sunflower County TANF Participants (1999)

	Mean	Range
Age	31.8	24 to 43
Number of children	2.0	0 to 4
Household size	4.0	1 to 7
Educational grade level	11.2	10 to B.S.
	Number	**Percent**
Currently on TANF	5	50
Obtained a job	9	90
Sanctioned off / left TANF without a job	0	0

NOTE: *N* = 10.

Table 14 Sunflower County TANF Participants (2002)

	Mean	Range
Age	37.9	20 to 58
Number of children	2.0	0 to 7
Household size	3.6	2 to 8
Educational grade level	11.1	7 to B.S.
	Number	Percent
Currently on TANF	8	38.1
Obtained a job	6	28.6
Sanctioned off / left TANF without a job	1	4.8

NOTE: $N = 21$.

APPENDIX B:
CLUSTER COUNTIES AND RESERVATIONS

Kentucky	Mississippi	South Dakota	Texas
Bell	Bolivar	Cheyenne River	Brooks
Breathitt	Carroll	Crow Creek	Dimmit
Clay	Coahoma	Flandreau	Jim Hogg
Floyd	Holmes	Lower Brule	Kinney
Harlan	Humphreys	Pine Ridge	La Salle
Jackson	Issaquena	Rosebud	Maverick
Knott	Leflore	Standing Rock	Starr
Knox	Quitman	Yankton	Uvalde
Laurel	Sharkey		Zapata
Lee	Sunflower		Zavala
Leslie	Tallahatchie		
Letcher	Tunica		
McCreary	Washington		
Owsley	Yazoo		
Perry			
Pike			
Pulaski			
Rockcastle			
Wayne			
Whitley			

REFERENCES

Albers, Terry O. 2001. Welfare to work final report, summer. Welfare to Work Program, Oglala Lakota College, Porcupine, S.Dak.

Anderson, Steven G., Anthony P. Halter, and Richard Schuldt. 2001. Support service use patterns by early TANF leavers. In *Outcomes of welfare reform for families who leave TANF,* ed. George Julnes and E. Michael Foster, 87–99. San Francisco: John Wiley & Sons.

Bane, Mary Jo, and David T. Ellwood. 1994. *Welfare realities: From rhetoric to reform.* Cambridge: Harvard University Press.

Beck, Elizabeth. 2000. The post industrial economy: An elephant in the living room. In *Early implications of welfare reform in the Southeast,* ed. Larry G. Nackerud and Margaret Robinson, 33–43. Huntington, N.Y.: Nova Science Publishers.

Berman, Tressa. 2003. *Circle of goods: Women, work, and welfare in a reservation community.* Albany: State University of New York Press.

Bernstein, Jared. 2001. Economic growth and poverty: Lessons from the 1980s and 1990s. In *Challenges to equality: Poverty and race in America,* ed. Chester Hartman, 91–97. Armonk, N.Y.: M. E. Sharpe.

Besharov, Douglas J. 2003. The past and future of welfare reform. *Public Interest* 150 (winter): 4–21.

Billings, Dwight B. 1988. The rural South in crisis: A historical perspective. In *The rural South in crisis: Challenges for the future,* ed. Lionel J. Beaulieu, 13–29. Boulder, Colo.: Westview Press.

Billings, Dwight B., Kathleen Blee, and Louis E. Swanson. 1986. Culture, family, and community in preindustrial Appalachia. *Appalachian Journal* 13 (2): 154–70.

Biolsi, Thomas. 1995. Birth of the reservation: Making the modern individual among the Lakota. *American Ethnologist* 22 (1): 28–53.

Biolsi, Thomas, Rose Cordier, Marvin Douville Two Eagle, and Melinda Weil. 2002. Welfare reform on Rosebud reservation: Challenges for tribal policy. *Wicazo Sa Review* 17 (1): 131–58.

Bisbee, Julie. 2001. "Lockheed Martin files lawsuit." *McAllen Monitor,* January 13. http://www.themonitor.com/.

Blank, Rebecca M. 1997. *It takes a nation: A new agenda for fighting poverty.* Princeton: Princeton University Press.

———. 2002. Evaluating welfare reform in the United States. *Journal of Economic Literature* 40 (December): 1105–66.

Blakeslee. Nat. 2001. The border bust boom: In Del Rio, the biggest employer is the drug war. *Texas Observer,* February. http://www.texasobserver.org/archives/asp/.

Bradshaw, Ted K. 2003. Theories of poverty and anti-poverty programs in rural and community development. Paper presented at the meeting of the Rural Sociological Society, Montreal, Canada, July 29.

Braudel, Fernand. 1981. The structures of everyday life: The limits of the possible. Vol. 1 of *Civilization and capitalism*. New York: Harper & Row.

Breaux, David A., Christopher M. Duncan, C. Denise Keller, and John C. Morris. 1998. Blazing the TANF trail: The Southern mind and welfare reform in Mississippi. *American Review of Politics* 19 (summer): 175–89.

———. 2000. Privatization and welfare reform implementation in Mississippi. In *Managing welfare reform: Updates from field research in five states*. New York: Rockefeller Institute of Government.

Brister, Bill M., Jessie Beeler, and Sharon Chambry. 1997. Implementation process study: Mississippi's temporary assistance for needy families program. Jackson, Miss.: Millsaps College Center for Applied Research.

Brustin, Stacy L. 2003. The intersection between welfare reform and child support enforcement: D.C.'s weak link. *Catholic University Law Review* 52:621–82.

Burt, Martha R. 2002. The "hard-to-serve": Definitions and implications. In *Welfare reform: The next act*, ed. Alan Weil and Kenneth Finegold, 163–78. Washington, D.C.: Urban Institute Press.

Buss, Terry F., and F. Stevens Redburn. 1988. *Hidden unemployment: Discouraged workers and public policy*. New York: Praeger Publishers.

Cancian, Maria, Robert Haveman, Daniel R. Meyer, and Barbara Wolfe. 2002. Before and after TANF: The economic well-being of women leaving welfare. Discussion Paper No. 1244-02, Institute for Research on Poverty, Madison, Wis.

Capps, Randy, Nancy Pindus, Kathleen Snyder, and Jacob Leos-Urbel. 2001. Recent changes in Texas welfare and work, child care and child welfare systems. *Assessing the new federalism*, State Update Number 1, June. Washington, D.C.: The Urban Institute. http://www.urban.org/.

Castille, George Pierre. 1998. *To show heart: Native American self-determination and federal Indian policy*. Tucson: University of Arizona Press.

Caudill, Harry M. 1962. *Night comes to the Cumberlands: A biography of a depressed area*. Boston: Little, Brown.

Cherlin, Andrew, Linda Burton, Judith Francis, Jance Henrici, Laura Lein, James Quane, and Karen Bogen. 2001. Sanctions and case closings for noncompliance: Who is affected and why. Policy Brief 01-1, Welfare, Children & Families: A Three City Study, Johns Hopkins University, Baltimore, Md.

Coates, Dan, and Gertrude Himmelfarb. 1996. Can Congress revive civil society? *Policy Review*, no. 75:24–34.

Cobb, James C. 1992. The most Southern place on Earth: The Mississippi Delta and the roots of regional identity. New York: Oxford University Press.

Colloff, Pamela. 2001. The battle for the border. *Texas Monthly*, April. http://www.texasmonthly.com/.

Cortez, Tricia. 2001. Officials: Workforce board overhaul showing results. *Laredo Morning Times*, July 15. http://madmax.lmtonline.com/mainnewsarchives/071501/s4.html/.

Deller, Steven C., and Thomas R. Harris. 1993. Estimation of minimum market thresholds for rural commercial sectors using stochastic frontier estimators. *Regional Science Perspectives* 23:3–17.

Dollard, John. 1957 [1936]. *Caste and class in a Southern town.* 3rd ed. Garden City, N.Y.: Doubleday.

Duncan, Cynthia M. 1992. Persistent poverty in Appalachia: Scarce work and rigid stratification. In *Rural poverty in America,* ed. Cynthia M. Duncan, 111–34. New York: Auburn House.

————. 1996. Understanding persistent poverty: Social class context in rural communities. *Rural Sociology* 61 (1): 103–24.

————. 1999. *Worlds apart: Why poverty persists in rural America.* New Haven: Yale University Press.

Duncan, Cynthia, and Stephen Sweet. 1992. Introduction: Poverty in rural America. In *Rural poverty in America,* ed. Cynthia Duncan, xix–xxvii. New York: Auburn House.

Duncan, Greg J., Kathleen Mullan Harris, and Johanne Boisjoly. 2000. Time limits and welfare reform: New estimates of the number and characteristics of affected families. *Social Science Review* 74 (1): 55–75.

East, Jean F. 1999. Hidden barriers to success for women in welfare reform. *Families in Society: The Journal of Contemporary Human Services* 80 (3): 295–304.

Edelman, Peter. 1997. The worst thing Bill Clinton has ever done. *Atlantic,* March.

Edin, Kathryn, and Laura Lein. 1997. *Making ends meet: How single mothers survive welfare and low-wage work.* New York: Russell Sage Foundation.

Ellwood, David T. 1988. *Poor support: Poverty in the American family.* New York: Basic Books.

Fagan, Mark, and Charles F. Longino, Jr. 1993. Migrating retirees: A source for economic development. *Economic Development Quarterly* 7 (1): 98–106.

Federal Reserve Bank of Dallas. 1996. Texas *colonias:* A thumbnail sketch of the conditions, issues, challenges, and opportunities. http://www.dallasfed.org/ca/pubs/colonias.pdf/.

Finegold, Kenneth, and Sarah Staveteig. 2002. Race, ethnicity, and welfare reform. In *Welfare reform: The next act,* ed. Alan Weil and Kenneth Finegold, 203–23. Washington, D.C.: Urban Institute Press.

Fisher, Robert. 1999. Get a job. *Texas Observer* (Austin), March 19. http://www.texas observer.org/archives.asp/.

Foster, E. Michael, and George Julnes. 2001. Conclusions: Implications for policy reform and policy research. In *Outcomes of welfare reform for families who leave TANF,* ed. George Julnes and E. Michael Foster, 125–30. San Francisco: John Wiley & Sons.

Gais, Thomas L., Richard P. Nathan, Irene Lurie, and Thomas Kaplan. 2001. Implementation of the Personal Responsibility Act of 1996. In *The new world of welfare,* ed. Rebecca M. Blank and Ron Haskins, 35–69. Washington, D.C.: Brookings Institution.

Gault, Barbara, and Annisah Um'rani. 2001. The outcomes of welfare reform for women. In *Challenges to equality: Poverty and race in America,* ed. Chester Hartman, 102–6. Armonk, N.Y.: M. E. Sharpe.

Gooden, Susan T. 2000. Race and welfare: Examining employment outcomes of white and black welfare recipients. *Journal of Poverty* 4 (3): 21–41.

Gorham, Lucy. 1992. The growing problem of low earnings in rural areas. In *Rural Poverty in America,* ed. Cynthia M. Duncan, 21–39. New York: Auburn House.

Greenberg, Mark, and Steve Savner. 1996. A detailed summary of key provisions of the temporary assistance for needy families block grant of H.R. 3734: The Personal Responsibility and Work Opportunity Reconciliation Act of 1996. Center for Law and Social Policy. http://www.clasp.org/.

Gueron, Judith M. 1995. Work programs and welfare reform. *Public Welfare* 53 (summer): 7–16.

Hansen, Karen V., and Anita Ilta Garey. 1998. Labor and family intersections. In *Families in the U.S.: Kinship and domestic politics,* ed. Karen V. Hansen and Anita Ilta Garey, 670–74. Philadelphia: Temple University Press.

Harris, Kathleen Mullan. 1996. Life after welfare: Women, work and repeat dependency. *American Sociological Review* 61:407–26.

Hartman, Chester, ed. 2001. *Challenges to equality: Poverty and race in America.* Armonk, N.Y.: M. E. Sharpe.

Haskins, Ron. 2001. Effects of welfare reform on family income and poverty. In *The new world of welfare,* ed. Rebecca M. Blank and Ron Haskins, 103–36. Washington, D.C.: Brookings Institution.

Hirschl, Thomas, and Gene F. Summers. 1982. Cash transfers and the export base of small communities. *Rural Sociology* 47:295–316.

Hochschild, Arlie Russell. 1998. Ideals of care: Traditional, postmodern, cold-modern, and warm-modern. In *Families in the U.S.: Kinship and domestic politics,* ed. Karen V. Hansen and Anita Ilta Garey, 527–38. Philadelphia: Temple University Press.

Holzer, Harry J., Michael A. Stoll, and Douglas Wissoker. 2001. Job performance and retention among welfare recipients. Discussion Paper No. 1237-01, Institute for Research on Poverty, Madison, Wis.

Hu, Wei-Yin. 1999. Child support, welfare dependency, and women's labor supply. *Journal of Human Resources* 34 (1): 71–103.

Hudson Institute. 1997. Kentucky TANF program. http://www.hudson.org/wpc/states/ky-tanf.htm/.

Isserman, Andrew M. 1980. Estimating export activity in a regional economy: A theoretical and empirical analysis of alternative methods. *International Regional Science Review* 5 (2): 155–84.

Jenkins, Dawn, and Deborah Miller. 1999. A reality check: How children are faring under welfare reform in Kentucky. Kentucky Youth Advocates. http://www.kyyouth.org/.

Jensen, Leif, Jill L. Findeis, Wan-Ling Hsu, and Jason P. Schachter. 1999. Slipping into and out of underemployment: Another disadvantage of nonmetropolitan workers? *Rural Sociology* 64 (3): 417–38.

Jones, Jacqueline. 1998. "My mother was much of a woman": Slavery. In *Families in the U.S.: Kinship and domestic politics,* ed. Karen V. Hansen and Anita Ilta Garey, 677–708. Philadelphia: Temple University Press.

Julnes, George, Kentaro Hayashi, and Steven Anderson. 2001. Acknowledging different needs: Developing a taxonomy of welfare leavers. In *Outcomes of welfare reform for families who leave TANF,* ed. George Julnes and E. Michael Foster, 73–85. San Francisco: John Wiley & Sons.

Kentucky Cabinet for Families and Children. 1997. Kentucky's transitional assistance program (K-TAP). http://cfc-chs.chr.state.ky.us/welfare.htm/.

————. 2003. Temporary assistance for needy families (TANF) Title IV-A State Plan. http://cfc.state.ky.us/reform/State_Plan_Final_August_03.asp/.

Kentucky Cabinet for Families and Children, Department for Community Based Services. 2003. Operation manuals. http://cfc.state.ky.us/cbs-pol-man/manuals/vol_iiia/ VOL%20IIIA%204310.html/.

Kentucky Department for Social Insurance. 1997. Facts about welfare in Kentucky. http://cfc-chr.state.ky.us/stats/htm/.

Kids Count. 2003. Data book online. http://www.aecf.org/kidscount/databook/.

Kirby, Gretchen C., Jerome L. Gallagher, LaDonna Pavetti, Milda Saunders, and Tennille Smith. 1998. *Income support and social services for low-income people in Mississippi: The new federalism.* Washington, D.C.: Urban Institute Press.

Krikelas, Andrew C. 1992. Why regions grow: A review of research on the economic base model. *Federal Reserve Bank of Atlanta Economic Review* 77 (4): 16–29.

Landale, Nancy S., and Daniel T. Lichter. 1997. Geography and the etiology of poverty among Latino children. *Social Science Quarterly* 78 (4): 874–94.

La Rossa, Ralph. 1998. The culture and conduct of fatherhood. In *Families in the U.S.: Kinship and domestic politics,* ed. Karen V. Hansen and Anita Ilta Garey, 377–85. Philadelphia: Temple University Press.

Larson, Jane E. 2002. Informality, illegality, and inequality. *Yale Law & Policy Review* 20:137–82.

Latimer, Melissa. 1998. Perceived barriers to labor force participation among welfare recipients in West Virginia. *Southern Rural Sociology* 14:67–90.

Lawrence, Sharmila. 2002. Domestic violence and welfare policy: Research findings that can inform policies on marriage and child well-being. The Research Forum at the National Center for Children in Poverty, Columbia University, Mailman School of Poverty, New York.

Levine, Daniel. 2001. Cheering for a team no longer on the field: Rhetoric and reality in American welfare history. *Journal of Economic Issues* 35 (3): 733–42.

Lichter, Daniel T. 1989. The underemployment of American rural women: Prevalence, trends and spatial inequality. *Journal of Rural Studies* 5 (2): 199–208.

Lichter, Daniel T., and Janice A. Costanzo. 1987. Nonmetropolitan underemployment and labor force composition. *Rural Sociology* 52 (3): 329–44.

Littrell, Jill, and Sadhna Diwan. 1998. Social workers' attitudes toward welfare reform: Comparing aid to families with dependent children to work programs. *Journal of Applied Social Sciences* 22 (2): 137–49.

Lobao, Linda, and David Kraybill. 2003. The emerging roles of county governments in metropolitan and nonmetropolitan areas: Findings from a national survey. Paper presented at the AAEA-RSS annual meeting, Spatial inequality: Continuity and change in territorial stratification, Montreal, Canada, July 27–30.

Loprest, Pamela. 2001. How are families that left welfare doing? A comparison of two cohorts of welfare leavers. *Federal Reserve Bank of New York Economic Policy Review* 7 (2): 9–19.

Maril, Robert Lee. 1989. *Poorest of Americans: The Mexican-Americans of the lower Rio Grande Valley of Texas.* Notre Dame: University of Notre Dame Press.

Marshall, Will, and Anne Kim. 2002. Finishing the welfare revolution: A blueprint for TANF renewal. Policy Brief, Progressive Policy Institute, Washington, D.C. http://www.ppionline.org/.

Mazzeo, Christopher, Sara Rab, and Susan Eachus. 2003. Work-first or work-only: Welfare reform, state policy, and access to postsecondary education. *Annals of the American Academy of Political and Social Science* (AAPSS) 586:144–71.

McAllen Monitor. 2001. February 11, p. 1b. Reps have rare meeting at Capital for open discussion.

Mead, Lawrence M. 2003. Welfare caseload change: An alternative approach. *Policy Studies Journal* 31 (2): 163–85.

———. 2004. *Government matters: Welfare reform in Wisconsin.* Princeton: Princeton University Press.

Mencken, F. C. 1997. Regional differences in socioeconomic well-being in Appalachia. *Sociological Focus* 30 (1): 79–97

Miller, Kathleen K., and Thomas D. Rowley. 2002. Rural poverty and rural-urban income gaps: A troubling snapshot of the "prosperous" 1990s. RUPRI Data Report P2002-5, The Rural Policy Research Institute, Columbia, Mo.

Mississippi Department of Human Services. 2003. Mississippi State Plan Temporary Assistance for Need Families Program. http://www.mississippi.gov/frame set.jsp?URL=http%3A%2F%2F www.mdhs.state.ms.us%2F/.

Murray, Charles A. 1984. *Losing ground: American social policy, 1950–1980.* New York: Basic Books.

Mushinski, David, and Kathleen Pickering. 2005. The impact of welfare reform on labor markets in impoverished rural areas. *Journal of Economic Issues* 39 (2): 401–8.

Mushinski, David, and Stephan Weiler. 2002. A note on the geographic interdependencies of retail market areas. *Journal of Regional Science* 42 (1): 75–86.

Myles, John, and Jill Quadagno. 2000. Envisioning a *third way:* The welfare state in the twenty-first century. *Sociology, Contemporary Journal of Reviews* 29 (1): 156–67.

Nelson, Margaret K. 1999. Economic restructuring, gender, and informal work: A case study of a rural county. *Rural Sociology* 64 (1): 18–43.

———. 2004. How men matter: Housework and self-provisioning among rural single-mother and married-couple families in Vermont, U.S. *Feminist Economics* 10 (2): 9–36.

Nelson, Margaret K., and Joan Smith. 1999. *Working hard and making do: Surviving in small town, America.* Berkeley and Los Angeles: University of California Press.

Newman, Katherine. 1999. *No shame in my game: The working poor in the inner city.* New York: The Russell Sage Foundation.

Nichols, Donald, and David Mushinski. 2003. Identifying export industries using parametric density functions. *International Regional Science Review* 26 (1): 68–85.

Nightingale, Demetra Smith, and Kathleen Brennan. 1998. The welfare to work grants program: A new link in the welfare reform chain. http://www.urban.org/.

Oglala Sioux Tribe (OST). n.d. TANF plan. Pine Ridge, S.Dak.

O'Hare, William, and Mark Mather. 2003. The growing number of kids in severely distressed neighborhoods: Evidence from the 2002 census. The Annie E. Casey Foundation and the Population Reference Bureau, Baltimore, Md., October.

Ownby, Ted. 1999. *American dreams in Mississippi: Consumers, poverty, and culture, 1830–1998.* Chapel Hill: University of North Carolina Press.

Partridge, Mark D., and Dan S. Rickman. 2005. Persistent pockets of extreme American poverty: People or place based? http://crerl.usask.ca/research/Partridge/Persist_poverty_Jan05.pdf/.

Pearce, Diana. 1997. The self-sufficiency standard for Texas. Wider Opportunities for Women, Washington, D.C. http://www.sixstrategies.org/.

———. 2000a. The self-sufficiency standard for Kentucky. Wider Opportunities for Women, Washington, D.C. http://www.sixstrategies.org/.

———. 2000b. The self-sufficiency standard for South Dakota. Wider Opportunities for Women, Washington, D.C. http://www.sixstrategies.org/.

———. 2003. The self-sufficiency standard for Mississippi. Wider Opportunities for Women, Washington, D.C. http://www.sixstrategies.org/.

Peck, Jamie. 2001. Workfare states. London: Guilford Press.

Pickering, Kathleen. 2000a. Lakota culture, world economy. Lincoln: University of Nebraska Press.

———. 2000b. Alternative economic strategies in low income rural communities: TANF, urban relocation and the case of the Pine Ridge Indian Reservation. Rural Sociology 65 (1): 148–67.

———. 2001. Legislating development through welfare reform: Indiscernible jobs, insurmountable barriers, and invisible agendas on the Pine Ridge and Rosebud Indian reservations. Political and Legal Anthropology Review 24 (1): 38–52.

———. 2002. Report to the Oglala Oyate Woitancan Empowerment Zone. Kyle, S.Dak., December.

———. 2003. Eagles, prairie dogs, and wild turnips: Lakota conservation values, economic fragmentation, and the politics of resource management on the Pine Ridge Indian Reservation. Presentation to the 102nd Annual Meeting of the American Anthropological Association, Chicago, Ill., November 19–23.

———. 2004. Decolonizing time regimes: Lakota conceptions of work, economy and society. American Anthropologist 106 (1): 85–97.

Pickering, Kathleen, and David Mushinski. 2001. Cultural aspects of credit institutions: Transplanting the Grameen Bank Credit Group structure to the Pine Ridge Indian Reservation. Journal of Economic Issues 35 (2): 459–67.

———. 2004. Locating the cultural context of credit: Institutional alternatives on the Pine Ridge Indian Reservation. In Values and valuables: From the sacred to the symbolic, ed. Cynthia Werner and Duran Bell, 185–205. Society of Economic Anthropology Monograph series, no. 21, Walnut Creek, Calif.: AltaMira Press.

Pindus, Nancy, Randy Capps, Jerome Gallegher, Linda Giannarelli, Milda Saunders, and Robin Smith. 1998. Income support and social services for low income people in Texas: Assessing the new federalism, state reports. Washington, D.C.: Urban Institute Press.

Piven, Frances Fox, and Richard A. Cloward. 1971. Regulating the poor: The function of public welfare. New York: Pantheon Books.

Pleck, Joseph H. 1998. American fathering in historical perspective. Families in the U.S.: Kinship and domestic politics, ed. Karen V. Hansen and Anita Ilta Garey, 351–61. Philadelphia: Temple University Press.

Powdermaker, Hortense. 1968. After freedom: A cultural study of the Deep South. New York: Atheneum.

Ptacek, James. 1998. Why do men batter their wives? In Families in the U.S.: Kinship and domestic politics, ed. Karen V. Hansen and Anita Ilta Garey, 619–33. Philadelphia: Temple University Press.

Quadagno, Jill. 1994. The color of welfare: How racism undermined the war on poverty. New York: Oxford University Press.

Rector, Robert, and Patrick F. Fagan. 2001. The good news about welfare reform. http://www.heritage.org/.

Reisch, Michale, and David Sommerfeld. 2003. Interorganizational relationships among nonprofits in the aftermath of welfare reform. *Social Work* 48 (3): 307–19.

A Review of Research on the Kentucky Education Reform Act, 1995 (KERA). 1996. Lexington: University of Kentucky / University of Louisville Joint Center for the Study of Educational Policy.

Richardson, Chad R. 1999. *Batos, bolillos, pochos, and pelados: Class and culture on the South Texas Border.* Austin: University of Texas Press.

Richardson, Chad, and José A. Pagán. 2002. Human and social aspects of cross border development in the McAllen/Reynosa area. Working Paper 2002-9, Center for Border Economic Studies, University of Texas Pan American, Edinburg.

Rickman, Dana K., and E. Michael Foster. 2001. Welfare reform and children: A comparison of leavers and stayers in Georgia. In *Outcomes of welfare reform for families who leave TANF,* ed. George Julnes and E. Michael Foster, 59–71. San Francisco: John Wiley & Sons.

Robinson, Margaret, and Larry Nackerud. 2000. The devolution of welfare: Assessing the first wave of impacts and anticipating what is to come. In *Early implications of welfare reform in the Southeast,* ed. Larry G. Nackerud and Margaret Robinson, 195–201. Huntington, N.Y.: Nova Science Publishers.

Rodriguez, Nestor, and Jacqueline Hagen. 2001. Transborder community relations at the U.S.-Mexico border. Laredo/Nuevo Laredo and El Paso/Cuidad Juárez. In *Caught in the middle: Border communities in an era of globalization,* ed. Demetrios G. Papademetriou and Deborah Waller Meyers, 88–116. Washington, D.C.: The Carnegie Endowment and The Brookings Institution.

Sabo, Jason, Carlos Romo, Patrick Bresette, and Chris Piper. 2003. Texas at work today and tomorrow: The case for sound workforce investment policies. A report by the Center for Public Priorities, September, Austin, Tex.

Savner, Steve. 2001. Welfare reform and racial/ethnic minorities: The questions to ask. In *Challenges to equality: Poverty and race in America,* ed. Chester Hartman, 97–102. Armonk, N.Y.: M. E. Sharpe.

Schiller, Bradley R. 1999. State welfare reform impacts: Content and enforcement effects. *Contemporary Economic Policy* 17 (2): 210–23.

Schwartzweller, Harry, James S. Brown, and J. J. Mangalam. 1971. *Mountain families in transition.* University Park: Pennsylvania State University Press.

Scorsone, Eric, and Stephan Weiler. 2004. New markets as informational asymmetries. *Economic Development Quarterly* 18 (3): 303–13.

Seccombe, Karen. 1999. *"So you think we drive a Cadillac." Welfare recipients' perspectives on the system and its reform.* Boston: Allyn and Bacon.

Seccombe, Karen, Kimberly Battle Walters, and Delores James. 1999. "Welfare mothers" welcome reform, urge compassion. *Family Relations* 48 (2): 197–206.

Shaffer, Ron. 1989. *Community economics: Economic structure and change in smaller communities.* Ames: Iowa State University Press.

Sharp, John. 1998. Bordering the future. Texas Comptroller of Public Accounts, Austin. http://www.window.state.tx.us/border/border.html/.

Smith, Anna Marie. 2002. The sexual regulation dimension of contemporary welfare law: A fifty state overview. *Michigan Journal of Gender and Law* 8:121–218.

Smith, Jordan. 2001. Welfare warfare: Fraud claims mar state's privatization push. *Austin Chronicle,* November. http://www.austinchronicle.com/.

Smith-FitzPatrick, Christina.1999. *Poverty despite work in Kentucky.* Center on Budget and Policy Priorities and Kentucky Youth Advocates. Washington, D.C.: CBPP.

Soss, Joe, Sanford F. Schram, Thomas P. Vartanian, and Erin O'Brien. 2001. Setting the terms of relief: Explaining state policy choices in the devolution revolution. *American Journal of Political Science* 45 (2): 378–95.

South Dakota Department of Labor. 2003. Labor market information center. http://www.state.sd.us/applications/ld54lmicinfo/labor/LFLISTPUBM.ASP/.

South Dakota Department of Social Services. 1997. State plan temporary assistance for needy families (TANF) program. http://www.state.sd.us/social/tanf/plan/.

———. 2003. State plan temporary assistance for needy families (TANF) program. http://www.state.sd.us/social/tanf/plan.htm/.

Spicer, P., J. Beals, C. D. Croy, C. M. Mitchell, D. K. Novins, L. Moore, and S. M. Manson. 2003. The prevalence of DSMIIIR alcohol dependence in two American Indian populations. *Alcoholism, clinical and experimental research* 27 (11): 1785–97.

Staudt, Kathleen. 1998. *Free trade: Informal economies at the U.S. Mexico border.* Philadelphia: Temple University Press.

Super, David A., Sharon Parrott, Susan Steinmetz, and Cindy Mann. 1996. The new welfare law. Center on Budget and Policy Priorities. http://www.cbpp.org/WECNF813.HTM/.

Taylor, Peter J. 1996. *The way the modern world works: World hegemony to world impasse.* New York: John Wiley & Sons.

Texas Department of Human Services. 1996. *Texas works: Your independence is our success.* Austin: Texas Department of Human Services.

Texas Department of Human Services. Texas works handbook. http://www.dhs.state.tx.us/handbooks/TexasWorks/.

Thorpe, Helen. 1998. The fall of the last patron. *Texas Monthly,* June. http://www.texasmonthly.com/.

Tickamyer, Ann, and Cecil Tickamyer. 1987. Poverty in Appalachia. Appalachian Center Data Bank Report 5, University of Kentucky, Lexington, March.

Under welfare reform: Are policy impacts different in rural areas? National Poverty Center Working Paper Series #03-7, Ann Arbor, Mich., September. http://www.npc.umich.edu/publications/working_papers/.

U.S. Bureau of the Census. American Fact Finder n.d. http://factfinder.census.gov/home/saff/main.html?lang=en.

U.S. Bureau of the Census. 1995. http://www.census.gov/hhes/www/saipe.html/.

———. 1990. http://homer.ssd.census.gov/cdrom/lookup/CMD=LIST/DB=C90STF3A/LEV=STATE/.

———. 1999. http://www.census.gov/population/www/estimates/popest.html/.

U.S. Commission on Civil Rights. 2001. *Race and ethnic tensions in American communities: Poverty, inequality and discrimination—Volume VII: The Mississippi Delta report.* February. Washington, D.C.: U.S. Commission on Civil Rights. http://www.usccr.gov/pubs/msdelta/main.htm./

U.S. Department of Commerce. 1997. Regional Economic Information System, 1997. http://gov.info.library.orst.edu/.

U.S. Department of Health and Human Services, Administration for Children and Families. http://www.acf.hhs.gov/programs/ofa/welfare/index.htm/ (accessed April, 29, 2004).

U.S. Department of Labor, Employment and Training Administration. 2003. Welfare-to-work grants. http://wtw.doleta.gov/resources/fact-grants.asp/.

U.S. Department of Labor, Bureau of Labor Statistics. 1999. http://www.bls.gov/.

Vila, Pablo. 2000. *Crossing borders, reinforcing borders: Social categories, metaphors, and narrative identities on the U.S.-Mexico frontier.* Austin: University of Texas Press.

Wagoner, Paula L. 2002. *"They treated us just like Indians": The worlds of Bennett County, South Dakota.* Lincoln: University of Nebraska Press.

Walsh, Margaret, and Cynthia M. Duncan. 2001. Race and poverty in the rural South. In *Challenges to equality: Poverty and race in America,* ed. Chester Hartman, 117–23. Armonk, N.Y.: M. E. Sharpe.

Walton, Gary M., and Hugh Rockoff. 1998. *History of the American economy.* Fort Worth, Tex.: Dryden Press.

Weber, Bruce, and Greg Duncan. 2001. Welfare reform reauthorization and rural America: Implications of recent research. Joint Center for Poverty Research, Northwestern University and University of Chicago, Evanston, Ill.

Weber, Bruce, Mark Edwards, and Greg Duncan. 2003. Single mothers work and poverty under welfare reform: are policy impacts different in rural areas? National Poverty Center Working Paper Series #03-7, September, Ann Arbor, Mich.

Weiler, Stephan. 1997. The economics of the struggling structurally unemployed. *Journal of Appalachian Studies* 3 (1): 71–97.

White, Lucie E. 2001. Closing the care gap that welfare reform left behind. *Annals* 577 (September): 131–42.

Wilson, William Julius. 1996. *When work disappears: The world of the new urban poor.* New York: Alfred A. Knopf.

Winston, Pamela. 2002. *Welfare policy making in the states: The devil in devolution.* Washington, D.C.: Georgetown University Press.

Wolfe, Barbara L. 2002. Incentives, challenges, and dilemmas of TANF: A case study. *Journal of Policy Analysis and Management* 21 (4): 577–86.

Ziliak, James P., David N. Figlio, Elizabeth E. Davis, and Laura S. Connolly. 2000. Accounting for the decline in AFDC caseloads: Welfare reform or economic growth? *Journal of Human Resources* 35 (3): 570–86.

Zylan, Yvonne, and Sarah A. Soule. 2000. Ending welfare as we know it (again): Welfare state retrenchment, 1989–1995. *Social Forces* 79 (2): 623–52.

INDEX

case workers/managers, 173–75

childcare, 103, 106, 146

child support payment system, 102

educational supports, 91–92, 131

job market, 90, 93, 96, 98

self-esteem, 88, 116, 118, 121, 147, 204

TANF compared to AFDC, 89, 90, 114, 184–85, 213

training, 92, 107, 114, 165–66, 170

work disincentives, 111–13

paternalistic dominance/paternalism, 12, 124, 215

Personal Responsibility and Work Opportunity Reconciliation Act of 1996 (PRWORA)

provisions, 1–5, 26, 28, 39, 43, 49, 61–62, 91, 151, 189, 209, 211, 218

policy implications, 19–21, 30, 33–34, 68–69, 76, 160, 185, 213–14

Pickering, Kathleen, 13, 19, 95, 96, 97, 110, 111, 114, 122

Pine Ridge Indian Reservation, 1–2, 8, 12–13, 21–22, 43–44, 87–104, 109–22, 212, 216, 218

plant closures, 83, 190–91, 196, 201

poverty

children, 72

extreme, 70

inequality by race and ethnicity, 69

persistent, 71, 76

pockets of persistent rural poverty, 1–2, 11–18, 151–59

rates in 1980, 1990, and 2000, 70

rural and urban differences, 69

single-mother families, 71–72

sub-families, 72–74

privatization, 9, 192–94, 216, 218

qualified work activity, 21, 24, 91, 105

qualitative research, 3, 5, 6–7, 8, 29, 81

race relations, 2, 4, 28–29, 30, 34, 50, 69, 96, 201–3, 215–16

Richardson, Chad R., 152, 153, 155, 156, 180

Rosebud Sioux Indian reservation, 1–2, 8, 12–13, 21–22, 43–44, 87–98, 104–22, 214

rural areas, 12, 18–19, 50–51, 76, 80

sanctions, 20, 29, 187, 197–98, 212–13, 214–15

harsh, 94–95, 98, 115, 164–65

increasing, 24–25, 89–90, 104, 112, 168–70, 182–85

last resort, 125

Seccombe, Karen, 3, 5, 31, 32

Self-esteem, 88, 116, 118, 121, 147, 204, 215

service economy/industry/sector, 49–51, 97, 124–25, 133, 210

shadow economy. See everyday economy

Shannon County, 1–2, 8, 12–13, 42, 70, 73, 76–77, 91, 93, 95, 96, 110, 111, 118

sharecropping system, 17, 30, 203

Sicangu Lakota. See Rosebud Sioux Indian Reservation

Sinta Gleska University, 92, 106–7, 114

Sioux. See Pine Ridge Indian Reservation, Rosebud Sioux Indian Reservation

social networks, 3, 31–32, 51–52, 180–86, 201–2, 211

South Dakota, 4, 7, 12–13, 21–23, 30–31, 40–42, 43, 53, 71, 72, 73, 87–122, 212–13

South Dakota Department of Social Services, 22, 42, 44, 98

staff reductions, 101, 108, 194

Starr County, 2, 8–9, 15–16, 42, 70, 80–82, 158, 159–60, 161–62, 167, 172, 180, 187, 212, 218

State Children's Health Insurance Program (SCHIP), 198–99, 213

Staveteig, Sarah, 28, 29, 30, 33, 34, 35, 39, 50, 51, 68

stringency, 4, 9, 190, 196, 207, 212, 215, 217

substance abuse, 116, 119–20, 125–26, 129–30, 191, 197, 211

Sunflower County, 2, 9, 16–18, 82–83, 196, 199, 201, 203–5